CHRISTIANS ALERT!

DEMOCRATS ARE ATTACKING OUR COUNTRY

2nd Edition

Richard Ferguson

CHRISTIANS ALERT!

DEMOCRATS ARE ATTACKING OUR COUNTRY

WHAT WE CAN DO ABOUT IT?

2nd Edition

*A*dvantage
BOOKS

RICHARD FERGUSON

Christians Alert! Democrats Are Attacking Our Country by Richard Ferguson
Copyright © 2019 by Richard Ferguson
All Rights Reserved.
ISBN: 978-1-59755-525-8

Published by: ADVANTAGE BOOKS™
                  Longwood, Florida, USA
                  www.advbookstore.com

Library of Congress Catalog Number: 2019948673

2nd Edition: August 2025
25 26 27 28 29 30   10 9 8 7 6 5 4 3

Introduction

This work is a deep look into the situation we as Christians find ourselves today in our beloved country. Our politics, government structure and place in this world is examined from a Jude-Christian perspective, using foundational Christian beliefs and principles as our guide to see what has happened to us as a society and culture. We as a nation have strayed ever so far from the foundational principles that created our country and in doing so, we have strayed far away from the will of Almighty God that He has for us His children. We are now seeing the resulting corruption, chaos and political corruption of our country being displayed every day we watch out news programs.

To understand more completely, a look is taken into the human minds and psychology our ourselves, especially our political leaders and their spirituality that propels them to say and do what they are responsible for. Why is it that leftist liberal politicians have become that way lurching toward socialism that has proven 100% of the time to bring pain, suffering and death to every nation that has tried it? Why is it that some politicians have implemented policies of domination over other nations using invasion and war to achieve their goals? We as a people do not want that. Why do some of our politicians?

In every instance, Judeo-Christian principles are used to measure the rightness or wrongness of what our leaders are doing and have done in the recent past. The teachings of Jesus Christ are used throughout this work to illustrate just how far we as a nation have gone astray from what Almighty God has intended for us.

Lastly, it is one thing to point out what is wrong today. That is not enough. Creative proposals for what we need to do as a country to restore this nation into a thriving Judeo Christian nation that takes into account the lessons we have learned since the foundation of our country and to solve many of the existing problems we face today.

We as Christians must always fervently seek the truth in all things. This I have done to the very best of my ability as objectively as possible. We live in a time of lies and deceit coming from all corners in our country, especially the media and both political parties. We as children of God must pierce the barriers that hide the truth from us and not be afraid to speak it, to write it and to act upon it. It is my hope in writing this it will take you to a deeper understanding of our current situation, why it is this way and what to do about it using the best truth we can find in these hostile anti-Christian times.

Table of Contents

Richard Ferguson

PART 1

The Christian Foundations of Who We Are

The Search for Ourselves

Knowing Who We Are:

We can know the nature of the universe and its laws through scientific inquiry such as astronomy, physics, math, and cosmology. We can know the relationship between mankind and the universe and God through the many writings of inspired people left for us to understand such as all the books in the Bible and other discoveries such as Dead Sea Scrolls.

We can know our relationship with God and his nature and our relationship with Him even through the writings of contemporary people such as John Templeton who established the Templeton Prize for Religious Progress. We can know our relationship with God and his laws just by living our lives. . . if we pay close attention that is and learn. Sadly, not nearly enough strive to understand both the world and universe they live in and themselves. Most people just stumble along in their lives choosing to remain ignorant and just watch TV. It is from all this collected knowledge and wisdom from the people who decided to strive to be their best that has made possible the best institutions to serve the needs of God's children while they are on this planet. Much of this discovered knowledge was already in place even before mankind existed. What was that like?

In order to have a fruitful life and grow closer to God and fulfill our potential it takes a lot of effort, dedication and learning through thought and observation. The object of our learning is to understand what the foundational pillars of our human existence are. What should be our world view that produces the most constructive positive results in our lives and those around us. What are these pillars, what are they like and what are their characteristics? Learning this will allow anyone to make intelligent, reasoned judgements during their life. For example, who should hold the ultimate power in a society. What is man's relationship with the physical world, the spiritual world and God Himself. What is the nature of man, his good side and dark side. How do you compensate

9

for man's dark side when designing a government that will allow freedom? There are many questions such as these. There is one major problem our founding fathers had to face directly, the good and evil sides of man. If we as Christians believe in an all loving God, then how do we explain evil and how do we compensate for that in government?

Before Creation: What Was It Like Before Creation?

To Understand Now We Need to Understand Before

For us to gain an accurate perception of how far we have strayed away from the intent of God for us in our beloved country, we need to go back to the beginning…the very beginning. Here we will see the magnificent beauty of where we came from and what it may have for us if we did not gain the knowledge of good and evil.

We will use the tool of midrash to explore our very beginnings to help us answer these questions. What are the foundational pillars of human existence in the universe? Why are we here? What is the nature of our Creator? What was it like for us before humankind came to earth. Where were we? What was it like there, where we were? What were we like? Knowing at least some of the answers to these questions gives us a solid foundation to measure"what should be"and therefore seeing how far we have gone astray.

I asked an elderly Jesuit Priest in graduate pastoral ministry school where were we before earth? I thought it was an insightful question. He laughed and said in a loud voice, "You did not exist!"How does he know that? After years of prayer and meditation God guided me gently to the answer. We did exist with Him. My Jesuit priest professor was completely wrong.

"Before I formed you in the womb, I knew you, before you were born, I set you apart; I appointed you as a prophet to the nations." Jerimiah 1:5 NIV

This Biblical quote is from the Old Testament. God is talking to the prophet Jerimiah. God says he knew Jerimiah before he was born. He existed before being born into this physical realm. Yet Jerimiah was a normal human being. Much can be learned from just this one quote. I cannot help but think that Almighty God loves all His children in the same loving manner as He does Jerimiah. The above thought does rest easy in my prayers and meditations with our Lord.

To understand who we are today we must know the very root of where we came from. We existed before coming to earth. This is gigantic It is absolutely necessary to do this to understand the situation we live in today, how we got here and what to do about it.

The Beginning of You, The Beginning of Me:

Before all that came to be was God, his children slowly born within all that was and yet to be. That which we know had not come to pass yet from His will but shall and from that is what we will learn who we are, who God is and all that will be.

It was a place of magnificent and inexorable beauty and love. Yet it wasn't a place. There was no up, no down, no left or no right. No here. No there. No within. No without. All of us children of God were of the One and only One. Intertwined together being born into the divine womb of that which was and is "I am". Each of us united completely within each other sharing all that was love. We loved knowing each other's thoughts, knowing everyone completely for each of us was all of us with rapturous love connecting all that was.

We were love an all encompassing love, a love beyond description which was also "I am", of all that was divine, sacred and holy. "I am" was and is perfect in the highest perfection, beyond all that was us, yet we were within the nursery of "I am". We were "I am"and"I am"was in us and all were one. For we were part of God. We had total freedom within creation. The infinite bliss which we were created in was beyond what we could understand for it was from"I AM".

God was within us and also beyond us in the silent fragrant calm of the angel's song of a luscious and succulent love, blessing their songs through all of that which was and yet going to be. We all were pregnant and bursting with that which was yet to come without time or space. Infinite loving potential was set before us for we were to enter that as individuals, something we knew not of. Our depth of happiness was delicious with gossamer breaths of life starting to surge within. We were exhilarated in an ecstasy of divine love that flowed through us all, in, out, through and around all that we were to be. This love was gentile as a butterfly wing caressing our very existence, all in the harmony of "I am". A fragrant divine love that touched our heart of hearts embracing the very idea of each of us in an endless wonderment of love.

Before creation all the multitudes of us were one with the Father. We were inseparable from all else. Our joy was beyond measure. Oh, the tingling infinite sounds of singing and us children giggling with the angels. It was complete and lacked nothing for there was not anything that was not already that which we were within our Father. Such a joyous existence, no wants, no needs, infinite beauty abounding in the pure light of love from God our Father.

There was no beginning as we would think. Space and time are inexorably inseparable and very flexible. It was when time had not started or even noticed by anyone of us in the brotherhood that we all were. All was and still is one and only one. We could hear all the angels singing and praising God almighty, the source of all that is good and just in all the dimensions of creation. There are many. It was an absolutely marvelous existence that all of us that were God's children. Born out of His loving thoughts into a realm of joy and love beyond anything we can describe with crude and primitive tools such as words.

The beginning of you is the same as the beginning of me. The beginning of us is the same as the beginning of the untold billions and trillions of all others in creation. Yet they are not really other as we would think. They too are us in ways that we cannot perceive. The cosmic intermingling of the one and others is the very nature of the one. Yet in this loving completeness God had planned for us to go even beyond that. Beyond that which we could ever understand or imagine in our sacred nursery of divine love. We were to be born now in a significantly different way.

The Beginning of Self Awareness and Consciousness:

Our awareness was something that came into existence by the thought of God. It is something that always existed but in a different way from what God has given unto us now. All of us are part of the divine completeness, and before God gave us the gift of individual identity, we were inseparable and part of from the divine whole. Yet I was me and you were you in the divine love within all that was. We were part of God and God was part of us. Nothing was not God. Everything was God. For God was, God is, and God will always be. The totality of all that ever was, is and ever will be is God our Father, the eternal One of love and light, from which all life and consciousness is given. We were part of God always before and forevermore throughout all dimensions, all creation, all time from the alpha to the omega. Yet mysteriously we all knew that the omega was also the alpha but different.

And God then said for all other living things, they will never violate my laws. It is because they will not have the divine gift of free will. It will be you my dear children that will have this gift and you will have the ability to go against my laws and my will. This gift I give to you is that powerful. But in doing so you will bring painful consequences into your lives. In this way the pain you will experience will teach you more clearly what is my will. It will teach you who "I Am". You will only be able see my physical creation through the lens of your senses. It is this way, so you may co-create yourself with Me as a fulfilled personal creation of yourself and Me as "I Am". You will have choices to make in the formation of your complete potential. But in doing so you will learn what effort and other necessary qualities are to be learned and experienced so as to form the complete beauty of who you will become.

The Physical Universe of Creation:

Before creation of the universe there were fundamental laws that would govern the universe that was to be made manifest in the physical realm. These divine laws pre-existed the physical universe we have today. Foundational truths were set into place that we all know about in our everyday lives. One overarching rule from God is that the closer you live to His rules the more fulfilled, successful (not necessarily money) and the more positive spiritual growth you will achieve. The more of God's blessings you can bestow upon and unto others of His children in this physical realm, the more you will grow in the spirit. After all, we are all spiritual beings in our essence. The farther you move away from God's laws the more pain and suffering you will experience and cause all that pain and suffering to spread to others as well. For you are inexorably connected with all in the brotherhood.

Remember, you and I as spiritual beings with separate identities within our vast brotherhood existed before the physical universe. During this spiritual period of our existence there was absolutely no need for rules of behavior. We were joyfully immersed in the pure love of God. We were guided in our existence by His love for all of us.

Today, your scientific discoveries match very well with these ancient accounts of creation's beginning. But they can never speak of the unmeasurable spiritual realm. For they can never measure that which is spiritual and unseen. Yet it is here in the realm of the spirit where almost all of My creation exists. This includes you and all the uncountable trillions of your brethren who I love as I love you.

God said, I will create a universe for you. But first there will be the universal laws that from which will this universe will come. From the very instant first heartbeat of creation, my laws will govern its coming into being, into existence. There will be absolute laws that will not, cannot and never be violated. It is these laws that will give you a solid foundation of life for your coming physical existence in that realm. What you will call nature and physics will by itself never violate my absolute laws. For they have no free will to do so as do you.

Yet if you understand, you will see that there are also laws that govern your life in this new physical realm. It will be these laws that will give you the freedom to become fully yourselves as I have intended. For my laws will govern your existence and make all things possible for you to discover and explore. For in your search for universal understanding you will also be searching for Me, creator of everything seen and unseen. For I have created you from my thoughts, each different from all the rest. But you will understand that you are not yet complete. Your inner most being will understand this deeply and silently. For we shall in our love for each other from that which will become you as co-creators in which you shall live for all eternity.

Individual Identities as One Brotherhood:

Then a most sacred event occurred. All of us, God's children, became individual expressions of God at His divine command, all unique, a one of only one, and we became aware as different facets of an infinite sided diamond. Each with exquisite beauty in a special way, shining our unique light of love into creation, different from the rest but also an inseparable part of the whole. The whole cannot exist if one part is missing. Each part is a unique reflection of the whole as "I Am" is the sacred loving light for all and through all. Within each child is contained all the attributes of the whole yet different from all the rest. How could one explain that which exists eternally and carries with it the infinite beauty of divine existence that was freely given without limitations or restraint of any kind? Yet that is exactly what God has done.

And God said it is you as an individual that will polish the diamond luster of your divine sparkling light that is Me which proceeds through you and toward the hearts and minds of all others in your brotherhood. Each of you are unique with different paths back to me. You have the freedom inside you to do this. Knowing my creation is part of knowing Me, like knowing a painting is knowing part of the painter. But my creation includes the unseen tapestry and fabric of loving connections between each of you who sing songs of creation with my angels. For it will be your love for others that will form the eternal bonds and form eternal relationships between you and all your kindred spirits.

And so, before the creation of this universe, God has given us another unspeakably sacred and wonderful gift. It is that of individual identity. Our Father said he was going to give us the gift of our own identities. We would become all that is within us, but we will also now have a name that is unique to each "one" of us. All that is within creation will still be within us, but we will not be aware of this. Yet we will now experience that as something to grow into. We all will be reflections of God in our own unique one of a kind manner of being. We were all that was and all that could be. Anything that interferes with this, God's plan for each of us, is evil and its author is Satan.

Our Journey into The Physical Realm, To Know Ourselves and God in a Different Way:

Our Father had also given us the power to create but in a limited way within the physical realm. We were loved and loved infinitely. Yet we did not know our own natures in that way. We needed to go on a journey of self-discovery. A journey that would teach us what we were, who we were and how we were so interrelated to all the others in creation including our Father. For we can only know our true selves through the eyes of the other, the other in the physical realm.

God told us that this would be a divine journey of our spirits. It would be a journey that had its challenges, full of hardships and sometimes pain and suffering, from others or ourselves. We did not know any of what He was telling us. We could not understand. All we knew was that our loving Father was with us, in us and we will journey back toward Him in bliss and love for those who love Him as He loved us. But there would be a danger too.

We became individuals, one of a kind, but still inseparable from the whole which was within God. Yes, we existed in some spiritual form before the physical universe came to be. [1] God has given us the gift of individuality. God said to beware of those who demean you as an individual. For in doing so, they also demean"I am". For all your physical life, it is you with your own individual identity that your existence is built upon. Beware of those who ignore this universal truth. They are of the fallen one.

We as humans in this time and place struggle with this oxymoron. We are all one yet with different identities. Identity is such a strange thing. It is basic to our existence as we now understand it. But it was not always that way. By its very nature it separates us from each other. There would be no need for identity if we were all one. But the conundrum is that we are all one and still have our own identities. One comfort for those who did not understand what individual is was that we all had complete freedom to go where ever we wished, we could have our own unique thoughts and love that we could share with all the rest. What a weird and wonderful part of existence this is. I can hear the loving echoes of God smiling at how we struggle with this oxymoron. Yet He is pleased in this as He knows our struggle ultimately leads directly back to Him our ultimate creator if we so choose.

---

[1] Jeremiah 1:5, "Before I formed thee in the belly I knew thee; and before thou camest forth out of the womb I sanctified thee, and I ordained thee a prophet unto the nations." (God was speaking to Jeremiah the prophet.)

Oh yes dear child God said, you must make a choice. Will it be to love others and "I Am", or to love yourselves at a cost to all others?

God Tells Us About Our Lives in The Physical Realm:

My dear children, you will exist in the physical universe as the individual I created you as. But you will only be able to see your real self in the eyes of the other, not the one you imagine yourself to be. Yet there is a collective consciousness that you will share with all your brethren throughout all of eternity. The more loving you become in the face of hardship and suffering the more divine fulfillment you will experience and the more painful the evil things that come from departing from my ways will feel to you. Seek always the truth for it is higher than anything else. I am the truth. If you decide to depart from the truth, you will pay the painful consequences. Embrace and pursue the truth and you will flourish.

My dear children I have created you out of my heart of hearts in pure love for all of you. My love for you means that you will in your hearts always desire freedom to pursue what you wish. This is foundational for your lives. Your wishes are an expression of your inner self. Pay attention to your desires. If they are holy, right and just then pursue them and manifest these desires into physical reality. In this way you will leave an imprint of my will in the history of your existence in the physical realm. Never let another stifle your desires for that is far short of my will for you. Remember that all that happens in time is your history forever as creation knows all that is and what events, decisions and wonderings turn into your history. Nothing is hidden, all is known throughout all of creation.

My dear children, you will be born into this physical realm as male and female. Just as you are incomplete without me, so too will you be incomplete without the other as one joined together as two in love as an eternal bond ordained by my divine will. And from this mutual love I will ordain others to join you not only in my image but also now yours as well. It is in this way that you will multiply and have dominion over all the earth and subdue it as you explore the beauty of love that creates eternal bonds going beyond what you will call time.

My dear children, I also give you my eternal guidance in your physical existence. I have made part of you, part of who "I am". In this way "I am" is always with you no matter where you are. In some ways you will call this conscience. I am your inner voice that guides you throughout all that you manifest, and all your choices set before you. Listen to My voice inside you in the love that I have created you from. For ultimately you are a unique expression of my love made to exist for a time in the physical realm where you will learn much about Me your Father, creator of all seen and unseen.

My dear children, I give you the freedom to set your eyes upon your unique path in life. Freedom to walk that path full of love, hardships, fulfillment, learning to love in different ways, being among your brethren and answering the big questions. Within the stress of physical life, will you put yourself above others of your kind. Will you continue faith in me? Will you continue to increase your knowledge? Will you combine these with your given ability to have faith, gain knowledge and reason so as to gain wisdom?

My dear children, the freedom I give to you is something you can lose very easily. For only virtuous and loving people are capable of freedom. Freedom requires the loving control of one's own self. Keeping the freedom that I freely give you will also require watchfulness from you. Guard your freedom with whatever force is required for freedom is something that is hated by the one who lost Heaven because he tried to put himself higher than Me. So, beware of the snake and his minions. Without these abilities I give to you, you will fall victim to those of the dark side that are among you.

My dear children I also give to you your sacred life. Your life for you to grow and fulfill our contract together. For your experience, your learning and your loving all those in the brotherhood. Like your freedom, you must also guard your sacred lives. Allow no one to take that from you. For if you do, all your goals, spiritual paths, fulfillment and learning will fall into dust. Your life is your gateway into the higher realms of existence within all creation.

My dear children, I will also give you the ability to reason, to understand what lays before you so you may choose wisely from the different paths that are put in front of you. Use your reason and understandings with love for all things. It is in this way that you will choose wisely in the realm that you will be for a time.

My dear children I will give to you the ability to imagine that which does not yet exist. You will have the gift of creation in the physical realm, to bring into being that which is in your mind and manifest that in your world which is to come. You will have the freedom to choose the nature of that which you bring into existence. It will be able to help all your brothers in life or hurt them. What you chose to do exposes who and what you are for all of creation to see. You will be judged for what you create along with your actions within your brotherhood of physical life. You must remember this for there is also danger for you in the physical realm. There will be a powerful question you must answer in your life to be. What path will you choose?

My dear children, the question you will answer for all the universe and its inhabitants to see is what path you will choose. Will you love yourself first and put yourself above others or will you choose to serve them? Will you humble yourself in the sight of your brothers and sisters or will you seek dominion over them? It is that question which is a fateful decision you must make. Seeking dominion over others is the path to separation from Me. It is the path of the fallen one cast out of the Heavenly Kingdom never to return.

My dear children, the fruitful loving answer is to always remember to love Me your Father and Creator above all else, and love others as you love yourself. All good things come from these two great commandments. In doing this you will be manifesting my will for you in this coming physical realm. Remember that a few angels before you have chosen the dark path of putting themselves on high only to fall from my divine grace. For it is loving yourself more than Me and all in your brotherhood that will result in your fall as well. If you love only yourself then that will be the only thing you will see in eternity, yourself which is what you loved the most. For it is all that you truly love that will follow you into the heavenly realm.

My dear children, this your physical universe is a mansion of coherent truths. There are many truths that you will discover. There are phenomena that you will believe to be true only to discover later that you were mistaken. This will be part of your learning experience. Disagreements will abound across all those of your brothers that wish to discover as you do. Work cooperatively with them as together you will come together in the truths that I have set forth for you. In doing this you will form a strong brotherhood founded in love, compassion and ever increasing understanding of who "I am". For the essence of my creation is the matrix of loving relationships and the intermingling of kindred spirits for all you my children that will be formed in another manner from the trials and opportunities that is being set before you.

And so, it was. God set forth and thought this universe into motion and existence. It is our home for at least now. For God has planned even greater things for us who love him, pursue him and increase in our understandings of Him our Creator. Most will fall by the wayside into a state unknown to this writer, but they will miss the complete ecstasy that is the ultimate will of God, union with Him as his anointed children, born as spirits and learning through the physical universe crafted for us.

God Prepares Us for The Nature of The Physical Realm:

The world I have prepared for you is a place of wonderment and joy, specially created for you and all your brothers and sisters to whom all are united as one within my arms of eternal love. It is there where you will recognize as a place like no other.

It is there you will see as a place that is but a dim shadow of my kingdom where you were brought into eternal existence. It is there you will see is a place of great learning and experience, from which you will participate in the formation of yourselves as you grow closer to who "I am" and who you will be. It is there that you will learn about yourselves and about a tiny part of the universe that this place is magnificent part of. It is there that you will grow into your own potential depending on how much effort you put into your own destiny. It is there that you will be tested about how much you grow in your love for Me and your brotherhood. It is there where you will progress in your understandings of who I am and who you are. It is there where you will grow in your abilities to learn, to love, to sacrifice for the benefit of all your brothers and sisters in the brotherhood of mankind.

It is there where you will learn that love is what you really are and grow to show that love outward to this world full of life of many kinds. It is there where you will be challenged to show that love through many different circumstances. It is there where you will have Me closer than your own breath but not be able to see me, hear me or feel my presence as you do now. For it is there where it is your own love that will propel you in your life journey towards the destiny that you chose through many small choices that will add up to fashion the trajectory of your eternal existence, your loves and who you become. It is there where you will explore the free will I have given you as one of the highest blessings and grace that can be given in my creation. For I have given you the power to shape what you become, to shape who you become and to shape what eternal relationships that you will form. For it is these bonds that will become an inexorable part of your inner being.

Only after you experience the hardships of love, its power and the wise use of the powers I have given you will you then after this kind of lives will you be then be prepared to experience the open door to the greater parts of creation. The utter magnificent parts of creation that you will then be able to take part in.

The danger for you will be exercising the power of making wrong choices. It is there where you will experience the consequences of wrong choices and the pleasures of right choices. Through this none will have an excuse for making wrong choices. All will be given to you to see the loving right choices and all the blessings that will bring.

Know that that the closer you live to My rules the more fulfilled, successful and the more positive spiritual growth you will achieve. After all, we are all spiritual beings in our essence. The farther you move away from My laws the more pain and suffering you will experience and spread to others as well. For this you will be responsible to Me.

The infinite creation will welcome you into its arms as you depart the universe of the physical. The unseen infinite creation will always surround you even as you are in the physical universe. It will guide you if only you ask for it. Guidance will be given freely to you as you journey through the lives that lay ahead for you. As you reach your potentials in love for me, your love for all your brothers and sisters you will see the arms of my loving creation opening for you even when you are still living there. When your days come to a close, you will reap your harvest as you have sown your seeds. If you have chosen wisely in love for others and with divine guidance, all parts of creation will open its arms to greet you in higher and higher depths of love that will glow its light within you and surround you. For that is another part of my infinite love for you my dearest children.

You will never be alone although by intent you will feel that way. For it is impossible for you to be apart from me unless you choose that path. Yet you will be masters of your choices, your abilities and your destiny. It is in this way that you will bring yourselves to the fruition of what you choose.

As I have said before, be wary of negative choices born of the worship of yourselves. This is the path to agony and eternal pain. It is this path that leads to separation from me my dear children. For I have also given you the power to choose to reject me. This is a fateful power that you must realize its consequences. For you may choose to fall from my grace and love. All you will need to do is to fall in love with yourselves. For in doing this you will be rejecting the brotherhood of all your brothers and sisters. You in doing this will be rejecting me. For I am the root of your lives. I am that which nourishes you in countless unseen ways. Loving yourself above me will detach yourself from my loving embrace, my power and grace that I freely give you if only you accept. That is all you need to do.

God said, my thoughts, my will, my heartfelt desire is that all of you choose wisely in the life I give you. That you come to recognize that which will be in front of you all the time you live in the physical world. It will be there for all to see if only you allow your eyes to see Me in all that there is where you will live. It will be very hard for you to not see me but choosing not to see will be within your power that I give to you.

What lays before you is to learn more deeply to love others as yourself. Therein is the kingdom of ecstasy. You will then be able to explore the other parts of my infinite creation. For there will be no time, no limits, nothing hidden. You will be able then to experience the lives of your brothers and sisters for you are eternally linked if you choose wisely. Remember it takes faith, knowledge and reason to attain wisdom. Pursue these with all your heart while loving all in your brotherhood.

It is past the open doors of my loving kingdom that you will be reunited with all that you have loved before. For that which you love becomes part of you. It is only through love that you can pass through the veils that are the doorways to higher and higher existence in the timeless place of infinite wonderment and joy that will remain beyond your physical understanding.

Lastly, if you fall in love with yourself that is all you will have in eternity. You will inhabit the darkness of only yourself with the light of my love not reaching you through your self-imposed veil that blocks out all that is good and right. You have the power to choose this path by manifesting and viewing yourself above others of your brotherhood, and in doing so you are placing yourself above Me. This is what the fallen one chose to do. You are wonderfully beautiful created as was the fallen one, but do not fall in love with your own beauty, that is a path my dearest children I warn you never to take.

Faith, Knowledge and Reason Leads to Wisdom:

Faith, Knowledge and Reason:

In addition to divine love, it is God that wants us to have faith, knowledge and reason which in turn develops wisdom during our lives. This is fundamental to His design for human existence in this physical realm. Each one of the above supplements the others within the arms of our love for each other. There must be a balance of these three or human life will not live up to its potential for us as human beings.

Faith:

It will be faith that can guide you to the answers that mankind seeks. Faith is that invisible gift I give to those who humble themselves before Me in love and heartfelt sincerity. For in adoring Me, all my children will come to their highest fulfillment within themselves and grow into the beloved child I have ordained from the beginning.

The blessing of faith increases the inner desire of more faith. It is a pleasurable succulent warmth of having strong faith. For it engenders the inner desires of spreading faith to all brothers and sisters as they live in the world. It also engenders a need to learn knowledge of my creation, of the nature of all living things and the inner nature of my other children who are also living.

But, for those who choose to have only faith, they will cast their eyes upon Me in adoration and love. This is very pleasing to me. For it is those who have faith in Me that will be by my side after the world comes to its natural physical end. Yet for those who only want faith and do not pursue knowledge, they leave themselves less than whole. They fall short of my intentions for them for they have not understood that both faith and knowledge is the key for what they search for.

Only faith, although good and true, is like a one-legged man standing. A wind will come and blow his faith over and he will lose what faith he may have. Only knowledge is also a one-legged man standing. His other leg only will also succumb to the wind and blow him over. For only knowledge will never inform him as to why he lives, what direction he should take his knowledge and why one path is better than the other. It is with faith and knowledge guided by reason that you can pursue truth for truth is higher than anything else which also leads to wisdom.

Knowledge supports faith. Remember that faith supports knowledge. It gives knowledge a framework, a context in which to be meaningful. But, faith without knowledge is fragile, subject to the winds of confusion, to the opinions of the ignorant masses who have neither faith or knowledge. For they will have not used their powers of reason as well. Reason will in many ways link together knowledge and faith in Me the "I AM" of all creation.

I have given all my children the gift of desiring knowledge but also yearning for faith as well. Reason is also inborn with you as part of your natural being. Remember that when something good and right is desired, it is I that has given that to you. It springs from that deeply hidden part of you that is the closest to Me. It is in this way that I live within you and guide you to your complete potential as my beloved child.

I say to you the complete person fulfilled in all manner of being will have knowledge of my creation, faith in Me so as to understand why creation is the way it is and reason to make sound judgements, which leads to wisdom and choosing the divine path with love that I wish for each of you my dear children. Pursue all of this my dear children. Pursue these with all your might. For in doing so you will draw close to me as "I am" and fulfill the promise of the individual and priceless unique you I saw at the beginning of your existence within Me and outside Me.

Knowledge:

God said there will be all too many of your brothers and sisters that will embrace the one only to reject the other. They will think that if they have knowledge there will be no need for faith. Knowledge of the physical is only part of a larger existence. Reason must be used to gain proper knowledge. It is this that will protect you from believing things that are untrue and lead you astray from your true spiritual path I have chosen for you. For if you increase your knowledge without faith in Me, you will falsely think that you do not need Me in your life. You will think that you are masters of your domain. You are not. For you will not know the infinite things that you do not know. This can only lead you to pain and suffering.

Knowledge by itself will only bring a dim light into the life of those who pursue only that. These people you will ᵃ¹¹ scientists will never be able to answe question of why all that is works the \ does. They will always have new que and new thoughts in their per blizzard of ideas that ultimately wil them nowhere. The answers for these brothers will only lead them to questions.

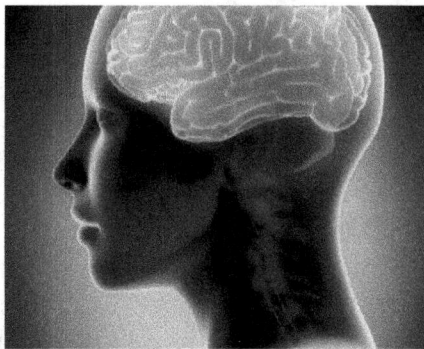

The pursuit of only knowledge ...... ultimately bring them to the point of asking why things are the way they are. It is this question of why that brings one to the edge of faith. It is the search for meaning and asking where everything is going that is the beginning of wisdom. Wisdom comes from knowledge guided by reason and faith in Me. For knowledge by itself is only one arm. I gave each of you two arms. The other is faith. Knowledge is the arm of how. Faith is the other arm of why and of meaning. Reason is why you have a brain. Together with experiences in life in the physical realm yields the precious fruit of wisdom. And your heart of hearts in faith leads to Me. It allows you to learn about Me through the creation I have brought forth for you to understand and see Me as the painter that is behind His painting.

Reason:

I have given you the gift of reason. Some will call this logical thinking with objective observation. It is with you, so you may understand knowledge and use it for your betterment in the physical realm. Reason will guide you to understand many of the questions of "why"and "how". Then you must put effort into applying your knowledge for the betterment of all your brothers and sisters in the brotherhood of mankind.

If you use your gift of reason, you will link both knowledge and faith. It is this with my inner voice of what you will call conscience that will guide you and make clear the path to take. Remember that "I am"the truth above all.

It is reason that will protect you from making fatal mistakes in the physical realm. For reason combines perception and discernment and logical thinking to provide you with correct decisions which you will have to do each day of your physical existence.

It is past the open doors of my loving kingdom that you will be reunited with all that you have loved before. For that which you love becomes part of you. It is only through love that you can pass through the veils that are the doorways to higher and higher existence in the timeless place of infinite wonderment and joy that will remain beyond your understanding, at least for now.

What lays before you as you learn more deeply to love others is the kingdom of ecstasy. You will then be able to explore the other parts of my infinite creation. For there will be no time, no limits, nothing hidden. You will be able then to experience the lives of your brothers and sisters.

Wisdom

Wisdom is more than the combination of faith, knowledge and reason. The whole of wisdom is most certainly greater than the sum of its parts. Wisdom is a quality of both heart and mind. It is faith, knowledge and reason that when they resonate together within our loving inner being, they complete each other and support each other to form what we call wisdom.

Wisdom is not attained easily or by accident. It must be pursued with all your mind, all your heart, all your love, all your faith, all your knowledge and all your reason that when combined with a deep sincere love for all of God's creation then you will attain a wisdom that few have achieved.

Wisdom will allow you to see different things in their relationships between each other that will give you deep insight into that which appears before you. These insights will allow you to make loving judgments that will benefit your brothers and sisters in a much higher way and is consistent with the will of God for his children.

True wisdom is attained within a deep sense of humility and service to others. It lifts up a wise person to see the higher truths that exist well beyond the details of the here and now. Wisdom allows a person to apply the higher truths of existence to different situations and identify actions or that which is needed to be manifest and be consistent with the will of God. And also, it will allow you to reach intelligent conclusions that would escape others that have not sought faith, knowledge and reason and intermingle these three under the guidance of God our father. It is wisdom that will guide a child of God without the use of a map.

Foundational Christian Beliefs

Rock Solid Foundational Core Christian Beliefs:

What are the foundational beliefs of the Christian faith our founding fathers taught and lived? What are the Christian principles they used to create the Declaration of Independence, Constitution and the Bill of Rights?

1. Love God above all else and love your neighbor as you love yourself. (Matthew 22:36-40)

2. The one true God Yahweh has created all that is seen and unseen. (Genesis 1, Nicene Creed)

3. Yahweh is all perfect, all knowing and infinite. He loves all humans who are created in His image. (Psalm 18:30)

4. God is eternal with no beginning and no end. God is unchanging, the same in the past, now and the future. (Deuteronomy 33:27; Psalm 90:2; 1 Timothy 1:17)

5. God is omnipotent, omnipresent, omniscient and is in, around and through us knowing everything about us including our thoughts. (Revelation 19:6; Jeremiah 32:17, 27)

6. God is one. There is no other. (Deuteronomy 6:4)

7. There is an objective universe that obeys the laws of God both physical and in the spirit, independent of human desires and understanding. These laws are absolute, physical, moral, ethical laws. Breaking these laws is sin and leads to pain. (Isaiah 37:16, Acts 14:15, Acts 17:24)

8. God is holy, perfect, infinite and ultimately a mystery. His greatness is beyond knowing (Psalm 145:3). The depth of His wisdom and His judgments are beyond knowing (Romans 11:33). His riches are boundless beyond understanding (Ephesians 3:8).

9. God is pure intelligent love for all creation and beyond our complete understanding. (John 3:16)

10. God is righteous, meaning that God cannot and will not pass over wrongdoing. (Exodus 9:27; Matthew 27:45-46; Romans 3:21-26).

11. Humans have fallen into sin because we gained the knowledge of good and evil. (Romans 5:12)

12. God's Son, Jesus Christ, came down from Heaven to save all humankind from the consequences of our sin of learning about good and evil.

13. We cannot go to God in our current fallen and unholy condition, we can only go to our Father through Yah'Shua, Jesus Christ. (John 3:16) Only good works is not enough.

14. We all are expected to and responsible to discern God's laws and uphold them in our lives. (Matthew 5:17-20)

15. Christian ethics are based on right and wrong in the light of the Biblical scriptures. This differs widely from philosophical ethics based on duty, pleasure, law, science etc. and all other religions [2]

16. Satan is a real spirit being and force, not symbolic, he fell from Heaven and desires human destruction. He actively works each day toward his goal of destruction. (Job1:8, Job 2:2, Zacharia 3:1, Matthew 4:10)

17. The Bible is an accurate representation of the Godly principles it teaches. [3]

18. We can know a part of God through His creation and Biblical scriptures. We are charged to make the effort to learn about this. (Proverbs 2:1-6, Colossians 1:10)

---

[2] http://www.christianityetc.org/morality.php
[3] https://bible.org/article/how-accurate-bible

To Know Ourselves

Knowing Who We Are:

To understand our problems that exist today we must understand the deep roots from where we came from. Knowing this provides a foundation from which we can further our understandings about ourselves and provide knowledgeable solutions to the problems we face. In my pursuit of truth, it is unavoidable to face the fact that 100% of us were not here a mere 110 years ago. All of us at one point were only a fertilized egg in our mother's womb. Not only that depending on our age, 50 years from now most of us will not be here again. We were not here before and we will not be here again. We will return to the place where we started from before we came here. During this very brief period of time while we are here, we are experiencing something magnificent. Theologians call it the eternal moment of "now". This moment is all we have yet it will always be with us.

While we are here the eternal moment of now provides us the opportunity to create memories, learn, expand our knowledge, grow closer to God, purify our spiritual selves, suffer for the sake of goodness, resist evil and a host of other godly endeavors all of which are recorded in our memories. Our organic brain memories will dim over time but the memories in our higher self will not. They will stay with us for eternity. This is part of who we are. We cannot see that for good reason.

Lucifer's Fall and The Resulting War of Good and Evil Inside Our Heads Today:

Let's face it. All humans including you, everyone you know, me and all others on this planet have a spiritual war going on inside our heads…all the time. This war is a spiritual one. It is very serious and has vast implications for all life on earth. It will determine your destiny. Our minds or brain and resulting thoughts are located at the intersection of the spiritual realm and the physical realm. All this happens inside our cranial cavity.

In our very beginning within the spiritual realm we had no knowledge of evil and going against the will of God our creator. God gave us free will and now we still indeed have free will. Then, how did evil enter this world? How did they get into our heads? The root cause of all evil in this world is a direct result of what Lucifer did when he was an angel in heaven. Lucifer's name meant "morning star". He was created by God as ever so beautiful; his splendor and wisdom were magnificent. He also had free will, just like you and me and all other human beings. Lucifer looked at himself and fell deeply in love with himself because of his great beauty. He felt that he then deserved his throne to be higher than God Himself. He used his free will to attempt to usurp for himself all the glory and honor that belongs to God.

The evil side came into existence when Lucifer "bestowal of God's divine favor" created inequity within himself with the powers given by God. He became then Satan loving his beauty corrupting his wisdom with his brightness. He created sin by attempting to put himself above God in the Heavenly Kingdom. Then he was cast down to earth after Adam and Eve were already here. God loved Adam and Eve and all their children. This is how evil came to earth and entered into the minds of humans. This is why he tempted them; Satan is trying to destroy what God had created in His image. [4] Christians, you know the rest of the story of redemption.

For Satan, in hateful revenge against God, wants to destroy all that is made by God and in the image of God. That means you and me for we are made in God's image. This destruction, suffering, pain and agony is played out within our spiritual existence and in all our minds which control all our actions in this physical realm. The earth is part this. It is the war that goes on inside our heads every day of our lives.

This also plays out above the surface in the physical realm in the form of personal relationships, personal actions and of course politics and wars, especially politics. For it is in politics that control of millions of the lives of God's children are played out. Many of us Children of God will succumb to the temptations of Satan. He is that intelligent and cunning. Remember there is the road to hell but a stairway to Heaven. Enough said.

This is how evil entered our universe. Lucifer chose through his free will to fall in love with himself and put himself above all others in creation. Thus, he and all the angels that followed him were cast down to earth with Lucifer becoming known as Satan, the adversary who seeks to destroy God's creation including all beings made in God's image. This means you and me.

Because of Lucifer's fall and becoming Satan, our human fall occurred by gaining the knowledge of good and evil when ignorantly giving in to temptation from Satan. Thus, the war in our heads is the battle of good versus evil. It exists right now, today in everyone's head including yours. We were not always like this. But what our ancestors did so very long ago has affected ALL of their human decedents. The root cause of all evil is Satan, it is not money or the love for money so many people proclaim. The love for money is the consequence and result of giving into the temptations inside of all of us.

---

[4] http://www.angelfire.com/mi/dinosaurs/lucifer.html

A Great Problem for Our Founding Fathers:

This caused great problems for our founding fathers when they were designing our government in such a way that evil would not gain unchecked power over us, God's children in the United States of America. They had to deal with it. Our founding fathers had a monumental task. How do you design a government that compensates for human dishonesty, corruption and evil? Also, how do you compensate for the well-known tendency of humans to seek domination over others? How do you design a government in order to have the best chance of avoiding all the negative and evil aspects of human nature?

One type of person that is very attracted to political power is the sociopath or psychopath. These people are the ones that will run over you to get what they want. They do this through manipulation. Any source of power over others is irresistible to these people. [5]

Not surprisingly, our nation's capital, Washington D.C. is the worst by far for the number of psychopaths there. Our genius founding fathers knew this would happen. It's human nature and they designed a government to mitigate these destructive human forces.

This is what was laid before our founding fathers. To complicate matters more, there were 55 very intelligent men at the Constitutional Convention, each with different views on most all the issues that faced them. The answers they created were an inspiration from God on how they did it.

They could not have done this alone. This writer can only understand the beauty of their design of our government by realizing that they were inspired by Almighty God. It was the divine guidance of God that carried this group of 55 highly intelligent men through the extremely difficult process of creating a government that would ensure the freedom of God's children during their lives on earth. When you read our founding documents, it becomes obvious just how much importance they placed on securing individual freedoms, just as God has intended for all His children.

---

[5] https://www.politico.com/magazine/story/2018/06/23/washington-dc-the-psychopath-capital-of-america-218892

What Is the Root of Our Political Behavior?

Fundamental Human Psychology Differences Between Liberals and Conservatives

On top of the existence of the battle between good and evil, there is another layer of human character. It is the psychology of human beings. There are common characteristics with individual expressions of personality that must be dealt with.

The root of our political differences, that of the left verses right, that of leftist liberal versus conservative, is our psychological differences and the foundational beliefs that we have been exposed to. To understand where we are today in the political maelstrom that we find ourselves in we must first look at our psychology as human beings.

To understand ourselves and why we are split between leftist liberals and conservatives we have to look at our own human psychological development. It is this that controls the manner and ways in which we think. To do this I have gone back to my graduate school studies in spirituality and psychology to answer the question of why we are so different from each other. I can now shed light on this, and it makes sense.

Interestingly enough, the works of the famous psychologists cited in this section of the book are all very consistent with the Judeo-Christian morality and ethics that form formed the pillars of our great nation of today. These professors and their life long works are used extensively in graduate level studies in theology, philosophy and psychology in our universities and are used as the basis of advanced studies of human behavior.

Understanding the works of these men and women go a very long way in unlocking the apparent mysteries of human behaviors in our society today in the private and public arena. This includes the horrific dysfunctions currently going on in our current political system at the highest levels of our government both state and federal. This systematic dysfunction is now of an extent that it seriously threatens like never before the very existence of our constitutional republic and our individual freedoms. We as a nation have already lost most of our freedoms and are about to lose what remaining freedom we still have at the ignorant altar of "so called socialist fairness". This is very serious business.

You will find in this section that there are systemic psychological differences between people who tend toward the left in the political spectrum versus the right. Even in Biblical Scripture it talks about differences in right versus left in both the Old and New Testaments. There are common differences in psychological makeup between people in the two major parties.

Each individual person goes through the normal emotional growth process as they mature there are both opportunities and dangers along the way. Unfortunately, some people stop growing and maturing before others, many times stopping well short of where others may achieve. This fact represents much of the differences we see in the political spectrum.

General Psychological Background:

In Jesuit Graduate Theological Pastoral Ministry school at Santa Clara University in Santa Clara California, we studied a lot about human psychology. Human psychology and spirituality are sisters within human behavior.

Why are liberals so different from conservatives? The real reasons must go deeper into the psyche of a person's mind both conscious and subconscious. To explore these areas hoping to shed light on the "why" people think the way they do, we need to understand the works of the great psychologists in the last 100 years. Their knowledge they left behind for us includes not only psychology but also stages of religious faith which is quite close to stages in psychology actually. The works I will summarize here of what is left and is right are from James Fowler [6], Jean Piaget [7], Erik Erickson [8] and Carl Jung [9]. There are many books written recently based on the works of Jung. The one listed here is a good place to start.

Each of these leaders in the field of developmental psychology bring a different light, a different angle, to understanding how human beings develop across their lifetimes. They all agree that there are definite stages of growth. Each stage brings with it both an opportunity and a danger. It is also true that different people progress to different stages before they stop growing. A large portion of our population stops developing psychologically at the adolescent stage. They stay here for the rest of their lives.

---

[6] Stages of Faith, James Fowler, HarperSanFrancisco, 1981, ISBN 0-06-062840-5

[7] The Psychology of Intelligence, Jean Piaget, Armand Colin, Paris, 1947, ISBN 0-203-25898-3

[8] Childhood and Society, Erick Erickson, W.W. Norton & Company, 1964, IBSN 978-0-393-34738-8

[9] Psychological Types, Carl Jung, Princeton University Press, 1971, ISBN 0-691-01813-8

The General Human Stages of Psychological Growth:

Infant: (Basic Trust) What a trauma being born is.

As an infant you slowly come to realize that you are separate now, not part of mommy anymore. You no longer feel the oneness that was constant in your existence up until now. Suddenly, that delicious oneness is gone forever. What a wretched, miserable shock to your entire being. You get hungry, you get cold, alien beings handle you, they make strange noises with their mouths, you get gas, you poop, you get wet, you have cloth that rubs against your tender skin. All of this is really irritating. Where the hell is mommy's nipple when I need it? Cry and cry some more. What the hell is going on here? I want to climb back into the place I came from. This new place sucks. Speaking of sucking, where the hell is mommy's nipple? I am still hungry. Infants must learn to trust that their needs will be taken care of. But this does not happen all the time in reality.

If mistrust is allowed to grow in an infant's psyche, this mistrust can and will manifest in future behavior patterns even into adulthood. This pattern becomes ingrained into a human's nervous system and brain patterns of thinking.

Early Childhood (2-6): (Autonomy, shame and doubt) This stage can take a while. Here a small child develops for the first time an egocentric point of view or perspective. Now he or she develops the capacity to understand that they themselves are a "self" a legitimate self. They have a viewpoint that is separate from others. It is also during this time when children start to develop mine versus yours. The idea of sharing is not on the list yet.

During this time a child's sense of self-worth develops depending on how they are treated by their parents and other adults. A parent determines a child's sense of self-worth, positive or negative. Great damage can occur to a small child at the hands of parents and others during this age that will last a lifetime.

Childhood (7-12): (Industry vs inferiority and competence) In this stage of development a child begins to learn the tools and knowledge necessary to be a productive and useful member of society. To contribute with others, teamwork, to a common goal that benefits all citizens and be rewarded for that behavior. The danger here is not learning to do so and becoming inferior to other children who do learn to create with others.

Learning skills during this stage of development provides a virtuous cycle of feedback where the child is encouraged to learn more positive skills and use them for still more positive feedback. The danger here is failure in learning is the cessation of attempting to keep trying to learn as the negative feedback is painful to the child. This sets up the child for future failure in a vicious cycle of failure in the future.

Adolescence (13-21): (Identity versus role confusion) This is a very big one. This is where many people stop developing psychologically. To progress it means accepting responsibility and thinking about cause and effect and a far deeper way. This is hard and sometimes painful. Many people shy away from this. The rudiments of the scientific method start to appear in the thinking process of adolescents. Experiments bear this out. [10] Piaget calls this formal operational thought process. The ability to think about thinking is emerging, said differently, intellectual transcendence. This sets the stage for the ability to reflect on the course of one's own life from above or beside it as it flows along its current trajectory.

This emerging ability sets the stage for the classic teenage years of who am I, where am I going and experimenting with all sorts of identities that drive parents crazy.

Peer pressure raises its head during this time. Adolescents like to bunch into groups around a common cause whether they believe in it or not. My wife says she during her university years was a groupie demonstrator. She ran around holding signs that said things she did not completely understand, stuff like that. She grew up to be a professor of theology and taught Christian Biblical courses for many years in at the University of Santo Tomas in Manila Philippines.

The big challenge during this time in life is understanding one's own identity from a selection of so many different possible roles. Hence, role confusion ensues, or "who the hell am I"becomes the preeminent question. Where am I going and where do I want to go? What can I hang on to?

Also, idealism sprouts during this time. That with not enough education or life experience to have solid foundations upon which to legitimize or delegitimize their ideals with long-held foundational principles like Judeo-Christian. Many Leftist liberals fall into this category and stay there.

---

[10] Stages of Faith, James Fowler, pg. 70, Harper Collins, 1995, ISBN 0-06-062840-5

Young Adulthood (21-35): (Intimacy vs. isolation, law and order) This is the sixth stage of psychological human development. It basically features how integrated a person becomes within society and how much structure do they believe is necessary both in their personal lives and in the culture in general. This has vast political overtones to it as those who tend against structure end up more liberal while those who recognize the need for structure tend toward the conservative right side of the political spectrum.

We find these differences in such slogans like the one used by Barack Obama in 2008 "Hope and Change". Hope for what and change what is left completely left undefined, yet people bought into that. With young adults you have a mixture of idealism and lack of reality based life experience. They then don't know what they don't know. So, they think they know everything. This summarizes the leftist liberal mindset. If you stop developing psychologically here, individuation also stops developing. This is why we have 40 to 70 year old adolescents and young adults. Bernie Sanders, Kamala Harris, Alexandre Ocasio Cortez, Cory Booker and many other top democrat leaders come to mind. But remember it is not only Democrats, these people are all around us in our society. But these people are very much attracted to the shallow thinking of the Democrat party. Much of it is a groupie kind of thing.

Carl Gustav Jung spent a lot of time on the development of the individual through the different stages of life as did James Fowler. Jung called the process of development individuation. In general, it is the process by which individual beings are formed and differentiated; in particular, it is the development of the psychological individual as a being distinct from the general, collective psychology. [11] This is opposed to the group think of the Democrat party.

Thus, we naturally seek law and order as best as we can understand it. At this age before real adulthood however, hormones also override other factors of behavior such as common sense and morality. There becomes a "groupie" mentality" that can take hold especially in the college years that rallies around a cause that sounds good that may not have much common sense behind it. Lots of energy of youth but not much brains or life experience. I remember the anti-Viet Nam war movement, free love, hippies, flower power, do it if it feels good, hate the cops (pigs) anti-establishment, pot, and drugs.

People that tend to level out right here and end up working in a motorcycle shop the rest of their lives or some other dead end job. Nothing against that but humans have much more potential than that.

---

[11] https://www.mindstructures.com/carl-jung-individuation-process/

Adulthood (35-60): (Generativity vs. Stagnation, social contract, individual rights)

This is the seventh stage of development according to Erikson. [12] Here, a person generally is raising children and concentrates on their future. As a parent myself I discovered that you never really understand what you truly believe until you start teaching your children what you think they should believe.

Generative adults who contribute to the next generation and avoid becoming overly self-indulgent develop the virtue of "care". This virtue of care is highly related to the commandment of God to love others as you love yourself.

One thing also happens during this time, as your generativity and love for others increases, your tolerance for evil decreases. Your tolerance for sin and the evil people do feels more and more painful to you. I know this from personal experience. I find that watching the news on TV these days is like experiencing a bursting sewer pipe spilling its guts all over the place.

Maturity (60+): (Integrity vs. despair, wisdom, universal ethical principles)

The eighth and final stage takes place during old age. At this point, people start to look back on their lives. If they can accept and find meaning in what they have done and accomplished throughout their lives, they will achieve integrity. If people look back and don't like what they see, this will lead to despair, and opportunity missed.

Artificial human politically imposed systems that feature top down forced at the barrel of a gun regimes (socialism and communism) always end in horrific tragedies and personal despair where people are robbed of the ability to achieve integrity in their lives. To the common person it becomes an empty life with no color or joy to it, no fulfillment as God intended. This I believe is one of the primary reasons that Patrick Henry said, "Give me liberty or give me death".

It is this that these idiot socialists like Bernie Sanders, Constantina Ocasio Cortez, Elizabeth Warren, Gavin Newsom and Pamela Harris offer us. A dark dreary lifeless existence where our lives have been taken away from us in the name of "fairness", where we cannot even control anything in our own existence. Are we as a people so stupid or apathetic to let this monstrosity happen???

It is only those people who have taken care of things throughout their lives in the previous stages of their lives that are able to reap the fruits of what Erickson calls ego

---

12   https://www.amazon.com/Identity-Crisis-Austen-Center-Monograph/dp/0393311449/ref=sr_1_1?ie=UTF8&qid=1548916676&sr=8-1&keywords=identity+youth+and+crisis+erikson+1968

integrity. (Hint: Liberals never get this far.) This is basically reaping the investment of order and meeting in one's personal life.

The absence of Erickson's integrity and the danger in this stage of life is a terrible sense of despair. The lack of integrity is then marked by a sense of emptiness, a fear of death and a deep sense of waste that what was that all about? Finding meaning in one's life in old age results in the virtue of wisdom.

It is in this way we may contribute a priceless gift to the following generation and allow them to achieve higher and higher levels of psychological and spiritual growth in their lives that they may have otherwise achieved. But I tell you leftist liberals do not cherish the elderly. In articles I have read I have run across the term" useless eaters" referring to old people. Liberals spit at the face of God when they say things like this.

Shouldn't "We the People" Test Political Candidates First?

People take psychological tests all the time for a myriad of reasons. These tests proved insight into the workings of a person's mind, mentality, personality and other aspects of their persona. They are largely valid giving professionals' clues to how a person might perform in various settings. Now, I ask the question, since being a senator, a representative, a president, a councilman, or other politician, then why do we not administer psychological test to candidates for important offices? These positions directly affect the lives of millions of people. I feel nothing could be more important to "test the merchandise" to see what we are getting before we make the purchase.

The psychological makeup of potential leaders of millions of people is so very important that I for one feel it important that in some objective manner we test each serious candidate for high office to determine their level of emotional maturity before being considered for political power. This would NOT be a test for political philosophy, rather a test for stability, rationality, healthy sense of self, awareness of others and objective reality.

Frankly "We the People" owe it to ourselves. We do it for buying cars and getting the keys handed over. Why not do it also for politicians before we hand over our lives?

The Shadow and Psychological Projection:

Nobody likes to think that there is evil inside their heads but there is. It is a natural human tendency to shove evil thoughts into the background. Too many people are very unwilling to acknowledge that a destructive side of themselves even exists. They rather want to view themselves only as goodness and light. This gives evil a chance to flourish within their subconscious having been being put there by the person's unwillingness to acknowledge it.

These evil impulses that has been pushed into the background starts to be seen in other people as psychological projections of themselves. Then we tend to see that same evil in others that resided in us. It is a psychological projection of ourselves and we condemn other people when in fact what we are seeing is a reflection of who and what we really are. Carl Jung calls this our shadow projection.

This is a very common human behavior in our society, and I have observed this within this political spectrum especially during campaigns when charges and counter charges fly back and forth between various candidates of political parties. Examples of this abound.

1. The demonization of Trump with no evidence after two years of intense investigation so it looks like the demons are Robert Mueller and the democratic party

2. The demonization of Putin being buddies with Trump with no evidence found so looks like the demons are in the democratic party

3. Qadhafi has weapons of mass destruction so said George Bush with no evidence ever found to start a war. He was supposed to be evil but looks like the evil was in Washington with president Bush instead.

4. Trump is a racist Islamophobe homophobe misogynist xenophobe anti-Immigrant insensitive unfeeling science-denier, all the very things liberals have created and trained their many divergent Social Justice Warriors to actually be.

5. Bill Clinton stared the at the entire nation and into our eyes and forcefully declared "I did not have sex with that woman", then his seamen stains popped up on her blue dress. He projected evil on Monica Lewinski ruining her life, but it was him that was completely evil even when Hillary declared that Bill never lied to her. Lots of evil projection going on in full public or should I say pubic view here.

6. Trump hates immigrants. This is a democrat psychological projection when in fact it is the democrats that hate the current voting system that is keeping them out of power. So, they wish to change the demographics by importing as many people as possible that will probably vote for them putting them into power

regardless of their sworn duty to uphold the constitution and protect the American constitution and its boarders from invasion.

There are many more examples but five will due to illustrate the point of psychological projection. Here are some references you can use for further research if you choose. [13] [14] [15]

[13] https://www.catholicamericanthinker.com/Political-Projection.html

[14] https://medium.com/@vinceperritano/projection-in-individuals-and-politics-68c14bd60c72

[15] http://www.libertariansolution.com/advocates/171/psychological-projection-in-politics

Richard Ferguson

Ultimate Morality

The Two Great Commandments in Christianity: Mark 12:(28-31)

The first great commandment. We are to love God above all else with all our hearts, our minds and our souls. Put God first. Simple.
The second great commandment. We are to love all others of Gods children as we love ourselves. In other words, we are all equal regardless of gender, race or all the other differences we may have. Also, simple. Both commandments are also elegant.
All laws must necessarily follow from the above two commandments.

Anything that confuses, detracts from, produces complexity or chaos surrounding the above two Great Commandments can be considered to be evil. This is Biblical. Thoughts about this have been written by many writers over a very long period of time 2,000 years ago and before that and since then till right now.

Our Government Goes Against God's Two Great Commandments:

In our society today there is a monstrous complexity and confusion. The government has inserted itself between all children of God. When Barack Obama was president there was a full 97,000 pages of rules and regulations in the federal government register that are to be obeyed by us all. This does not even include state government. Think of all taxes paid, licenses demanded, permissions to seek to live your life. That amounts to a definition of evil complexity.

Thanks to Pres. Donald Trump this monster load upon God's children in the United States of America has been reduced to 67,000 pages in the Federal Register. He did this within the last two years. This accomplishment is magnificent and has lit fires of our economy, created jobs, made production more efficient, and is taken the monster burden off the backs of us the American citizen. President Trump is acting according to the two great commandments.

Yet nobody in the media will ever tell you this. Why? Because the top management in media companies are leftist liberals who frankly hate Donald Trump. Who is the author of hate? You will never hear anything good from our mainstream media about Donald Trump. It is these people too that need to be removed from their office for the betterment of the American people.

Our government has put itself above God's children in this country, the average American citizen. Our government has become horribly immoral in so many different ways. Of this there is no doubt. Remember that all of us are made in the image of God. When our government in the United States has put itself above us to control us it also tries to put its throne above Almighty God. This cannot and will not stand.

Our government has committed the identical sin that Lucifer committed so long ago when he was still an angel in heaven. Lucifer's fall becoming Satan is the same thing that will happen to our government. It cannot stand the way it currently is. It will fall. I only hope and pray that none of God's children will be hurt in that process.

These two great commandments really are the ultimate morality for God's children while we are here on planet Earth. Our government has willfully and purposely chosen to violate these two great commandments and in doing so has produced ever so much pain, suffering and death in our country. Just look at all the killings of developing fetal human beings under the guise of women's reproductive rights or women's reproductive health. This is monstrously evil no matter how you look at it. And there is ever so much more on top of this.

When the Hebrews in the Old Testament broke their covenants with God really bad things happened to them. Why should we be any different?

Richard Ferguson

The Fundamental Psychology of People on the Left

A Careful Analysis of People on the Left:

It became interesting to me to think that democrats of 40 years ago acted and behaved just like the ones we have today. Today we have democrats fighting tooth and nail to keep our southern border open in spite of mountains of data that says this situation is killing many thousands of American citizens each year. This is because of a flood of dangerous drugs, MS-13 gang members, illegal aliens here committing horrendous crimes against citizens and other awful statistics readily available to anyone that is interested. Why would supposedly sane rational human beings be against protecting our own citizens? What kind of mind does it take to purposely want to put American citizens in the way of killers and drug death? Democrats must know that people will die directly because of their policy. WHY?

I started my search to find out. I went back to my graduate studies in Spirituality and psychology. I found my answers there. It will open your eyes. It did mine and explained so many things we see today from Democrats.

The Answer:

People who tend toward the left of the political spectrum are indeed psychologically different than those on the right side. Psychological studies have borne this out. In my search for objective truth I have no axe to grind regarding this but only to understand what is and what is not. I have always wondered what drives a Democrat versus what drives a Republican. So, I conducted an evenhanded objective analysis in as scientific manner as I could the five renowned psychologists mentioned earlier along with more modern commentary from other psychologists.

There are 11 major characteristics of adolescents. Most of them have to do with changes in biology. I will skip those. It is the mental and emotional components of lingering adolescence that we must be concerned about in our leftist liberal democrats. Remember that adolescence is quite age independent. Most adolescents mature into adults. However, many do not. We see this behavior from them over and over again in what they say and what they do. To me, Bernie Sanders is an adolescent. He does exhibit much of the 11 traits shown below. Constantina Ocasio Cortex is the poster child adolescent. Do we want a bunch of adolescents having the nuclear codes?

"Adolescent behavior has been studied from very early times. Plato characterized the adolescents to be argumentative and easily excitable while Aristotle described them as

impulsive, prone to excess and exaggeration and lacking self-restraint. The period of adolescence in the life of an individual is characterized as problematic and has been studied for a long time."[16]

Adolescents are characterized by:

1. Anxiety

2. Mood swings

3. Confusion/Indecision

4. Lethargy

5. Argumentation

6. Anger/Irritability

7. Experimentation

8. Problems with personal identity

9. Self centeredness

10. Strong emotions

11. Volatile self image

12. Insufficient knowledge how the world works

13. Inability to reason issues through

14. Thinking they know more than they really do

I remember growing up being aware of the two political parties. One was for "big corporations" and the other was for "labor unions" against the selfish, dirty rats in "management". Democrats were always for unions, going on strike, pay increases, better working conditions and that list goes on and on. Republicans always seemed to be for stuff like profits, investments, the stock market. It was "white collar" versus "blue collar". Yet during the time of people like Everett Dirksen the Democrats and Republicans sat down and compromised their differences and passed legislation for the good of the American people. Even growing up I was aware of this. No compromises anymore. So sad.

---

[16]   http://www.preservearticles.com/2011111517256/list-the-characteristic-features-of-adolescent-behaviour.html

All of this was happening during a time of great competition between Communism and Capitalism. Nikita Khrushchev of Russia famously took off his shoe at the UN and kept yelling that the USSR was going to bury the United States. A huge nuclear weapons race was on going along with the race to the moon to win the prize of claiming whose economic system was better.

Then President Ronal Reagan decided on a master stroke to beat the USSR in the arms race. He announced a vast new space based weapons system for the defense and offense of the United States. This meant spending a monster amount of money. In doing this, he forced the USSR to spend money it did not have thus bankrupting them and subsequently the USSR fell apart and became no longer a threat to the United States.

This was a divine master stroke of genius because Reagan won the cold war for us without firing a shot or worse yet, ICBM's loaded with nuclear weapons. Of course, Reagan was called a complete fool by all democrats. They called it the Star Wars fiasco. They actually challenged his sanity and the attacks against him were vicious and constant. It was very much like what the democrats are doing to President Trump today. Over the years, the behavior of the democratic party seemingly has not changed. Why? Was not all these proposals intended to protect ALL Americans? Was not this the prime responsibility of all presidents? Why would a political party be so vehemently against self-defense, from a country that promised to "bury us"? This made no sense and gave aid and comfort to our avowed enemy, the Russians. Treason?

Democrats of 40 years ago acted and behaved just like the ones we have today. Today we have democrats fighting tooth and nail to keep our southern border open in spite of mountains of data that says this is killing many thousands of American citizens each year. The drugs coming in from the south alone kill between 30,000 to 50,000 Americans each year and This is because of a flood of dangerous drugs, MS-13 gang members, illegal aliens here committing horrendous crimes against citizens and other awful statistics readily available to anyone that is interested. Why would supposedly sane rational human beings be against protecting our own citizens? This is complete insanity to allow the killing of American citizens.

Something is terribly wrong, systematically defective and dangerous to the health and wellbeing of the United States of America. Plato and Aristotle both observed the same problem with adolescents. What could this explosive problem be? Could it be genetic or psychological or learned behavior?

Leftists are Mentioned in the Bible:

It turns out that this kind of thinking is not new. It existed in Biblical times as well. Even though I have a Masters Degree in Theology, and Pastoral Ministry I was not familiar with the following verses:

It is fascinating. As it turns out even back into biblical times differences were noted in the way in which people thought of things and conducted themselves. Back then, they did not have the understandings of psychology and philosophy that we do today, but they certainly understood the outward characteristics of human nature.

With this in mind there are a number of biblical quotes and facts that compare the left versus the right of things. This is very serious business. Pray for them.

First, please remember that Jesus Christ sits at the Right Hand of The Father in Heaven, God and Creator of all that is seen and unseen. Yes, he sits on the right hand. This is foundational to all Christian theology. There are things that have happened in my personal life that lead me directly to know this is true, yes true. That has been partly documented in my previous book, "The Divine Resting on My Shoulder". This is a theme of the right goes throughout the entire bible. It is the "right" that is good and the left that is bad. For example, in the Gospel of Matthew (25:33-36) NIV Jesus Christ says:

33 He will put the sheep on his right and the goats on his left. 34 "Then the King will say to those on his right, 'Come, you who are blessed by my Father; take your inheritance, the kingdom prepared for you since the creation of the world. 35 For I was hungry and you gave me something to eat, I was thirsty and you gave me something to drink, I was a stranger and you invited me in, 36 I needed clothes and you clothed me, I was sick and you looked after me, I was in prison and you came to visit me.'

I cannot begin to express how monumental this is for it affects everyone's eternal destiny. This is part of objective reality, part of the unseen creation that exists whether we want it to or not. We can choose to ignore it. We can choose to disagree. But I ask on what foundation, on what basis do you have to ignore, to disagree with what is biblically and objectively real?

In the Gospel of John (21:6), He said, "Throw your net on the right side of the boat and you will find some." When they did, they were unable to haul the net in because of the large number of fish. Here again the bible shows that it is fruitful to be on the right side of things. Remember that Jesus used allegories and parables to teach people. The right side of things has eternal meaning is the message.

There is another biblical verse in the book of Ecclesiastes 10:2. The heart of the wise inclines to the right, but the heart of the fool to the left. Thus, saith the Lord. Amen NIV this again is completely consistent with the previous thoughts are right versus left. I cannot add anything else to what has already been said.

The Adolescent Psychological Aspects of The Left are Determinative:

The psychology of human behavior is mostly controlled by their psychological makeup. This does also include spirituality as these two disciplines are separate but joined at the hip. As I stated earlier regarding the works of Piaget and Jung, every human goes through multiple stages of psychological and spiritual growth. Each stage has an opportunity and a danger to it. Most people do not make it to ultimate maturity but stop growing somewhere short of that.

As stated earlier a lot of people for many personal reasons have elected to opt out of further emotional and spiritual growth because it involves taking on more responsibility in becoming more serious about life in general. Growing up is not fun. It in fact is very hard. It involves pain, fortitude and determination. So, somewhere along the line, very many people decide they like it better not to become full adults or reach their full potential as mature adults or reach full maturity either.

There are consistent behavioral markers for adolescents' in that stage of human development that can be observed. It is predictable but does vary from individual to individual to a certain extent. Nonetheless the following traits are indeed observable. Being adults in age with adolescent mindsets does not stop them from engaging in adult activities such as politics and say very misguided hurtful things in the process. We will see that there is a direct connection between the liberal political belief system and the adolescent mindset.

The Liberal Adolescent Mindset Connection:

Through observation of a liberal's behavior in the political realm I see that they are consistent with what James W Fowler describes as adolescent behavior. We need to note that James Fowler was a preeminent psychologist along with Sigmund Freud, Carl Gustav Young, Eric Erickson and Jean Piaget, all of whom are quoted in this book regarding the behavioral analysis of liberals and their mindset. So, this analysis stands on a rock solid foundation in its assertions about the things that liberal politicians say in public. In his book Stages of Faith, Fowler describes the following:

The adolescent... Able imaginatively to transcend empirical experience, formal thinking can construct ideal states or regulative norms. In social terms, formal operational thinking can be utopian. With its ability to extrapolate or imagine perfection, the adolescent mind can be quite harsh in judging... Now able to conceive of the possibility of the infinity of perspectives on a problem, the adolescent shows both a marked improvement and taking on the perspective of others and a tendency to overconfident distortion of other's perspectives through over simulation of them into his or her own. [17]

"*I have on a multitude of occasions watched the Progressives undergo an abrupt personality change in reaction to something – anything – which violates the precepts their fanatic religion holds at the moment. The term in psychology is Dissociative Identity Disorder. It enables them to hold polar opposite beliefs simultaneously as exemplified by the "Believe the Accuser"maxim as long as the accusation is not against one of their own ikons, in which case the mantra is "Demonize the Accuser."*

Francisco Machado October 25, 2018 at 9:10 pm Fox News

The Fairy Tale Adolescent:

Let's parse the thoughts above. Adolescents are *"Able imaginatively to transcend empirical experience".*

Other psychologists prefer to call it, Flights of Imagination, "rising high above the limitations of realities"[18]

This means they can replace reality with fantasy at will. WOW! In a sense, this is one form of insanity people. If they cannot tell the difference between reality and fantasy as us parents wonder about as our kids go through this stage of development, just how dangerous would it be if we set our kids loose running our country with the nuclear power of the government over our lives. Simply put, this means adolescents are able to ignore reality and make decisions based on their preferred fantasy.

"Able imaginatively to transcend empirical experience"[19] *James Fowler*
Women have always been the primary victims of war. Women lose their husbands, their fathers, their sons in combat. Hillary Clinton

This shows Hillary Clinton's adolescent fantasy. Gee, what about the men Hillary? Hillary loses all connection with reality and completely ignores the horrific deaths men suffer and catastrophic wounds the suffer both physically and mentally. She acts as if they just do not exist at all. My God, and she wanted to be commander in chief.

---

[17] Stages of Faith, James W Fowler, pg71, HarperSanFrancisco, 1995, ISBN 0-06-062840-0

[18] http://www.psychologydiscussion.net/child-development/11-major-characteristics-of-adolescence-child-development/1111

[19] Stages of Faith, James W Fowler, pg71, HarperSanFrancisco, 1995, ISBN 0-06-062840-0

Every month that we do not have an economic recovery package 500 million Americans lose their jobs. [20] Nancy Pelosi

Another fantasy from an adolescent. In Nancy's case she has achieved adolescent grand motherhood. Well, in a little over one year the whole world will be unemployed according to her calculations. You just cannot make this stuff up. But then again, they are not all Americans, does she know that?

It takes a village to raise a child. Hillary Clinton

BS, it takes two good parents, besides, God knows who is in the village. Creepy uncle Joe Biden might be there, or Hillary's husband or Harvey Weiner etc. Did you see the video tape of Biden wrapping his arms around a senator's wife on stage during a speech and putting his lips next to hers right in front of everybody? Only leeches do that. Eeech! I did see that and was disgusted.

Corporations and businesses [don't] create jobs. Hillary Clinton.

Adolescents do not know what they don't know. In this case the ignorance is of economics. Spoken like a true socialist bureaucrat Again, she completely has no understanding of how economics work. Has not a scintilla of understanding of where and how jobs are created and yet she wants to lead the largest economy in the world. God help us. If business does not create jobs Hillary, then who does? This again is pure adolescent behavior on display, a complete departure from reality transcending empirical experience as James Fowler explained a long time ago.

During my service in the United States Congress, I took the initiative in creating the Internet. [21] Al Gore

Al Gore has a number of fantasies. He invented the internet and global warming flooded New York in 1988. No Al, the first workable prototype of the Internet was

---

[20] https://townhall.com/columnists/johnhawkins/2013/08/17/the-25-stupidest-liberal-quotes-of-the-last-decade-n1666619

[21] https://townhall.com/columnists/johnhawkins/2013/08/17/the-25-stupidest-liberal-quotes-of-the-last-decade-n1666619

ARPANET in the 1960s funded by the department of defense. Al did not enter politics until 1977 as a representative from Tennessee. Let us also not forget that Al predicted on December 13, 2008 that the North Pole would have no ice by 2013. When confronted by a question her about this failure, Al responded, "Well, we gotta keep working." [22] And this adolescent in fantasyland was the vice president of the United States to Bill Clinton chief skirt chaser in command with the nuclear codes.

The conventional viewpoint says we need a jobs program and we need to cut welfare. Just the opposite! We need more welfare and fewer jobs. Jerry Brown

Another ignorance laden fantasy from Jerry Moonbeam Brown. And where does the money come from Jerry? This is more of the same departure from reality. A long time ago Jerry Brown was called Jerry Moonbeam Brown because frankly people thought he was crazy. He still is. He was an adolescent, is an adolescent and will always be an adolescent. Yet there are enough adolescents and ignorance in California to get people like him elected and many thousands of people are leaving California as a result. And now Gavin, "not afraid to make glorious mistakes" Newsom is our new governor.

Unemployment benefits are creating jobs faster than practically any other program. Nancy Pelosi

This is a complete departure from reality and economics. So, sitting on your ass watching TV generates jobs. She was not an economic major. This does not even rise to adolescence.

You cannot cut your way to deficit reduction. Nancy Pelosi

Oh, Dear God, please help this deluded woman of yours…please! Again, this is kindergarten.

I have so many more of these quotes that it is frankly sickening, and I am getting depressed writing this part of the book. I have to go get some Tums or Pepto-Bismol right now.

---

[22]   http://www.climatedepot.com/2017/01/22/inconvenient-question-gore-asked-about-failed-10-year-tipping-point-refuses-to-answer-enters-suv-in-snow/

All of the above quotes are from people who are truly living in a fantasy world divorced from reality. This is systemic to the adolescent stage of human growth. Although these people look like adults, THEY ARE NOT. What they say, their behavior and what they do betrays their true mental condition. They are indeed adolescents. Given political power they are then in a position to bring suffering pain and death to millions of people by what Democratic governor Gavin Newsom calls "Making glorious mistakes and the willingness to do so". Are these the kind of people you want to be pulling the levers and pushing the buttons of power in our country?

"I remember landing under sniper fire. There was supposed to be some kind of a greeting ceremony at the airport, but instead we just ran with our heads down to get into the vehicles to get to our base." [23]— Hillary Clinton

More fantasy from Hillary Clinton. She made up this fantasy story about her trip to Bosnia. I saw the real video of her arrival. It was completely normal. Pure adolescent behavior coming from a very old person. Yes, that is very possible. It is the Peter Pan syndrome.

We will continue on now to other aspects that prove this point even more, sadly so.

Adolescent Behavior in Debates:

I have noticed in watching many debates in news programs a highly repetitive behavioral pattern with regards to the person representing liberal leftist Democrats. A particular issue or question is put forth to both sides of the debate. On the conservative side I have noticed that the person representing conservatism always tends to focus on the issues at hand and discusses why their particular point of view is the best and is consistent with the way in which our country was founded.

On the other hand, the Democrat representative almost uniformly attacks the character and motivations of the person representing conservative values. I have seen time and time again the host of the program or moderator attempt multiple times to get the leftist liberal representative to address the issue directly and get clear answers, mostly to no avail. This is totally consistent with adolescent behavior.

"Believe the Accuser" maxim as long as the accusation is not against one of their own ikons, in which case the mantra is "Demonize the Accuser." [24]

---

[23] https://townhall.com/columnists/johnhawkins/2015/06/16/draft-n2012995

[24] Francisco Machado October 25, 2018 at 9:10 pm Fox News

Francisco Machado October 25, 2018 at 9:10 pm

Just last evening I was watching Laura Ingraham. The discussion point was about how Candace Owens was unfairly treated during her testimony in front of the judiciary subcommittee. The head of the committee, Democrat Nadler, accused her falsely of calling Democrat representative Ted Lieu stupid. She clearly did not and objected to Nadler. In the interview by Laura Ingraham, Candace Owens restated what she had said in front of the judiciary committee. The Democrat representative in his response then went on to attack her credibility, her personality and her motivations while never once addressing the point of the whole conversation. He only attacked her personally.

This is ever so common behavior that is completely consistent with an adolescent stage of psychological development. Adolescents are well known to be argumentative and have a lack of ability to recognize a different point of view. Adolescents have not yet achieved an adult perspective with the ability to comprehend that there are legitimate differences of opinion between different people. Adolescents get quickly frustrated and do the only thing they know how which is to attack the other person while not addressing the issue at hand.

The video of this exchange is in the footnote. [25]

Adolescents Slip into Utopian Thinking:

"In social terms, formal operational thinking can be utopian." [26] James Fowler

This means they can rearrange social arrangements and imagine that everything will be absolutely great with no thought whatsoever to the reality of human nature or any downside at all. *"the ability to extrapolate or imagine perfection, the adolescent mind…"*

Other psychologists put it in a different way. They use other terms, but the thought is the same. Flights of Imagination, "rising high above the limitations of realities"[27]

This is what the adolescent mind does. Years ago, my 21 year old son dated a 24 year old woman with 4 kids and insisted that everything would work out just fine. Right! I could not stop him. He had his dream, and nothing could convince him otherwise. His head was firmly planted in the clouds or his ass depending on your point of view. Common sense flew out the window. I could not convince him it would be a disaster. It turned out that I now have two illegitimate grandchildren and he pays horrific child

---

[25] https://www.youtube.com/watch?v=DGVdD_QxuEc

[26] Stages of Faith, James W Fowler, pg71, HarperSanFrancisco, 1995, ISBN 0-06-062840-0

[27] http://www.psychologydiscussion.net/child-development/11-major-characteristics-of-adolescence-child-development/1111

support. Reality is a bitch. He lived in his utopian dream and reality delivered him a cursed blow that he still lives with.

The problem with adolescent politicians no matter what their numerical age is that it is"We the People"that have to live with the wreckage they cause long after they are gone. And remember all of them are far wealthier than we are so they are sheltered from the disasters they cause for the rest of us wage slaves. Their utopian dreams become our real life nightmares. We have to pay for.

"My dream is a hemispheric common market, with open trade and open borders." Hillary Clinton

Yet another fantasy. Now isn't she so forward and farsighted? I bet all the ignorant people get goosebumps hearing this. This is the single best way to export jobs out of the United States I can think of and make our nation just like Mexico and Honduras. Anyone who took Econ 101 knows this. There are many different cultures involved here and many different local economic systems involved as well in many different ways of doing business. Yet she ignores all of this reality. She ignores all of this completely as any fantasy minded adolescent would.

The poorest of the poor would flock to the richest of the rich which is the United States and Canada. Tent cities would spring up all over the United States. Crime would go to horrific levels in the United States and we would become just another Third World country. This would be the reality of her socialist dream. Hillary is completely unable like all adolescents to think and see past the end of her nose. This fantasy will not affect her personally because she is a zillionaire with all the money she made as Secretary of State during the Obama administration, especially with the $145 million payoff from Russia for selling them 20% of our country's uranium reserves. It is people like you and I that will live the nightmare of Hillary's socialist dream. Again, Hillary is a 70 year old adolescent that just does not know any better, apple cheeks and all.

"Anything is possible". (Only if you are God) Alexandria piano teeth Ocasio Cortez

When we talk about the word 'socialism,' I think what it really means is just democratic participation in our economic dignity and our economic, social, and racial dignity. Alexandria Ocasio Cortez [28]

---

[28] https://www.brainyquote.com/topics/democratic

So, socialism is *"democratic participation"*. We have that already Ms. Cortez. It is called voting and purchasing goods and services in and open and free market.

Socialism is *"Economic dignity"*. Adolescents like to invent words with no meaning to sound intelligent. This does sound utopian though. High and mighty for sure. If you were to ask her the definition of "economic dignity"she would dance around that like a sombrero with more meaningless words and smile a lot with her piano teeth.

Socialism is *"our social, and racial dignity"*Well, who gets upset about social and racial dignity? But this is a complete fantasy. Socialism is an economic system at its heart with no dignity for anyone. Here Ms. Cortez shows complete ignorance about socialism. She certainly does not let mere facts stop her from stringing meaningless words together that sound good to her.

The Utopian Socialist San Francisco Example:

These adolescent leftist Democratic childlike politicians live in the mental equivalent of the San Francisco Haight-Ashbury district of 1967. It was called "The Summer of Love". Everything is lovely. Everything is possible. In fact, this last sentence is a quote from Alexandria Ocasio Cortez in February 2019. There was dancing in the streets. Flower power was bountiful, singing could be heard everywhere the sweet smell of marijuana wafted in the air, free love could be had at the wink of an eye. If it felt good go ahead and do it. People were young, there were orgies every night with no admission charged, if you were friends with anybody come on in. It was the age of the hippies. VW buses were everywhere with paintings on their sides. The Mommas and Pappas were so popular. Drug songs abounded. The world was carefree. Vietnam what?

Please understand that this is exactly what the Democrats are trying to sell to you right now. It is nothing new. It is the same old pie in the sky bull that has existed since mankind discovered that he did not want to grow up. Growing up is a pain in the butt. It is hard. It sucks frankly. Let's go have a beer instead.

But regarding the summer of 1967 and love, everything has a price. The party stopped somewhere in 1968. All the money was spent. People started to scrounge for every scrap they could find. They did not know how to work. They had no skills. They started to steal from each other. Sex was no longer free, girls started charging. They had to eat. It's called prostitution folks. Ugly arrived. The marijuana caused addiction to harder drugs like heroin. People started shooting up. Crime also shot up. Trash lined the streets of this once free love paradise. And everything went to hell in a hand basket. Free love turned into"buddy can you spare a dime?"

And so, ended the false promise of free everything. Just like what the idiot radical leftist socialist adolescent Democrats are promising to our entire nation. You have to be a blithering idiot and complete fool to vote for these people to take the nation down the sewer of San Francisco 1968 because that is precisely where we will go. Venezuela is already there if you care to look. San Francisco has yet to recover people. Due to idiot democratic policies, that stinking city spends $60 million per year to clean feces and drug paraphernalia off the streets. Thank you, Gavin Newsom who was the mayor of San Francisco and is now our shiny new governor of California, who says he is "not afraid to make glorious mistakes". I can hardly wait.

Medicare for All and The Green New Deal:

Both these ideas are completely utopian fantasies. They have no connection with reality. If implemented either one will completely destroy family finances in this country. No joke. It is real. When put together it will cost $338,000 per taxpayer over the next 10 years. Again, that is per person. For a family of four that will be $1.4 million. This analysis is provided to us by Newsmax. [29] They are a levelheaded news organization that I have observed over the years. Alexandria Ocasio Cortez and her supporters will completely destroy the United States of America and put us all into slavery if they even come close to enacting their plans. For even coming close it will require a horrific number of rifles being pointed at American citizens. For that is the only way things like this have happened in world history.

The Green New Deal is a bomb that will destroy the entire United States as we know it. Russia and China and Iran will fall over in pure delight to watch this happen. The only threat to them will be the loud sounds of our implosion reaching their capitols. Alexandria Ocasio Cortez the wide eyed piano toothed fantasyland liberal democrat has this as her dream like Hillary had NAFTA as hers. Here are a few fun facts about dreamy Cortez's plan for all of us. Calls for getting rid of all aircraft in 10 years. Calls for getting rid of cows because they fart too much, no kidding people. Calls for every building in the United States to be retrofitted "to achieve maximum efficiency" etc. Calls for zero carbon emissions in 10 years. Calls for no gas powered cars in 10 years. Calls for paying a living wage to those who are "unwilling to work". Yes, you read that correctly. Where do I sign up?

This woman has serious congestion of the corpus collosum, with one complete brain hemisphere completely missing. This is way beyond psychology, this gets into physical brain malfunction. Just how many brain cells don't work at all or are misfiring? It must look like a scatter gram inside her skull.

---

[29]   https://www.newsmax.com/platinum/climate-change-green-deal-donald-trump-ocasio-cortez/2019/02/19/id/903397/?gdpr_consent=&gdpr=false

Adolescence is characterized by making risky decisions...See above about that. This suggests that decision-making in adolescence may be particularly modulated by emotion and social factors, for example, when adolescents are with peers or in other affective ('hot') contexts.

Excerpt from: https://www.nature.com/articles/nn.3177

"Be willing to make bold decisions and be willing to make glorious mistakes. Learn from your mistakes, but you've got to be willing to make them first." Gavin Newsom

This is pure adolescence in action made to sound great by a professional politician.

When I was in Arroyo high school in San Lorenzo California, I had a friend who was known to be a little wild. He had a motorcycle. He was killed on that motorcycle in the hills above Hayward. He never made it into the senior yearbook. He made a glorious mistake and killed himself. Adolescent risk-taking was obviously the cause. Gavin wants to do the same kinds of things with the entire state of California affecting the lives of all Californians.

"...able to conceive of the possibility of the infinity of perspectives on a problem, the adolescent shows both a marked improvement taking on the perspectives of others and a tendency to be overconfident distortion of other's perspectives through over simulation..."

In other words take a socialist idea, amplify it and be extra confident about it while distorting it in a manner that they like better. This is particularly irresponsible and dangerous.

What this simply means is that the adolescent has an overactive imagination and has a very loose relationship with reality and is not bound by any kind of logic or realistic thinking or logical thinking for that matter. They are not yet able to discern the difference between fantasy and realism to the necessary degree in their thinking process. This is one foundation why kids this age constantly makes bad choices that end up creating damage in so many ways both to themselves and others.

Put into a position of political power this is highly destructive and has the potential of destroying entire societies. This is nothing short of a hydrogen bomb that will bring horrific pain, suffering and death through a lens of utopian insanity. This is the psychological condition of the Democratic Party as we observe it today and 2019. There are so many examples of this today that I would need another book to address this point alone. This is the majority of the democrats led by adults that are adults with demonic character inside their inner being. More on this point later.

We have a bunch of adolescents dressed up as democratic adults where their minds are something less than 20 years old. This is horrifically sad, but it is true as near as I can tell with all the education and life experience I have brought to bear on this topic. You will do well to listen and act accordingly. If you understand these few paragraphs, it will explain ever so much regarding the things they say and their behavior.

This will explain why they name call so much. The adolescent mind does not know how to deal with logical opposition to their political positions. So, their circuits overload and they instantly resort to verbal or physical violence while grouping together like high school clubs do. Adolescents always band together behind a common cause it is part of their mindset. And the cause is usually simple in nature things like "free the nipple", "my body my rights", "I hate Trump", "Save the Climate", and so on. There is never more than three maybe four words. Complexity is not their strong point.

As adolescents, they are typically ignorant because when asked questions they usually have no factual answers. This has been demonstrated again and again when interviewers go to the streets with a camera and a microphone. They giggle a lot when this happens. How sad. They will be teaching our children soon.

But now you understand the foundational psychological basis for ever so much that underlies and generates the Democratic Party's behavior and its ideas like the Green New Deal. That is a fantasy that will completely destroy the United States of America and the lives of every man woman and child that lives here under the control of the lunatic adolescents that want to assume power over us.

As an aside, the higher up democrats know all this. Why do you think they are against the southern wall? It is because they desperately need more ignorant people in this country that will fall for their brand of utopian fantasy and vote for them. They care NOT about America. These adolescent reptilian democrats would rather have power over an infested dung heap than participate in a sparkling culture and society. Power and money are their goal, nothing else. Lies, misrepresentations, and all the other demonic and Satanic tools of the trade are what they freely use to get what they want.

Our weapon is truth and logic. It all is just that simple.

According to psychologist Carl Gustav Jung, all of us really do resist growing up. We don't like the idea of going from childhood to adolescence to adulthood to maturity. There is just no fun in that. Dr. Jung says:

"Something in us wishes to remain a child, to be unconscious or, at most, conscious only of the ego; to reject everything strange, or else subject it to our will; to do nothing, or else indulge our own craving for pleasure or power." [30]

A lot of us succeed in not growing up to the full extent that we could have. Growing up means taking on responsibility that is frankly quite scary. Motorcycle clubs are filled with these kinds of people. They remain children of God with broken potential.

But as the leftists languish in their stupor of meaningless slogans and hate filled animus toward their fictious enemy they are doing real damage to both themselves and the country they live in. They are being used by those higher up in the Democratic Party who in turn are filled with demonic desire of power and domination over the citizens of the United States of America.

This is precisely what Satan has always wanted since the beginning of creation. While Jesus Christ was on this earth Satan even tempted Him with all the principalities Jesus could rule over if only Jesus would bow down to Satan himself. Obviously, he refused even in His weakened physical state. But now Satan continues on working through the Democratic Party who works tirelessly to reach dominion over the last powerful standing Christian nation in the world, the United States of America. He will fail.

On the brighter side, we all need to be thankful for Christianity. Liberals hate Christians for many reasons. The sum of it though is that everything they want to burden society with violates Christian principles. So, Hillary Clinton took the following position:

"I have to confess that it's crossed my mind that you could not be a Republican and a Christian."

First notice her use of Christian words, "cross" and "confess". Nice touch, but very evil in its intent. You do know that Satan knows Jesus, don't you? This is pure demonic evil at work. She aimed this satanic remark at the ignorant among us to purposely form horrifically wrong ideas in their minds and sway their votes to give her more power in hopes of dominion over all of us. That is the same thing that Satan has craved for ever since the beginning of time. It is really that simple my dearest people, children of God. Hillary Clinton thinks, how could you be a Christian and lower yourself to not be a democrat? Just how sinful are you anyway? You miserable deplorable heathen are going to hell if you do not vote democrat! So says Satan's handmaiden.

---

[30] The Structures & Dynamics of the Psyche, University Press, 1970, ISBN 0-691-09774-7

Other Psychological Characteristics of an Adolescent: [31]

Self Absorption or egocentrism and confusion with their feelings about their feelings themselves with what they think of others. They construct a personal fable about themselves as very important for the eyes of others. Think of Elizabeth Warren being a native Indian and Hillary Clinton being under sniper fire. Also, there is hero worship like in how Democrats idolized Barack Obama

It is all Not Pure Adolescence but Domination Thrown in Too

"The money has to go to the federal government because the federal government will spend that money better than the private sector will spend it."

"We must stop thinking of the individual and start thinking about what is best for society."

"We are going to take things away from you on behalf of the common good."

"The only way to make a difference is to acquire power."

"Corporations and Businesses Don't Create Jobs"

"My husband may have his faults, but he has never lied to me."

Hillary Clinton

"I have never had sex with that woman, Miss Lewinski."

President Bill Clinton speaks to the nation

Adolescence:

This is the root cause of the things we see in the Democratic Party today. This is the root cause of the behaviors we see within the Democratic Party. This is the root cause of the political programs being proposed by the Democratic Party. This is the root cause of the opposition the Democratic Party mounts against Pres. Trump these days. This is the root cause of all the name-calling they use against those they disagree with as well. It is all adolescent behavior in nature and now we will go into specific examples of this. This is not a new phenomenon. This has been going on for a very long time, sad but true.

---

[31] http://www.psychologydiscussion.net/child-development/11-major-characteristics-of-adolescence-child-development/1111

In the case of the left they try to tear down the very structures of our society much like what termites do to wooden buildings. The fundamental value proposition they put forward is that if they do not like something, they want to change it to their liking for everyone whether or not everyone likes it or not. They will ram it down everyone else's throats at the end of a barrel of a gun. This is how leftists have always operated throughout history. This is completely opposite of the foundational Christian principles of love God first and love your neighbors as you love yourself. When they have an idea they like, they shove it down their neighbor's throat and say you should be happy about it.

They try to eat away silently at the very foundations of the structures are society depends upon. However, I have noticed lately the quality of their dental plans because their mouths have been far more open, and they have been baring their teeth a lot more than they have in the past.

In the End:

We are all born with different abilities and predispositions. We are born into different circumstances, some better than others. But we are all equal in the eyes of Almighty God. The problem is that Democrats want to make all thing equal for everyone. They want equality of outcome by taking away from the achievers in our culture. How demeaning. This goes directly against the will of God.

"The worst form of inequality is to try to make unequal things equal."[32] Aristotle

Remember that Democrat policies intend to provide universal income to people whether they work or not. Think about this. You can decide to not work, and you will get a monthly government check just by sitting down and watching TV.

"Ignorance is Satan's playground, so too are idle hands" Anonymous

---

[32] https://www.brainyquote.com/authors/aristotle

Our Right Wing Republican Party's Mindset

As is always the case, we must keep Christian foundational truth, and Christian principles in our minds at all times no matter what we read matter what we see and no matter what we do. And so as using that as our lens let us look at the right side of our political equation in this country and we will find that the stench is of a different flavor but a stench, nonetheless. It is just as caustic, just as harmful, just as deadly to human beings but only the mechanisms are different. In the case of the left they try to tear down the very structures of our society much like what termites do to wooden buildings. They try to eat away silently at the very foundations of the structures are society depends upon. However, I have noticed lately the quality of their dental plans because their mouths have been far more open, and they have been baring their teeth a lot more than they have in the past.

But I digress, let us look at the right side of the political spectrum again and see their favorite ways of self-admiration and domination of others. During my research for this section I wanted to give the right-hand part of our political spectrum equal treatment. So, I looked all over the Internet for topics such as the political right's morality, the political rights ethics, the political rights moral foundations and so on. I was shocked with what I found. There were two things in general. First, our journalists do not know what morality is. They actually have no idea what the word morality means or its definition. This is sadly clear by reading what they write. The amount of backward talking I ran into is astounding.

In an article published by The Federalist July 5, 2016 by Paul David Miller, the title of the article was "The Moral Collapse of The Republican Party. Good, just what I am looking for. In the following 22 paragraphs he says embracing Donald Trump for president is a colossal world historical vast mistake, and inexplicable failure of moral courage and a repugnant act of institutional suicide. He then goes on to talk about political strategy like somehow that has something to do with morality. Lastly, he claims that "this is a morally clarifying moment", Trumpism is unjust, foolish and un-American. How is "Make America Great Again" un-American I ask"? I can only conclude sadly that this is just bigot thinking. I was hoping for something far better.

Okay, nowhere in sight is any basis for any of his claims and all of this is just accusations with his feet firmly planted in midair like my philosophy professors used to say. One thing you learn in philosophy, in logic and in spirituality is that you must, you must have a foundation upon which to speak. If you do not have a solid foundation you must keep your mouth shut! It is far better to be silent and to have people suspect you are an idiot than to open your mouth and remove all doubt. That is what Mr. Miller has succeeded in doing. By the way he teaches your kids at The University of Texas at Austin. Who in the hell hired this doof?

One article by Jennifer Rubin titled "The GOP's moral rot is the problem" looked like it would discuss the Republicans moral issues, good. Instead, she launches into six paragraphs of disjointed sentences featuring words like gobsmacking, flim flamers, and only in the last sentence accuses the GOP of being in opposition to reality and any external moral truth or ethical code. That's it, this passes for an article on morality in the Washington Post on July 14, 2017. Disgusting. This was a form of journalistic goo. It oozed all over the place with a stench to it.

I hate to say it, but this reminds me of a quote from the great Henry Ford who said, "Thinking is the hardest work there is, which is probably the reason why, so few engage in it."The above leftist trash talk is certain evidence of that.

This unfortunately was just the top of the mess I happen to discover. Believe it or not, this was par for the course. So, in desperation I turned to historical accounts of Republican presidencies and measured them against Judeo-Christian morality and ethics much like an average American citizen would and should do. I decided to start about 30 years ago. But in the case of LBJ I went a bit farther back.

So, I was forced to go to fairly objective historical new sources that described presidential events on the world stage that I have lived through. That dredged up a lot of memories. I chose to start with George Bush the 41st president of the United States.

George H. W. Bush:

First, he was a graduate from Yale and a member of a secret society called skull and bones. Secret societies by definition are never a good thing. I repeat never, ever a good thing. If something good is going on why do you want to keep it a secret? John Kerry who put together the worst deal in the history of the United States with Iran regarding nuclear weapons is also a member of skull and bones. Get the idea? This is not bipartisanship. John Kerry suffers from terminal pot brain disease. This man cannot think his way out of a wet paper bag.

One huge problem that George H. W. Bush decided not to foresee was NAFTA. This writer believes that any freshman in college that took economics 101 could see that large trade deficits would occur against the United States with NAFTA.

He had economics professors on staff that could figure this out on a napkin for God's sake. Let's be real about things. Under its rules that is precisely what happened. John J Sweeney president of the AFL- CIO said the deficit increased 12 times its former annual size reaching $111 billion in 2004. Something had to be going on behind the scenes. Someone was making a lot of money behind the scenes. And no one was talking.

The American people were being silently shafted, and our government was remaining silent about it. The very people who we hired to protect our best interest had done the shafting to us all. Remember, not telling a meaningful truth is the same as a lie. It is called a lie of omission. This is simple Foundational Christian morality. Our government, specifically, George H. W. Bush, decided NOT to tell us Americans how we were being screwed. Now that is the truth. And we all wondered why life was getting harder. The word dishonest is one word to describe it. Treachery comes closer in my opinion.

However, that was not his big mistake. He told all the American people to "Read my lips no new taxes ". Right, guess what, new taxes came anyway. And the people voted his butt out of the White House and rightly so. So, he lied to the people and paid the price because he lied to openly and upfront. You would think being a member of a secret society he would have known better, but he didn't. Not the brightest bulb in the box.

In keeping with an awful so called presidential tradition, president Bush during his last days as president pardoned six senior government officials from felony convictions regarding the Iran Contra scandals. These guys were guilty as sin, but the good old boy club was operating effectively. I do not know how many people died because of these felons that Bush pardoned.

Other recent scandals involving people on the right mention three.

"In New York, Rep. Chris Collins has been indicted for insider trading. In California, Rep. Duncan Hunter is also facing charges for allegedly using his campaign's cash to pay for a lavish personal lifestyle. In Iowa, Rep. Rod Blum is under investigation by the House Ethics Committee over his role in an internet company whose work is directly related to the federal government." [33]

Chris Christie GOP's poster boy 2016 presidential nominee created "Bridgegate." Christie collaborated to create traffic jams in Fort Lee, NJ, along the George Washington Bridge, as retribution against Fort Lee Mayor Mark Sokolich for not endorsing Christie in the 2013 gubernatorial election. Good God, this is elementary school stuff.

Over many decades of observation, it is this writer's opinion that this is the mode of operation of immorality on the right hand side of our political spectrum. It is either election rigging which both sides do in very amateurish ways or has to do with moolah

---

[33] https://www.vox.com/2018/11/5/18064466/republican-corruption-scandal-midterms-2018

and boatloads of it. On the other hand, the left side already has sex covered in an entertaining wide assortment of ways and positions depending on your particular preferences. The top three Virginia State Officials including the governor all democrats are under investigation for sex and racial crimes as of the time this is being written. So, the only thing left is money for the right side to indulge in.

George Bush Our 43rd President:

Now here is something we get to take a bite out of. In an article published by Sidney Blumenthal on September 6, 2007 [34] he categorically states that CIA director George tenet briefed Pres. Bush in the Oval Office on top secret intelligence that Saddam Hussain did not have weapons of mass destruction according to two senior CIA officers. President Bush unilaterally dismissed this information as worthless. What was going on here?

This information was not included in documents given to Congress that needed to vote on the authorization to use our military force in Iraq. This was never told the American people either. Rather there was a orchestrated campaign to do quite the opposite which was to paint a picture that Saddam Hussein had many weapons of mass destruction including chemical biological warfare and SCUD missiles to deliver them.

As for his part Mr. Tennant knowing the real truth of things kept his mouth shut and allowed the charade and lies to Congress and the American people to continue and the March toward war to continue onward as well. This charade of lies even included the lies of omission to the then Secretary of State Powell and his preparation for a speech to the UN spending days at CIA headquarters where he was never told the truth either. Secretary Powell's speech ended up being a series of falsehoods.

An insider named Subri was paid hundreds of thousands of dollars by both the CIA and French intelligence to give us documents on Saddam's weapons programs. The information detailed that Saddam did not I repeat did not have any chemical or biological weapons or any fissile material for anything nuclear. Our entire CIA infrastructure checked on everything Sabri revealed and it was all validated.

President Bush for reasons unknown had already made up his mind and would not listen to anything else other than to pound the drums of war. He was obsessed on going

---

[34] https://www.salon.com/2007/09/06/bush_wmd/

to war with Iraq and overthrowing Saddam Hussain. Then a new report about Saddam Hussain was written by unknown sources by someone in the CIA. They knew what the president wanted so they gave it to him. The report contained all the falsehoods that the president wanted and stated that, "Saddam was aggressively and covertly developing nuclear weapons and that he already possessed chemical and biological weapons."

This was a complete boldface lie but it is exactly what Pres. Bush wanted to hear so he could justify invading Iraq. From the appearances of things Bush wanted dominion over this part of the middle east. It is never ever a good thing to want dominion over anything. This is the way of evil, the way of Satan. It is the way of attempting to put yourself higher than other people, of other children of God. It is what Lucifer did or try to do eyed as a result he was cast down to this earth and hell. Do any of you really wonder what will happen to the person that caused all this or the people that allowed all this to happen. It is just as bad to allow evil to occur and watch it happen as it is to be perpetrated. Think about that. Christian morality is very much involved in all of this. It is a wise person that learns from the mistakes of others so they do not have to learn the hard way as the others will. Mr. Tennant will have to answer to God just as much George Bush will.

In terms of what happened as the result of these lies by George Bush, 600,000 people died. Most of them were innocent civilians killed either directly or indirectly by the militaries fighting each other or by such things as starvation and other ways of horrific death. When elephants fight people want to get out of the way so it's no wonder you have a lot of Muslims heading north into Europe. This is especially true considering the unrest in Syria these days. But that is another matter and not for this book. But suffice to say the politicians involved are royally messing that up too.

So here we have one grandiose lie of omission by our president George W Bush leading to a war in Iraq that has caused horrific instability within measurable amounts of pain, suffering, dislocation, and death in an entire region of this world we live on. Why did he do this? That is the big huge question of the century. The answer could possibly be in the words of our great president Dwight D Eisenhower. First, we all must remember that there are deep and hidden connections between the highest politicians in our federal government and state and very large corporations in both commercial and defense industries. It is especially true between government and defense industries. It is almost a revolving door. Dick Cheney the vice president is well-established with Halliburton and God knows what other defense companies. Let me state this simply. War is profitable for our defense industry. This is ugly, ugly but a true statement. With this in mind let's get back to what Pres. Eisenhower warned us of.

On January 17, 1961 Pres. Dwight Eisenhower gave our country a sincere and dire warning about a deep and serious threat to our democratic government. He called it the military industrial complex, and intricate union of defense contractors and our military. This is in part what he said:

"In the councils of government, we must guard against the acquisition of unwarranted influence, whether sought or unsought, by the military-industrial complex. The potential for the disastrous rise of misplaced power exists, and will persist."

Remember that when things don't make sense on the surface, look underneath the table and follow the money. And while you're doing that always look at this objective reality through the foundational lens of Christian morality and ethics. I will let you connect the dots on why president George W Bush decided to completely ignore all the evidence he had at his fingertips that Iraq had no weapons of mass destruction and instead knowingly sent our military to overthrow Saddam Hussein and knowingly allowed the deaths of hundreds of thousands of human beings. Yet today, he is walking around and smiling. Why is this man not in prison? I for one put this into the hands of God and it is God alone that will deal with this for it is well beyond any human capacity.

This is identical to what Lyndon Baines Johnson did regarding the Vietnam war. He wanted the United States to enter that war but needed an excuse. So, his staff manufactured the completely false Gulf of Tonkin incident where one of our destroyers, The USS Maddox DD-731, was supposedly attacked a North Vietnamese patrol torpedo boat. That never happened. Yes, there was action in the gulf involving torpedo boats and US destroyers in recent days. But Johnson got a weasel worded bill past congress with the lying help of Robert McNamara that he described as "like Grandma's nightshirt, it covers everything".

But if they used all the reports available to them, "The overwhelming body of reports, if used, would have told the story that no attack occurred." So, this is the same thing as president Bush with Iraq. Ignore what you do not want to see because it interferes with your agenda toward war. You want war, you want killing, you want blood, you want pain and suffering, and most of all you want domination. Can you smell pure evil here? Who is the author of evil?

This means he now had the legal power to make all the war he wanted. Pres. Johnson used that as his excuse to send hundreds of thousands of our military men and women to Vietnam to fight the North Vietnamese communists and untold tens of thousands, mostly innocent women and children died at the hands of our military including many thousands of our military. That caused the rise of pole pot who slaughtered millions to firmly establish communism in South Vietnam and Laos. It is amazing what one stinking lie leads to. But this is the case for George W. Bush, and Lyndon Baines Johnson.

I can only imagine as a Christian how God will handle these people when their time comes with all the blood they have on their hands from uncountable numbers of people and all the pain and suffering that they have directly caused and for what? As I said above, Christian morality is always involved in everything we say and do.

We as children of God must always follow two simple guidelines to the best of our ability. Love God first and above all else and love all other of God's children as we love ourselves. This is ever so simple, ever so beautiful and elegant. But many times, it is ever so difficult to apply into various situations. It is then we must rely on our true and loving intentions to guide us in the proper ways to act. It is the love in our hearts that will lead us to the proper way of doing things. And if we make a mistake, so be it. It was a mistake filled with love and we will do better next time. That is the way of this life and just a bump in our path to God.

However, in the actions of the politicians mentioned above I can find zero influence of God anywhere in anything whatsoever. I do however find the evidence of evil dripping all over the place. And these people through their lifelong desire to have dominion over the American people have succeeded in fulfilling that obsession. But that was not enough for them they wanted to conquer other parts of the world as well all the while thinking of themselves as great leaders of humankind killing innocent people and using people as they went. In my humble opinion we will not be sharing heaven with these kinds of people. I think God for that.

I do have to say that I am very disappointed in my sincere efforts to hang the right side as high as I hang the left. I feel it's only fair to see both of them strung up staring at each other face-to-face. But the ugly and objective truth of things is that it just is not to be. The left just seems to love its sex and the right just seems to love its money and both love to cheat especially in elections and of course both love to lie their asses off to you and me.

However, there is one gargantuan take away that you need to understand. The good old boys from the right hand side work within the existing framework of our culture and our society and government. They pretty much leave things stand as they currently exist. So, you and I can count on our society moving forward with a political system much as it exists today.

With our friends on the left however, nothing could be further from the truth. Besides the sex thing which is actually only the very tip of the iceberg for them and that frankly is the most innocent part of things, the leftists among us have a program that will inexorably destroy this nation down to its very foundations and replace it with some flavor of socialism or communism which has 100% of the time in human history resulted in genocide, mass death and destruction on a scale that will be in the many millions in the United States of America. This is not an exaggeration.

So, before you vote for: piano keys mouth Ocasio Cortez. Pocahontas Warren, Tight Lips Booker, Scary hair brain Sanders, Creepy Joe Biden, kill'em Andrew Cuomo, or any other Hillary Clinton clone, or even the real swamp thing you better think long and hard about how you want your children and grandchildren to live. Because how you vote will determine how they live their lives. I hope you realize that because your parents and your grandparents did. Now it is your turn to do the same thing.

Also, do any of the above creatures fit with foundational Christian values and morality? I mean the foundational values that this nation was created upon. I highly doubt it. Well, the answer is a resounding NO! This is a rogue's gallery of self-indulgent, say anything, do anything, attack anybody to get elected and deal with the aftermath later kind of people. You do not want to be standing downwind from these people. Or you do not want to be hunting with people like Dick Cheney vice president of George Bush who was out hunting birds. You might get a load of birdshot in your face like his friend Harry Whittington got which included a subsequent heart attack and collapsed lung. Shockingly, it was Whittington's family who apologized to Cheney for any trauma the incident may have caused him (Cheney) that interfered with his relaxation in Texas. Now is that backwards or what? [35] Sick!

Our Left Wing Democratic Party's Mindset

Their mindset is born out of their psychology just as it is for all human beings.

I remember growing up being aware of the two political parties. One was for "big corporations" and the other was for "labor unions" against the selfish, dirty rats in "management". Democrats were always for unions, going on strike, pay increases, better working conditions and that list goes on and on. Republicans always seemed to be for stuff like profits, investments, the stock market. It was "white collar" versus "blue collar".

All of this was happening during a time of great competition between Communism and Capitalism. Nikita Khrushchev of Russia famously took off his shoe at the UN and kept yelling that the USSR was going to bury the United States. A huge weapons race was on going along with the race to the moon to win the prize claiming whose economic system was better.

---

[35] https://en.wikipedia.org/wiki/Dick_Cheney_hunting_accident

A number of years later, I got my graduate degrees, a job and a family to raise. We beat the USSR to the moon quite easily because their main rocket engine to take them there kept exploding. Then President Ronald Reagan decided on a master stroke to beat the USSR in the arms race. He announced a vast new space based weapons system for the defense and offence of the United States. This meant spending a monster amount of money. In doing this, he forced the USSR to spend money it did not have thus bankrupting them and subsequently the USSR fell apart and became no longer a threat to the United States.

This was a divine master stroke of genius because Reagan won the cold war for us without firing a shot or worse yet, ICBM's loaded with nuclear weapons. Of course, Reagan was called a complete fool by all democrats. They called it the Star Wars fiasco. They challenged his sanity and the attacks against him were vicious and constant. It was very much like what the democrats are doing to President Trump today. Over the years, the behavior of the democratic party seemingly has not changed. Why? Were not all these proposals intended to protect ALL Americans? Why would a political party be so vehemently against self-defense, from a country that promised to "bury us"? This was back 45 years ago.

It became interesting to me to think that democrats of 40 years ago acted and behaved just like the ones we have today. Different people, same circus. Today we have democrats fighting tooth and nail to keep our southern boarder open in spite of mountains of data that says this is killing many thousands of American citizens each year. This is because of a flood of dangerous drugs, MS-13 gang members, illegal aliens here committing horrendous crimes against citizens and other awful statistics readily available to anyone that is interested. Why would supposedly sane rational human beings be against protecting our own citizens?

Something is terribly wrong, systematically defective and dangerous to the health and well being of the United States of America. What could this explosive problem be? Could it be genetic or psychological or learned behavior? This kind of thinking is not new. It existed in Biblical times as well.

In the case of the left they try to tear down the very structures of our society much like what termites do to wooden buildings. The fundamental value proposition they put forward is that if they do not like something, they want to change it to their liking for everyone whether or not everyone likes it or not. They will ram it down everyone else's throats at the end of a barrel of a gun. This is how leftists have always operated throughout history. This is completely opposite of the foundational Christian principles of love God first and love your neighbors as you love yourself. When they have an idea they like, they shove it down their neighbor's throat and say you should be happy about it.

They try to eat away silently at the very foundations of the structures are society depends upon. However, I have noticed lately the quality of their dental plans because their mouths have been far more open, and they have been baring their teeth a lot more than they have in the past.

Richard Ferguson

PART 2

The Christian Foundations of The United States of America

Our founding Fathers and The United States of America:

As Christians we know evil entered this world because of the fall of Lucifer. Theologically speaking we do not know for certain if the fall occurred before or after Almighty God put humans on this earth into the garden of Eden. My opinion, the fall occurred after Adam and Eve existed here on earth. Why? Because I do not think God would send His children to a planet where Satan was waiting for them. But, the tree of the knowledge of good and evil was placed there by God. The temptation obviously occurred after. So, my vote is that the fall occurred also afterward. Nonetheless we all live in a bifurcated world where the clash of good versus evil occurs in all of our minds every day.

Our founding fathers were all Christian and were well aware of this and had to account for the evil in the minds of men as designers of a government to serve the needs of the people. Their fundamental answer was to disperse political power among different branches of government as widely as they could so no one person with an evil mind could destroy our country. This is why our government is designed the way it is. We call it checks and balances. It accounts for and compensates for the fall of Lucifer and the fall of Adam and Eve in the nature of the human mind. Our founding fathers were indeed extremely intelligent, knowledgeable and devoted to the long-lasting success of our country.

They pledged their lives, the reputations and all their wealth to create the foundations of what we have today. Remember this. It is like you putting your house, all your other assets, your life and your reputation in serious danger in order to create a far better government for all the people that you obviously love very much.

As I stated before, our founding fathers addressed the two sided nature of man during their lives before they wrote our founding documents. They were deeply concerned. We are the beneficiaries of just how right they got things. Too few people bother to realize the beauty and Godliness of our form of government even with all our problems which there will always be. As we get farther away from the formation of our United States of America the more ignorant, we as a people have become by not understanding the great inheritance that we have received from generations past. The children of God today do not understand or appreciated all that it took in spilled blood to give us today the freedom and equality we have in this country and the form of government we have that compensates for the dark side of human nature.

How did they do it? Fundamentally, they did it by creating multiple branches of government and other checks and balances within the mechanisms of our government in order to prevent any single person or small group of people to usurp power over all of us. Our founding fathers were successful. The government they designed has served us very well for the first 200 years of our country's existence. That is right up until the time enough people figured out that using the ballot box, they could vote themselves government benefits paid for by taxing other people.

FOUNDING FATHERS

Our founding fathers addressed questions such as these during their lives before they wrote our founding documents. We are the beneficiaries of just how right they got things. Too few people bother to realize the beauty and Godliness of our form of government even with all our problems which there will always be. As we get farther away from the foundational principles of our United States of America the more ignorant, we as a people have become by not understanding the great inheritance that we have received from generations past. The children of God today do not understand or appreciated all that it took in spilled blood, pain, suffering and death to give us today the freedom and equality we have in this country and the form of government we have that compensates for the dark side of human nature.

We as a collection of God's children have lost our way from the road to success and fulfillment both on an individual level and national level. We have not bothered to teach our children the reasons this country, the United States of America, is as great as it is and is a place where most people in the world want to come to. We through our own laziness have relegated the education of our children to leftist liberal teachers who have propagandized our children away from the Judeo-Christian foundations that have made this country so successful in the past few hundred years.

There are now all too many people within this great country that actually hate America and are actively working toward its destruction. Our young people today want socialism which has been proven to be 100% a disastrous failure in the world. This is not at all what God has designed for us to live and grow to our fulfillment. The Democrat party is the biggest proponent of the immorality and evil that exists in our country today. The tactics these people use to spread their Democrat lies are well worn like things such as propaganda, mobs, violent protests, speeches, censorship, intimidation, outright violence against those who disagree, and they tell groups of people their troubles are the fault of another group fostering hatred within the hearts of those who cannot think for themselves.

They spread division among God's children. All these are the tools of Satan and the Democrat party wallows within these tools and uses them against anyone that does not go along with their plan of dominating the United States of America under a central government that controls every aspect of our lives. There have already been speeches by Democrats saying that government should control every aspect of our individual lives. They want to crush every freedom God has given us. It is my strong opinion that if any Christian votes Democrat, they are a complete and disastrous fool. For they are voting against the very foundational beliefs that they say they believe in.

Our founding fathers crafted founding documents that are indeed inspired by Almighty God Himself. In these documents, the Declaration of Independence, The Constitution and the Bill of Rights they show just how consistent they are with the stated will of God for his human children, with the natural characteristics of man and with recognition of the dark side of man while compensating for that in the design of our government. It is for these reasons that the United States of America has stood out on planet earth as a model to be followed by other nations due to our freedoms as willed by God, due to our economic success by creating a system that allows anyone to rise above and become a leader in industry, science and a whole host of other fields of endeavor and due to the Judeo-Christian morality and ethics that guide us every day of our lives.

I urge all of you to go online and read the original documents of our nation, the Declaration of Independence, the United States Constitution and our Bill of Rights. It is also my belief that if you do not do this, I cannot help but think that you will be held accountable by Almighty God for your apathy and lack of action to do something to protect others of his children. There are two kinds of sin, the sins of commission and the sins of omission. Apathy is the latter sin. Enough said.

A Constitutional Republic with Free Market Capitalism:

This is the winning combination of government and economic policy that has brought the United States to the highest levels of human achievement in the history of the world. The free market capitalism is an ingenious economic policy. In socialism and communism, quotas are forced down the throats of the citizens. Everything is planned in one central organization. The governments have control over every aspect of everyone's lives.

We have our Christian founding fathers to thank for this. They saw first hand all the government burdens and force applied to people in Europe to keep them in line. This domination by kings was starting to infect the United States. This is why there was the American Revolution against the British empire. This is the reason we have the freedoms we do today. Their focus was on individual freedom, the free exchange of goods and services, small government and few regulations. The opposite follows.

Carl Marx envisioned a worker's paradise. Stalin implemented his ideas and to do that 20 million Russian citizens were murdered. Many more died from starvation. People became cynical about life over the long years. This is why vodka is so very popular in Russia. Both these disastrous political/economic systems go against the very nature of God's children. They remove the freedom we need to prosper in our spiritual growth, mental health and wellbeing.

Why is free market capitalism so successful? The reason is that it is an economic system that is consistent with the will of God for His children. It takes into account and rewards the creative powers, skills and labors of people without restrictions. If you create a better mousetrap, you will get the monetary rewards for that when people pay you for producing your product and sell it to them. No government to tell you no or give you a quota to meet.

The genius of free market capitalism is if a person wants to be successful, he or she must provide goods or services that other people want or need. Other people vote with their money going to the ones who provide the best products or services. In this way everyone in society in order to provide for the necessities of life for themselves and their families, must meet the needs and wants of other people. This is a self-regulating economic system that rewards creativity and hard work. Participating in this economic system also promotes a person's spiritual growth by fostering connections between people. This is part of God's creation.

Quotes from Our Founding Fathers:

"And to preserve our independence, we must not let our rulers load us with perpetual debt. We must make our election between economy and liberty or profusion and servitude"
Thomas Jefferson

"The end of democracy and the defeat of the American Revolution will occur when government falls into the hands of lending institutions and moneyed corporations".
Thomas Jefferson 1816

When the people fear their government, there is tyranny. When the government fears the people, there is liberty.
Thomas Jefferson

"I prefer dangerous freedom over peaceful slavery". Thomas Jefferson 1787

Government is instituted for the common good, for the protection, safety, prosperity and happiness of the people, and not for profit, honor, or private interest of any man, family, or class of man. Therefore, the people alone have an incontestable, on alienable, and in feasible right to institute government, and to reform, alter, or totally change the same when their protection, safety, prosperity and happiness require it ". John Adams 1776

"How little do my countrymen know what precious blessings they are in possession of, and which no other people on earth enjoy!" — Thomas Jefferson

"It already appears, that there must be in every society of men superiors and inferiors, because God has laid in the constitution and course of nature the foundations of the distinction." — John Adams, Thoughts on Government, 1776

"Public affairs go on pretty much as usual: perpetual chicanery and rather more personal abuse than there used to be... Our American Chivalry is the worst in the world. It has no Laws, no bounds, no definitions; it seems to be all a Caprice." — John Adams, letter to Thomas Jefferson, April 17, 1826

"Those who expect to reap the blessings of freedom, must, like men, undergo the fatigues of supporting it." — Thomas Paine, The American Crisis, No. 4, September 11, 1777

Our Founding Documents and Christian Principles:

Our founding fathers crafted founding documents that are indeed inspired by Almighty God Himself. In these documents, the Declaration of Independence, The Constitution and the Bill of Rights show just how consistent they are with the stated will of God for his human children, with the natural characteristics of man and with recognition of the dark side of man while compensating for that in the design of our government. When you compare our founding documents with the two great Commandments in the law as Jesus said:

Matthew 22:37-40

37 Jesus said unto him, thou shalt love the Lord thy God with all thy heart, and with all thy soul, and with all thy mind. 38 This is the first and great commandment. 39 And the second is like unto it, thou shalt love thy neighbor as thyself. 40 On these two commandments hang all the law and the prophets.

You will find that they are in complete agreement. So, when Democrats attack the United States of America, they also are attacking Christianity. When they attack our founding documents or ignore them for their own political gain they are also attacking and ignoring Almighty God. This you must remember. Lastly remember who is it that is the author of lies and attacks against God? We all know the answer is Satan. I will let you connect those two dots.

It is for these reasons that the United States of America has stood out on planet earth as a model to be followed by other nations. It is due to our freedoms as willed by God so we may follow our individual paths of spiritual growth as we co-create ourselves with Almighty God into the fulfillment of his original vision for each of us. It is also due to our natural blessed economic success by creating a system that allows anyone to rise above and become a leader in industry, science and a whole host of other fields. We become more of what God intended for us due to the Judeo-Christian morality and ethics that guide us every day of our lives. Our government will last for an extremely long time because of its Godly foundations. But we must defend it as vigorously as our founding fathers did against the British. And as our beloved military has done in World War I, World War II, the Korean War and all the other conflicts from our enemies.

Now however, thanks to leftist liberals and their infiltration into our education system, we as a collection of God's children have lost our way from the road to success and fulfillment both on an individual level and national level. We have not bothered to teach our children the reasons this country, the United States of America, is as great as it is and is a place where most people in the world want to come to. Thomas Paine warned us NOT to ignore this. But we did.

When we are planning for posterity, we ought to remember that virtue is not hereditary. Thomas Paine, Common Sense, 1776

There are now all too many people within this great country that actually hate America and are actively working toward its destruction. All of them are in the Democrat party. I find this disgusting and horrible. We as Christians MUST RISE UP IN RIGHTEOUS INDIGNATION AGAINST THIS AND HAVE OUR VOICES BECOME A THUNDERING CHOROUS AGAINST THOSE WHO WANT TO DESTROY OUR COUNTRY.

Those who expect to reap the blessings of freedom, must, like men, undergo the fatigues of supporting it. —Thomas Paine, The American Crisis, No. 4, September 11, 1777

Richard Ferguson

The Pillars of Our Godly Inspired Founding Documents

Foundations:

Everything in this life rests on some sort of foundation. If you think all this is obvious then you are one of the few philosophers with deep understandings about the nature of life and reality. If you fancy yourself as a philosopher then answer this question, what foundation is the earth resting upon? Now you must think out of the box.

A good question for everyone to ponder: what is the foundation that your life, your existence rests upon? You don't know? Well, think about it. You do have a foundation so start to identify it. This exercise will do you good. It will shed more of God's light into your life and you will lift the veil that currently blinds you to so many existential truths. You cannot "have your feet firmly planted in mid-air" a favorite slogan of one of my philosophy professors. So, have at it my dear courageous one lest you get blown over with the slightest puff of wind.

Our great founding fathers had to search for the best foundations to rest the design of our government. They did not have brainiacs like P-Diddy, Kanye West, Tupac Shakur or Jay-Z and "impeach 45" Maxine Waters to give them celestial great advice to build a nation. Thank God for that!

Our Foundational Documents Judeo-Christian Philosophical Basis:

Philosophy is the study of fundamental phenomena about reality both seen and unseen, the nature of existence, knowledge, relative and absolute values, reason, analytical thinking, logic, mind, and language. Philosophy is a pillar or foundation on which all advancement and intellectual thought is built. [36]

Every opinion or feeling you express in language has an unsaid philosophical premise or foundation underneath what you say. Most people are blind to the underpinning philosophy that they express in the opinions and feelings that they articulate into the common physical world in which we all exist for now.

Most people do not realize the deep source of what they say but rather "rest upon the idea that it seems right at the time". In doing this they are rejecting their very own potential to make positive contributions to all of mankind. Blind thought leads ultimately to chaos and destruction of those good things created by others of mankind for the benefit of all peoples. Thoughtless words coming from a human not based on a solid foundation are as thin as a worn out paint job on a rusted out 55 Chevy Bel Air.

---

[36] https://www.answers.com/Q/What_is_philosophy_of_man

"Every single theory, concept, belief, doctrine, word, phrase, term, and claim can be attributed to philosophy. In a way, philosophy is the basis that defines and develops everything, from God to Atheism and Capitalism to Communism. Each and everything you touch, think, feel, believe, and know is associated with the all-encompassing idea of philosophical thought. [37]

Secondly, the word theology comes from the word "theo" meaning God and "ology" means "the study of". So, theology means the study of God. This subject explores every morsel of our existence much like philosophy but has God or Source as its focal point. If you have an open mind you will see both inside your mind and outside into the physical world.

A Christian philosophy of life is intrinsically positive. In a world full of evil how in the heck can that be? It is simple. The Christian philosophy can see beyond the physical realm and all of its sham and drudgery. Christians are able to put things into proper perspective knowing that what we see in the "here and now" is not all that there is. In reality the spiritual realm is far greater, far more loving and complete than this physical realm we now occupy for a short time.

One secular and scientific hint of this is that recently astrophysicists, cosmologists and astronomers have discovered "dark matter" and "dark energy". Without this our universe as we know it would not exist. Here is the point. The universe we see, feel and touch makes up only 4% of all that physically exists. Dark matter and dark energy make up the rest. Yet we cannot measure these directly with our instruments, but we know it is there by the effect it has on what we do see. So, it is completely reasonable that Christians are correct when we say that the spiritual realm is far larger that our physical realm.

Cutting edge theoretical quantum physics of today says that the reality you and I perceive could be nothing more than a 3 dimensional holographic projection. That agrees with Socrates. They have the mathematics to back this up. Ask people like Prof. Lawrence Krauss (he is an avowed atheist, I have to talk to him and set him straight), Prof. Leonard Susskind at Stanford (my hero), Prof. Roger Penrose, Prof. Peter Higgs (famous for predicting the Higgs Boson regarding gravity), Prof. Stephan Hawking and others. This modern idea is very parallel to what Socrates said 2,300 year ago. [38] Think about that before you dismiss the Greek philosophers because "what could they know so long ago?"

---

[37] https://www.answers.com/Q/What_is_philosophy_of_man
[38] https://en.wikipedia.org/wiki/Holographic_principle

The Foundation of American Cultural Philosophy:

So, here is the big question. What is the foundational basis of our American cultural philosophy? It is elegant and understandable. The following articulates the basis for why the United States became the greatest country in the history of mankind. The following explores the different aspects of our Christian philosophical foundations we use in this country:

Almighty God:

First, God is the ultimate source of everything real, everything that has potential and the source of the essence of all things seen and unseen. There is nothing above or greater than God. It is God that has created all things and sustains all things. Legitimate sovereign power flows from only God to the individual citizen, to the individual human being, NOT governments. We all need to burn this fact into our minds and NEVER allow anybody to tell us any different.

Democrats get big government confused with God. They think that if they are in control, government is surely God. They then go about their business, taxing the hell out of everyone to give that money to their favorite constituents in order to buy their votes and maintain power. This is a very old game I have observed since the 1960's.

We are His children all created as individuals as expressed in the first chapter. Governments cannot have a relationship with God, only individual children of God can do this. It is impossible for a government to have a relationship with God. It is vital that you remember this.

God's Children:

Second. All of God's children are loved equally. All His Children however are NOT born with the same abilities, attitudes, aptitudes, IQ's or circumstances. This is in accordance with the sacred will of God. Some leftists think this is terrible. What do they know about God anyway? Not much if anything. Does God judge like humans do? Of course not. God does not have a cookie cutter that produces His children.

The best reason I have discerned why these differences exist is because each of us being different also have different reasons and different lives to live while we are on this planet earth. Somehow there is a divine reason that some of God's children are born Eskimo, some French, some Brazilian, some black, some white and so on. Therefore, we cannot all be the same. Our physical bodies are also all different. Even twins are born different. Each of us are born different so as to live different lives and learn different things in our spiritual journey during the time we spend in this physical world.

It is for these reasons that socialism and communism cannot be successful. For by their very nature, the government must treat all people the SAME, not equally but the very same. It is "one size fits all". Look around you. That is impossible for everyone is different by God's design.

God's Blessings to Us:

Third. Beyond this, our philosophy of existence is that we must secure all of the gifts that God has bequeathed to us, His children. This means that we must protect and hold tight to the gifts God has given to us for there will always be those evil dark entities disguised as humans who will always want to take these gifts away from us in their Satanic lust for power of all kinds. This means first, the freedom to be and express our unique personhood in this objective reality. Each of us is different so we must be able to express our uniqueness outward into this physical world.

When we express our unique love that comes from ourselves to other people, we are enriching their lives as well. We are giving them the gift of the uniqueness of who we are as God created us to be. We must have the freedom to set a direction in our lives and live in pursuit of what God intended for us whatever that may be. Anything that forces human beings into a predetermined mold of sameness (socialism and communism) is an attack against the sacred will of God for us His children. Remember this always. We find this "sameness" attack against God in forms such as socialism, dictatorships and communism where the different natural inclinations of people are extinguished by the force of guns by governments. More on this point later.

We Are Spiritual Being First:

Fourth. As already described in the first chapter, we existed before we came to earth. We have an individual reason for being here, a mission to perform for both our own spiritual growth and to benefit our brothers and sisters while we are here. It is for this reason we have all been created differently with different abilities and circumstances. While here in the physical, it is up to us to discover what our mission is and perform it to the best of our abilities.

Logic, An Indispensable Skill for God's Children:

Fifth: This is ever so important. I tell you now that ignorance and the inability to think logically are two of Satan's most deadly weapons against God's children. Low IQ is another so throw away ALL iPhones and the average emotional IQ of school age kids will go back up to where it should be. Bill Gates has an agenda that is not in the best interest of human beings across the world in my "humble observations".

We must understand that our brains are made for perceiving, discerning, logical thinking, problem solving and a magnificent list of things it does automatically that result in us, being spiritual beings, to live in a physical world. Yes, our brain is the interface between the spiritual and physical realms. There is a mountain of evidence regarding this and here are a few footnotes to get you started if you are interested in further research. [39] [40] [41] Note however what you could get doing a random search on the internet is the materialistic secular scientifically prejudiced and atheistic view of things. Be very careful of the sources you use.

Today people actually DO NOT know how to think. This is not an insult, it is a terrible fact. Our public school system has seen to that. Logical thinking has no axes to grind. By definition it cannot be due to its very nature. Logical thinking leads us to truth, the truth of objective reality. Logical thinking will make you immune to propaganda and other political lies that stink up our country. A very good resource to consult in advancing your skills at logical thinking is the following footnote. [42]

The Dangers of Not Thinking:

I warn you that if you pay no attention to your ability to think you will remain ignorant in so many ways. You will believe any and all candy coated turds of political manipulation propagated by both democrats and republicans. The leftists that pollute our population are famous for promoting illogical thinking. This is the only way they can entrap the unwary of God's children into believing lies, lies of Satan.

Here is but one popular example. "Well your truth may be that, but my truth is this", prime example of relativistic thinking that completely ignores the basic structure of the objective reality we live in. In that last sentence, the objective truth is that both

---

[39] https://serendipstudio.org/bb/kinser/Structure1.html

[40] https://en.wikipedia.org/wiki/Brain

[41] http://www.2012-spiritual-growth-prophecies.com/chakra-symbols.html

[42] http://www.blackwellpublishing.com/content/BPL_Images/Content_store/Sample_Chapter/0631
227105/Bonevac.pdf

participants in that discussion are ignorant with their thinking process firmly planted in midair.

Two more examples of real leftist statements showing a complete lack of cogent thought process:

"Free speech is meant to prevent censorship, to allow people to express any ideas in public, however unpopular or unsettling. It does not imply that these ideas must be expressed anywhere, anytime, under any conditions." [43]

This is a raging example of "internal contradiction", the second half of the sentence contradicts the first half. This is from a professor at of course the University of California Berkeley. I call it Berserkly for good reason.

By the way, leftists also purposely pervert our vocabulary to entrap the stupid among us. The coined word "Antifa" is supposed to mean "anti-fascist". So, you think they are against fascism. WRONG! Well, it is this Antifa group that has been acting exactly like a fascist would act. They beat up people, smash windows, make threats to those with they disagree and are responsible for a number of deaths. They have taken a page directly out of the book from Joseph Goebbels, propaganda minister for Adolph Hitler during WWII. [44] He promoted demonizing your opponent with lies and then doing the very same thing you accuse your opponent of. Goebbels must have had a very close relationship with Satan.

I strongly encourage you to start reading the material on the following website. It is clear thinking, logical and no axe to grind pumping propaganda. [45] It is called The American Thinker. Your IQ will go up and you will begin to see through the dense fog of lies from both political parties.

The Only Legitimate Excuse for Government:

This physical realm has been created by God for all His children to learn a number of things that can be learned no where else. Government's only excuse for their existence is to facilitate this learning process by structuring society in a way that provides order, opportunity, protection as necessary and other services to the population. Governments are to serve "We the People" as necessary then get the hell out of the way of God's children

---

[43] https://www.americanthinker.com/blog/2017/05/leftist_language_and_logic.html

[44] http://www.psywarrior.com/Goebbels.html

[45] https://www.americanthinker.com/

because it is His children that are here each to live a special life ordained for them by God Himself.

This means maximum freedom for the people. It means protecting the people from evil people sent here by Satan and don't ever believe this does not happen. It means helping people recover from terrible misfortune like fires and floods. It means locking up people who have done criminal acts. It means protecting all of society from invasion by foreign powers. It means protecting trade routes with other nations. It means performing the will of the people through the representative process in legislation. It means keeping the currency strong so as to protect the savings of the people for their old age.

It is these activities that justify a government "of the people, for the people and by the people". Lastly it means that the federal government must be small but just large enough to protect our nation's interest while leaving the more detailed activities to the states for they are the closest to the different needs of the people in the different areas of our beloved country.

Unfortunately, there are people that have inbred obsessive mental problems called psychopathic and sociopathic illnesses. Others are just plain greedy and have huge egos. The list is big. These people crave power over other people and desire to control others of God's children.

Washington DC has the highest concentration of sociopaths and psychopaths in our country. [46] [47] All this plays out in the physical realm that we live in. But remember that the physical realm is only one realm and is not all that big. It is a learning ground that prepares God's children for bigger, better and far more loving things to come for those who love God first with all their heart and love all others as they love themselves.

Learning in the Physical:

What else can be said about this physical universe we live in for a short while? The physical realm has been created by God for a purpose. What is that purpose then? We do not know all the reasons, but we do know some. From an anthropomorphic perspective, we know that the physical gives us humans a platform to learn things we could not learn in other dimensions as mentioned earlier. The physical automatically limits us to not allow us to do anything we wish. We are not allowed to be a loose cannon in other words. This is the reason some commentators call our earth the "prison planet".

---

[46] https://www.politico.com/magazine/story/2018/06/23/washington-dc-the-psychopath-capital-of-america-218892

[47] https://personalliberty.com/psychopaths-congregate-washington-dc/

The physical gives us a place to learn many lessons of interacting with other children of God. It gives us the opportunity to do good or make mistakes and get feedback in the form of pleasure or pain. We learn from that. If we do what is right and good, we get pleasure from that. The physical then is a teaching tool God has designed for us. Eastern religions call this karma. Christians call it "the wages of sin".

There really is an objective reality that exists regardless of what we think or feel. Generally speaking it starts at the end of your nose and proceeds out from there. But it also includes our physical bodies. This reality does not care what you think of it. It does not care about your opinion or your feelings. Facts do not care one iota about your feelings or being offended. If you are offended by the law of gravity, lodge your protest by jumping off a building to demonstrate against that awful law of gravity and show how unfair and offensive it is. It is certain that gravity will not kill you. But the sudden stop will.

Objective Reality:

First is "the closer you are to God's will and rules when you create or manifest things with your own co-creative powers, the more successful and fulfilled you will be", money is not a measure of success. God does not give a damn about money. Remember that! This is an absolutely important principle of existence in this objective reality. If you take sincere time to understand the rules of this reality you will find that the ten commandments describe them very nicely.

These ten commandments are not there to torture you or keep you from having a great time. No! They are the keys to the divine heavenly realm where total love and fulfillment exist for you. Much to the complete dismay of our leftist Democrat friends, there are walls around Heaven and entry requirements to get in. If you are a leftist and insisting on getting into heaven without approval, good luck. God created another place for you. If you ever forget this rule of existence, our objective reality will quickly remind you in very memorable ways. It is a four lettered word called pain.

Secondly, within this objective reality are all the connections between everything. One truth of creation is that everything is connected. There is nothing that is not connected to everything else. As said in chapter one, there is no real distance, no real separateness and all of God's children are a brotherhood connected by the bonds of love for each other. I know you do not feel that way. That is by design for our benefit.

Third, there is a veil between heaven and earth. God believes in walls, fences and other devices of separation. Only sincere love can penetrate this veil. You cannot just waltz into heaven and claim government benefits. Walls exist to separate different kinds so as to maintain peace. I know this for certain from personal experience. The physical realm and the spiritual realm are separated by a veil that is impenetrable. But again, sincere love makes is permeable.

To emphasize again, there is one exception by design…love. It is pure love that freely penetrates the divine veil. In my third book, "The Divine Resting on My Shoulder", I describe just a few of the uncountably many divine mystical experiences I have had during my life. One example, I was able to communicate with my wife Marilyn after she died of cancer. She gave me advice about things I should avoid. Good thing too. What she told me came true and allowed me to avoid an awful mess with another woman.

Fourth, one thing you will learn is that if you truly love someone, that love will never die. It will exist for all eternity. My late wife and I still love each other to this day even though she passed away more than 10 years ago. In"The Divine Resting on My Shoulder" I document her mystical appearances to me over many years. If you are interested, you can purchase the above book at Amazon or Barns and Noble. In summary, there is an objective reality that we live in both physical and spiritual and we must come to understand what it requires of us. It is in this way we learn and become better spirit beings. If you screw up your life, you probably will have to come back and take the learning course again. The Hindu's know all about this.

Fifth, you will want to be separated from the evil and destructive people. God has provided for that for His children. Heaven has walls, gates and strict entry requirements.

Sixth, heaven is up, hell is down. Good is to the right and fools are to the left. This is biblical. I worry about people who ignore the rules of God and wonder if they will be going down instead of up when their time comes. One day I had an unexpected mystical experience. A very close relative of mine went down and after a time appeared to me by coming out of an inky black cloud out of the floor. I told him to go back to hell where he belonged in the name of Jesus Christ. He was forced to obey because of the power of the name Jesus Christ has across all creation. During his life he was a very cruel man. Yes, this is a true story.

Seventh, regarding left and right. This is an important point that almost everyone misses. Ever wonder why republicans are on the right and the democrats are on the left? History books say this dates back to the French revolution and seating arrangements. Maybe, but there is a deeper theological connection that goes back much farther. It is Biblical. Remember, God does indeed separate different kinds from each other. Who is to argue with infinite intelligence?

The Biblical Left and Right:

After reading the following, does anyone want to be on the left?

Remember what Jesus said: 'Goats on the left, sheep on the right' (Matthew 25:33).

He said, "Throw your net on the right side of the boat and you will find some." When they did, they were unable to haul the net in because of the large number of fish. John 21:6

"The heart of the wise inclines to the right, but the heart of the fool to the left." Thus, sayeth the Lord. Amen. Ecclesiastes 10:2

32 All the nations will be gathered before him, and he will separate the people one from another as a shepherd separates the sheep from the goats. 33 He will put the sheep on his right and the goats on his left. Matthew 25: 32-33

41 "Then he will say to those on his left, 'Depart from me, you who are cursed, into the eternal fire prepared for the devil and his angels. Matthew 25:41

(Notice here that contrary to our neo-leftists, God separates people one from another as sheep from goats) Today, leftists want no such separation except for themselves. They demand no boarders so as to change the demographics of our beloved country such that the new illegal aliens will out vote those of us who built this nation and it gets turned into a socialist paradise which has never existed. Socialism only brings death and destruction. There are walls around heaven as well dear reader. I know.

"Jesus said to him, "You have said it yourself; nevertheless, I tell you, hereafter you will see THE SON OF MAN SITTING AT THE RIGHT HAND OF POWER and COMING ON THE CLOUDS OF HEAVEN." Matthew 26:64

"He is the one whom God exalted to His right hand as a Prince and a Savior. Acts 5:31

"which He brought about in Christ, when He raised Him from the dead and seated Him at His right hand in the heavenly places." Ephesians 1:20

"Therefore, if you have been raised up with Christ, keep seeking the things above, where Christ is, seated at the right hand of God." Colossians 3:1

The above treatment of left versus right is consistent across the bible written across many hundreds of years from different authors, This does not seem coincidental to me.

The Alignment of Our Founding Documents with Almighty God:

When I read our country's founding documents, I see great connections between God's will and His intent for His children. For example, our constitution gives us freedom. God gave us freedom from the beginning. He gave us free will. God's will is that we have full freedom to work out our spiritual goals. Therefore, our Constitution does indeed reflect the will of God. There indeed is a direct linkage between our founding documents and the values, principles and ethics of Christian theological philosophy. So, there is a real and profound linkage between our Constitution, Bill of Rights and Declaration of Independence, foundational Christian principles and the Christian Philosophy of man. This is enormously important.

Our Constitution has a specific world view, a philosophy of man and government. It recognizes the downfalls of man that need to be compensated for in a healthy long lasting government that must serve "We the People". There is no other legitimate reason for any government to exist other than this, to serve "We the People". God's children are NOT born to serve the government no matter what form it takes.

The following is a Judeo-Christian fundamental. Power and legitimacy must be recognized by mankind that legitimate sovereign power flows from God to us as individuals. This is extremely important. Sovereignty flows to you and me directly from God. Why? We are in our essence a sparkle of God's light and love. Nothing supersedes that, nothing. It does not flow from God to government of any kind, no!

Because each of us are "made in the image of God", legitimate government power then can only come from the governed, the people. "We the People" temporarily lend our sovereignty to our representatives in government to make rules and enforce laws. Our 13 colonies were stiffly ruled by England and their troops stationed here in America. King George tried to dictate laws to Americans through the barrel of a gun held by British soldiers. We had a revolution and the United States of America was born.

A Cohesive Whole:

We need to know about the character and nature of mankind, the philosophy of our Constitution and other things like this.

So, what exactly are our founding documents standing on?

1. Our Foundational Judeo-Christian Philosophy and belief in our Christian God

2. The One True Objective Physical Reality:

3. An objective reality that is both seen, and unseen is connected together. Everything in this universe is known to everything else. All is known and the one affects the all.

4. Humans are rational beings but are torn between good and evil.

5. Knowing the will of God through the Judeo-Christian Biblical tradition and history

6. Understanding how things are connected in our objective reality. It goes something like this: God--His Children—Human Nature—Freedom is required for all individuals—freedom is one focus in founding documents.

7. In depth understanding of Greek and French philosophy

8. The design of our government is very much the opposite of kingly rule over the people. It is the people who have sovereignty from God.

9. Understanding an accurate picture of mankind's nature, good and bad and most importantly know how to compensate for that yielding maximum freedoms for all citizens

10. Understanding how different forms of government work, strengths and weaknesses and why they fail producing suffering and death.

11. Lastly, our founding documents are founded upon the Judeo-Christian philosophical answer to the question of why we are here on earth.

Then we can better appreciate the brilliant wisdom that is contained in our founding documents that has resulted in the greatest country this world has ever seen. Why is our country the best? It is because its design is the most compatible with the will of God for us His children.

Government Must Get Out of Our Way:

Getting back to government, this then simply means that government in any form MUST get out of the way for individuals to reach their various fulfillments and destinies as determined by God Himself. If government gets in the way of these individual fulfillments, then government must be necessarily be labeled as evil for it goes against the will of God. This simply means the individual child of God MUST have individual freedom to pursue his or her reason for being on this planet. To the extent that a government interferes with this is to the same extent that the government is evil inspired by Satan himself. Is this strong language? Yes, and it is accurate. Think about this and this idea will become clear.

Many forms of government by their very nature fly in the face of Christian fundamentals and hence the obvious will of God we see in this physical reality every day of our lives. Governments that prevent individuals from pursuing their missions to learn and experience here on earth are by definition evil.

Remember Satan wants to dominate, Jesus Christ wants to set you free through knowing the truth.

It really is just that simple. Governments that dominate children of God are by definition, evil doing the work of Satan. Our precious United States of America is well on its way crumbling toward tyranny. We will explore this in the chapter "Our Perverted Government".

Core Human Philosophical and Theological Fundamentals For our Founding Documents:

To understand and really appreciate our founding documents and realize just how wonderfully constructed they are while being aligned with God's will for mankind, we must first have a little discussion about both the philosophical and theological fundamentals we find in them.

In the following I have purposely mixed, philosophy, metaphysics and theology. The reason is because statements about total existence in the universe touches all three disciplines. To design a successful government, you must understand and incorporate these major points.

1. Individuals have been created in a part of the image of God, not His totality. Each of us has at the center of our inner being a "unique sparkle" of the light and love of God. His children celebrate this divine gift of identity and spread His love each day of their lives.

2. For those who are evil at heart, they have chosen to destroy this divine sparkle by putting themselves higher than others and God himself. They fell in love with only themselves at the expense of anything or anybody that may get in their way. This is exactly what Lucifer did. He fell in love with his beauty and tried to put his throne above God's. As a result, he was thrown down to earth and ended up in hell. So too will these people who are numerous in this world. The Bible calls them goats. This must be recognized and compensated for in any government. Remember that government is a powerful attraction to people who want to dominate others. The best defense against this tragedy is a well-educated citizenry.

3. But, those of us that carry the sparkle of God's love in our hearts are all equal children of God. Differences of race, gender and other superficial distinctions are of no consequence except that these different aspects play an important role to assist individuals fulfill their personal reasons for coming to this earth and live a human life. Therefore, everyone must have the freedom to pursue their reason for being on earth.

4. We are all born equal in the sight of God. But we all are not born into this earth with equal circumstances. Also, we are all not born each with the same gifts or talents as determined by God. Each of us are different with different circumstances and different abilities as given by God to us. It is this mix of circumstances and talents that will allow us to learn the lessons each of us need to advance in our personal spiritual maturity. Aristotle was wrong. We are each not born with a"tableau rasa".

5. We are all equal under the laws and commands of God. As such so too are we bound to Gods laws here on earth. The ten commandments are NOT actually restrictions forced upon us. Rather these commandments are the keys to the eternal kingdom of God. It is these commandments that are the true source of human freedom. It is violating these commandments that enslave us in painful prisons of our own making separating us from God our Father.

6. Within the minds of every person there exists a war of good verses evil. Each of us experience this battle in our thoughts and feelings. It is our free will decision to go one way or another, good or evil and this decision is then acted out in this physical world for all the universe to see and record

7. The universe is a unity, a singularity where everything is known to all in this universe. Nothing is hidden, everything is known by all. Everything is this universe, seen and unseen is inexorably connected with God at its center of existence. Theoretical quantum physicists would call this "entanglement". Albert Einstein called it "spooky action at a distance". The point here is that both Judeo-Christian theology and cutting edge quantum physics appear to agree with each other.

8. Therefore, every thought, feeling and physical act is known in its entire detail by all else in this universe. Think about this and its implications.

9. We as individuals are here on earth to learn about our true selves as spiritual beings, to learn the virtuous morals that are blessed by God, and to learn how to identify the slithering stench of evil and how to avoid it and fight against it. This book is a weapon against evil as it promotes and blesses all who read it to come closer to God who created all of us within His womb of infinite love for each of us as His child.

10. We each have complete free will as ordained by God as His child. We can choose our own path, our own thoughts and actions. From our actions we will either be blessed by loving choices or suffer the consequences of bad choices. This is the very nature of life on earth. In a real sense, pain is a very effective teacher if we pay attention. The sacred desire of God is a loving relationship with those who chose to love Him. He does not want robots with no free will.

11. Life does not appear to be consistent with the human understanding of what is "fair". But what is forgotten is that we do not and cannot see the big picture of why this is. We are limited in our perception of things. Just like our eyes can only see a very tiny portion of the electromagnetic spectrum, we can only perceive a very small portion of the much larger unseen part of creation. This is by God's design so as not to overwhelm us by perceiving the whole of creation all at once which includes all the unseen spiritual realm which is far greater in dimensions than this small physical existence we are to deal with in our lives today. This author believes that once we see the bigger picture including the spiritual realm, all the "unfairness" of this life will then be understood to be actually fair as those unfair conditions will be perceived to exist to aid those children of God to grow closer to Him through the lessons they must learn.

12. One evil temptation that exists for all humans is to "put yourself above others of God's children. The thought that you are somehow 'better" than others is a shortcut to hell. There are many people who set themselves above others on earth in their pursuit of domination over others of God's children. This temptation is strong such that many people who succumb to this find their way into society's positions of government power. They seek to dominate others, not to serve others to increase other's health and well-being. They will promise free stuff only if they can obtain power over other people by doing so. They forget or refuse to acknowledge that nothing on earth is free and thus by necessity they are promoting the confiscation of the labors of others of God's children. In doing so they are stealing the very lives God has given to His children. They will answer for that when their time comes. It is this where they set their throne above all others. This is the very thing that Lucifer did when he fell in love with himself and attempted to set his thrown higher than God. He was thrown out of Heaven into eternal damnation and now seeks to destroy all of God's children for his revenge. You and I are his demonic targets.

13. The temptation to fall in love with yourself at the expense of others through your own free will is the single cause of all human suffering on this planet. Do this and hell is certain for those who choose this path of torment. It is this that Lucifer did. This is quite a far reaching statement. It is simple yet global in its application. Here is the Satanic danger. It is these kinds of people who have a poor sense of right or wrong, a defective conscience in other words. Empathy for others is either weak or non-existent. This combined with a desire to obtain social or political power with control over the lives of others many times propel these types of people into real positions of power in our society. It could be in the corporate world, military or the political sphere.

14. Lastly and bluntly, God's children are NOT here to serve government. You are not here to serve government. This is the way of dictatorships, socialism and communism. Those forms of government are built on the foundations of the graves of hundreds of millions of innocent people murdered for either saying the wrong thing or being the wrong type of human being. If you want to live under communism, go to either Russia or China.

The Government of God:

I must describe something regarding the government of God. I mean God's government in heaven. Is there even a need for one? Nobody talks about this, yet it is a very important subject if you want to understand what form of government is the best and how to craft laws that will enhance the lives of "We the People".

Government like we have on earth is just plainly not needed in heaven. God is within us and we feel His love all the time wanting for nothing. Doing something wrong or against another is completely unheard of. It is basically you and God and all that you have loved with unlimited opportunities within all creation.

There is a hierarchical government of sorts with God as King. There are multiple levels as well that I do not understand. This works perfectly since the King has infinite intelligence and love for all His children. His children love him perfectly as well in an environment that know no evil so nothing but goodness can prevail.

Human Government, Why Have One?

It is the role of human self-government to provide a platform and set of laws that promote the health and wellbeing of "We the "People". This is the only excuse for needing any form of government. It is the fundamental role of government to protect the people, make laws that ensure equality of opportunity, ensure the Godly inalienable rights of all people are protected, ensure the inalienable right to life and stay out of the way so each individual can work out their spiritual reason for coming to this earth.

Here on earth the security business is a very profitable one. And thus, we sadly need government to maintain the peace here on earth. It is because of the spiritual war that is going on around us and in our minds.

Satan is real. He lives inside all levels of our government. I have been attacked multiple times by him and his demons. His demons are real too. I describe one encounter with the dark evil forces in my third book, "The Divine Resting on My Shoulder". Get used to this fact and you will be better off in your personal battle. So, if we do need a government what role should it play in our lives and what are is proper goals for us?

Our Government Has Usurped Illegitimate Power Over Us:

Government will say they are "taking care of us".

"I predict future happiness for Americans, if they can prevent the government from wasting the labors of the people under the pretense of taking care of them."[48] — Thomas Jefferson

"We must stop thinking of the individual and start thinking about what is best for society."[49] — Hillary Clinton

This statement is pure poison to the health and wellbeing of our democratic republic. Clinton has forgotten that it is the individual sovereign person that IS society. She has it backwards much to the horrific danger to all of us citizens. She does not have the faintest idea what Christianity really is. Here is another notable quote.

"I have to confess that it's crossed my mind that you could not be a Republican and a Christian."[50] — Hillary Clinton

The opposite is true. Because of the Democrat policies and anti-Christian hate, no Christian should ever vote for any Democrat, no exceptions. This Satanic statement indicates that she actually thinks she knows the bounds of what being a Christian is. Good Lord, even the Pope cannot comment on that in objective terms. This is proof that this woman is anti-Christian.

In other words, taking almost half of people's lives who work and give to those political constituents that vote for her is the real Christian way according to Hillary. Only a rabid socialist or a communist could say those words and mean it. Socialism and communism have always 100% led to mass starvation and death to hundreds of millions of people in the last 100 years of human history. Another part of this book documents just some of the horrific death and suffering these monster forms of government.

"The state is that great fiction by which everyone tries to live at the expense of everyone else." — Frederic Bastiat

---

[48] https://www.goodreads.com/quotes/tag/government
[49] https://www.azquotes.com/author/2997-Hillary_Clinton
[50] https://www.azquotes.com/author/2997-Hillary_Clinton

Mr. Bastiat's description of socialism promoted by the Democratic National party is accurate. The Bernie Sanders, Hillary Clintons, Ocasio Cortez's, the Corey Bookers and on and on ad nauseum of our country destructively insist on a society that can be described as a snake eating its own tail. Death comes quickly after that.

We are becoming too ignorant to know we are ignorant. So, they will vote for the candidate that will promise them the most free stuff. Who pays for this free stuff? It is the American taxpayer who is having ever increasing parts of their sacred lives stolen from them through the mechanism of tax policy. Hillary Clinton promised just exactly this. If you want more and more of your sacred existence confiscated by our government, then vote for Bernie Sanders or Ocasio Cortez or any other Democrat. You will be sorry.

Our Inspired Constitution

People have never really appreciated the tight connection between, our God's rules for living, our founding fathers and our Constitution of the United States of America. Remember that God has told us that the closer we are to his divine will, the more successful and fulfilled we will be. The Constitution is very close to the will of God for mankind. Let's take a look at some of the words in our Constitution and compare how that fits with God's will for man and what we already covered earlier in chapter 1.

To begin with we must remember what John Adams said:

"Our constitution was made only for a moral and religious people. It is wholly inadequate to the government of any other".

This is a magnificently insightful comment. To have a successful constitutional republic each citizen needs to share in the work necessary to make the society and culture vibrant and alive with loving values for all to share in. We as a people have ignored this for the last 50 years and now, we're starting to pay a monstrous price for that.

"Don't interfere with anything in the Constitution. That must be maintained, for it is the only safeguard of our liberties. And not to Democrats alone do I make this appeal, but to all who love these great and true principles."

—Abraham Lincoln, running for election to the U.S. Senate as a Republican in 1856

Notice even back then when Lincoln was alive people already knew the danger Democrats posed to the sacred freedoms provided to us God's children. President Lincoln was shot in the back of his head by a Democrat actor John Wilkes Booth.

It was Abraham Lincoln that saved our United States from ripping apart and ended the scourge of slavery in the face of the fact that slaves were all over the world at the time. Also notice how Lincoln singled out Democrats as the ones most likely to mess with and change our Constitution, true then and still true now. Disgusting. Another example, after losing the 2016 election Democrats now and again want to change the election rules. Disgusting!

They now have gone so far as to create phony documents as the basis for attacking President Donald Trump for collusion with Russia. This after two years of intense investigation has proved that all the charges against him are false. Democrats will lie, cheat and corrupt anything to get power over the people. This behavior is a horrific sin against Almighty God.

Who Has Ultimate Sovereignty?

It is "We the People". We are children of God, sovereign of all creation and this physical world. We carry our sovereignty with us no matter where we go. The first three word of our Constitution are absolutely bursting with deep meaning and point out universal truths of God's creation that almost all people overlook. Mankind is now so deluded into thinking by constant propaganda from the leftist Democrat party that the normal human being is supposed to work and slave for the benefit of "those above him or her", that they never question who really has power. It is NOT the damned government! It is "We the People". Our inspired Constitution cannot make it any more clear.

There are 24 different verses in different books in the Bible written across thousands of years that address freedom. They proclaim freedom for all individual people. This is just one.

17 Now the Lord is the Spirit, and where the Spirit of the Lord is, there is freedom. Saint Paul 2 Corinthians 3:17 (NIV)

Our beloved Abraham Lincoln was completely consistent with the will and laws of God when he said.

"We the people are the rightful masters of both Congress and the Courts, not to overthrow the Constitution but to overthrow the men who would pervert the Constitution"Abraham Lincoln

Thomas Pain said in "Common Sense" 1776 that government "at best is a necessary evil".

Major Themes of Our Constitution:

The major themes of the design of our American Constitutional Republic is to ensure a few very important things:

1. The people are the true sovereign in all political matters. It is the will of the people that must be carried out by their duly elected representatives in all levels of government.

2. There must be checks and balances imbedded within the structure of government that ensure no one person or small group of people can acquire large amounts of power in order to bypass the will of the people.

3. Government power must be diversified across three branches of government which serves as a check and balance.

4. To enact legislation the legislative branch and the executive branch must agree and sign bills into law. The judicial branch if necessary, can strike down laws that do not follow the Constitution according to its original intent. This has not been the case lately however due to leftist liberal judges with their own agenda.

5. We must not allow people to stay in government too long for that can develop into a ruling class very much like the nobility in Europe. Therefore, there are term limits in both the legislative and executive branches of government. However, there are not enough term limits. We need to expand them.

6. Create a set of laws that allow trials against members of government that are accused of criminal activity and removal from office and other punishments.

Please realize that all this is aimed at preventing the dark side of human nature from taking over the reigns of power in government. If there were no dark side to human nature by knowledge of good and evil, we would still have Eden on earth.

James Madison said that whenever things get to where we are today:

"That whenever any Form of Government becomes destructive of these ends, it is the Right of the People to alter or to abolish it, and to institute new Government, laying its foundation on such principles and organizing its powers in such form, as to them shall seem most likely to affect their Safety and Happiness." — **James Madison, <u>The Constitution of the United States of America</u>**

The design of a legitimate government must be such that the will of the people is what drives the action of the government. Government is legitimate only to the extent that it serves the best interest of all the people while not favoring one group over another. Citizens must be educated and informed to current events.

Ignorant voters are much more easily lied to, propagandized and conditioned to vote a certain way. It is the duty and responsibility of every voter to understand the issues and all the candidates and select that choice that will do the most good for the most people. If we do not, remember this:

"One of the penalties for refusing to participate in politics is that you end up being governed by your inferiors"– Plato

In more modern times: "The ignorance of one voter in a democracy impairs the security of all". – John F. Kennedy

We have not done this. Think about why our children's scores in standardized tests keep falling in the public school system. Think common core! My daughter is a teacher. Likewise, the term "special interest group" is an insult to the very foundation of our government. They pay lobbyists to pay off government officials in various ways so as to get laws written in their favor, mostly by definition at the expense of others of God's children who work for a paycheck to support their family.

These are the fundamental pillars of truth in this world. The only way for a government to be legitimate is to adhere to the above principles and truths. If ever a government starts to rule and control the people by threat of force, it is then that the government becomes illegitimate and must be replaced by "We the People". This my dear fellow Americans is why we all should keep and bear arms. It is the LAST guarantee that we as a people will retain our God given freedoms.

Our Inspired Constitution Creates a Legitimate Government: [51]

Article I:

This part of the constitution designs the houses of congress. There are two separate houses in congress. Because us human beings took the "knowledge of good and evil", the design of our government disbursed power across three branches of power. This is to provide protection against too few people acquiring too much unilateral power. Power corrupts. The main points are as follows:

"Legislative powers are vested in Congress of the United States which shall consist of a Senate and a House of Representatives."

The Senate shall consist of two senators from each state regardless of population or land area. The term of service shall be six years for each senator elected by the people. Candidates must be US citizens and at least 35 years of age.

Vice president shall be the President of the Senate, have no vote unless to break a tie. The Senate shall try all cases of impeachment. A two thirds majority is required to convict such impeachment and remove the person from office.

The House of Representatives shall consist of elected representatives in proportion to the population of the State. The term of service shall be two years. Candidates shall be US citizens and be at least 25 years of age.

The House of Representatives shall have the power to impeach.

All bills for raising Revenue shall originate in the House of Representatives. Each bill must also be passed by the senate before it is submitted to the president for signing. Upon signing the bill it then becomes law. If rejected the bill shall be sent back to the House of Representatives where a 2/3 majority to pass the bill to the Senate for its reconsideration. If there is a 2/3 majority then the bill becomes law without the signature of the president.

Congress shall have the power to levy and collect taxes, duties imposts and excises. Congress shall pay the debts and provide for the common defense and general welfare of the United States. Congress has the power to borrow money, regulate commerce with foreign nations, establish rules of Naturalization, to coin money and regulate the value

---

[51] http://constitutionus.com/

thereof. Congress shall establish Post Offices, promote science and useful arts by what we call today issuing patents to the inventors of new technology or art. Congress has the power to declare war, to raise and support armies, maintain a navy.

No title of nobility shall be granted by the United States. No state may enter into any treaty, alliance or confederation. No state may create or support its own army or militia. This is to eliminate any possibility of a return to the dreadful feudal times where there was no freedom.

Notice how power is split between two houses in Congress. The House of Representatives has representatives from each state in the union in proportion to its population size. Large states get more influence in congress. The Senate has two senators from each state regardless of its size and population. This is to ensure that small states are not dominated by the larger states. The good news is that it takes BOTH houses to pass legislation before it goes to the president for his signature and become law. Remember that it is "We the People"(God's children) that choose the persons we want to represent us thus carrying with them the decisions of the people on various topics. This is the mechanism that allows for the will of the people to generate legislation accordingly. If the president agrees and signs the legislation, it becomes law. If he does not agree he can veto the legislation and send it back to congress. This is an important check and balance for congress.

Our forefathers had great wisdom, reasoning, knowledge and faith in order to design a government with so many checks and balances in the system. They also studied the Greek philosophers and the history of the recent medieval times in Europe. They were perfect for the task at hand, to design a system of government that was in alignment with God's will for human being.

Article II:

The president is in the executive branch of the federal government. He has to take an oath to "faithfully execute the Office of President of the United States, and will to the best of my ability, preserve, protect and defend the Constitution of the United States."

The president shall be the Commander in Chief of the Army and Navy and other branches of our military. He shall have power to make treaties with 2/3 vote of the Senate, appoint ambassadors, Judges of the Supreme Court. The president shall inform the congress regarding the State of the Union. The president shall preserve the laws of this nation and maintain proper police and other forces to maintain peace and tranquility. The President shall conduct foreign relations activities and strategies consistent with policies of the United States. The president has the authority to negotiate treaties with other nations. He can appoint ambassadors. The president is responsible to protect the entire nation from foreign incursions whatever the form.

The president is elected by the electoral college with a majority vote for a term of four years. A person may serve a maximum of two terms in office. This is also true for the vice-president. Most people do not know this. The United States of America is NOT a democracy as most believe. No, we are a constitutional republic. The ultimate law of the land is our Constitution and Bill of Rights.

We citizens do not directly elect the president for example. Voting for president is not a popularity contest across all states in the union. Rather based on voting results in an election we are actually electing "electors". It is these electors that officially vote for president and they declare the winner. If our founding fathers did not design our government this way, then only the big coastal states would have enough population to control the entire nation. This would ultimately break up the United States of America into small pieces and we would fall from being the shining star that the people of the world look up to and want to come here.

Article III:

The Supreme Court is the highest court in the land. It is the final decision maker in issues that involve the interpretation of the US Constitution. There is a large system of inferior courts in the land that make almost all judicial decisions. However, there are times when an issue needs clarification related to the intent of the Constitution. Then the issue is presented in the supreme court.

This article creates the Supreme Court of our land. It has nine judges appointed for life by the president and ratified by a vote in the senate. This judicial body is supposed to be the height of impartiality immune from the politics of the day. They are to interpret what the Constitution says without political influence. However lately, the political forces in play have been seeing the Supreme Court as a battleground to install judges that are far more leftist and liberal socialist in philosophy. This is a dangerous insult to all the American people. Also, lately Democrats have been applying a litmus test against Christianity for nominees for federal courts. This is both unconstitutional and immoral. But they do it anyway as documents elsewhere in this book.

Article IV:

This article describes the relationships between states and the federal government. It provides that the federal government shall protect all states from invasions and sets law regarding extradition for law enforcement. Lots of other important but boring stuff here.

Article V:

This article creates the Constitution as a living document where amendments may be included with the original Constitution to reflect the changing needs of the population. To add an amendment to the Constitution it takes two thirds in favor vote of the states in the union.

Article VI:

Treaties made with foreign powers by Congress shall constitute the supreme law of the land. All states shall adhere to this. All elected senators, representatives in State Legislatures shall be bound by an Oath of Affirmation to support the Constitution.

Article VII:

The ratification of the Conventions of the States shall be sufficient to the establishment of this Constitution of the United States.

A General Discussion:

This Constitution may be amended by a 2/3 favorable vote in each of the two houses in Congress and ratified by ¾ of the states in the union.

Our Constitution designed a government that was founded on Judeo-Christian beliefs and experience. As God made his children sovereign within the universe so too has the Constitution made individual citizens sovereign in the affairs of government.

It is the primary duty of a government to always protect the best interest of its people. If not, it needs to be replaced by"We the People". George Washington himself said this. Democrats today fiercely oppose to secure our southern border. They willfully are ignoring their sworn duty to protect American citizens from all the drugs, gangs that kill, illegal aliens that suck up the resources our taxpayers need and paid for. Why? Votes somewhere down the line. Disgusting. Remember this. Democrats want power over everything else. They would gladly rule over a dung heap than participate in a sparkling society. If you are a professing Christian, you must vote against the onslaught of the Democrat party in 2020.

The Bill of Rights: Compensating for the Human Darkside:

These first 10 amendments to the Constitution were ratified December 15, 1791. When I read our founding documents, I am struck by all the ink used to define those characteristics of our government that are specifically designed to be there for addressing and compensating for the dark side of human nature. Our founding fathers were keenly aware of corruption in government and actively pursued ways to forestall or prevent as much as possible the opportunity for evil minded people in government to dominate American citizens by having too much power so as to serve themselves above the people.

They recognized the war of good versus evil that rages within everyone's head and took steps to defeat evil in the minds of those in government. It is this that is a shortcut to hell in the eyes of God, giving in to evil and using government power to dominate, to control and manipulate the rest of His children. It forms the basis of ALL sin or wrong doing and very serious.

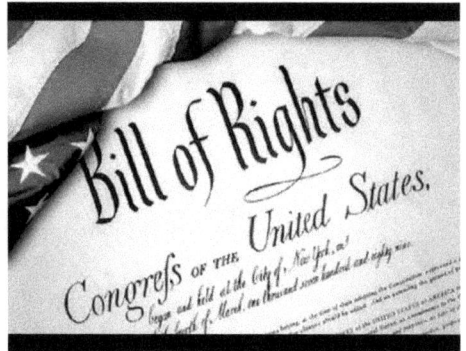

Regarding the first ten amendments, they protect individuals from their own government. That is exactly what was intended. For if left unchecked, any government will grow and spread its control over all the people into every aspect of their lives. This would destroy the very fabric of freedom in America and the foundations our sacred country is built upon. We all can thank Thomas Payne for this. He was the most revolutionary of our founding fathers and mistrusted the idea of government the most.

Now, it is Democrats that are actively promoting "limitations" on free speech that is protected by the first amendment. We also have democrats constantly attacking the "right to keep and bear arms" using a false premise that guns are "the" danger while ignoring the human being that animates the inanimate object into violence. More on this later.

So, it is natural that Thomas Payne and the other founding fathers would want to codify into our founding documents provisions that are there to protect the individual citizen from their own government. Thomas Payne was a very wise man. His love for the individual citizen is a sacred gift from our Almighty Father in Heaven. Remember as I described in the first chapter. God created all of us as unique individual expressions of his love. Our founding fathers were so deep in their love for this country and all future citizens that they provided for us the necessary protections we need from our own government. The problem today is that people either take these protections for granted or in the case of leftist liberals, attack the very basis for the freedoms we still have. One tangential note, we are not nearly as free as we were 40 years ago in this country due to our monster government confiscating our productive lives and forcing every so many regulations on us in the name of "protecting us". BS!

Amendment I:

Congress shall make no law respecting an establishment of religion or prohibiting the free exercise thereof; or abridging the freedom of speech, or of the press; or the right of the people peaceably to assemble, and to petition the Government for a redress of grievances.

The first amendment gives every citizen the right to free speech. It guarantees everyone the right to speak their minds and state opinions in the marketplace of ideas. It matters NOT if someone is offended by what another person says. Do NOT in any way believe the sewage like stench filled blather coming from the left about "offensive speech"is bad and free speech must be controlled including our common vocabulary. This is the drumbeat of tyrants who want dominion over others of God's children!

All this talk about "politically correct"speech is a direct offense against all citizens and God Himself. It is the vocabulary of tyrants who set themselves higher than all others of God's children, the very same thing Lucifer did causing him to be cast out of heaven into eternal hellfire. From my very personal experience, I know he is there to this day. Please think about this.

Free speech is completely necessary for a democratic republic to exist. Why? It is because we must have a free market of ideas that are openly expressed by the people in our country. This is one of the most important foundations of our country. If there are seven ideas that come forth in order to solve a societal issue, let them be openly expressed. Let all the people know what these ideas are. This alone recognizes the sovereignty of the people as the ultimate and legitimate source of political power.

Then through voting the people express their decision on which idea wins to be implemented by the representatives of the people. This is completely consistent with the will of God and is the highest form of human self-government however imperfect this may be in its manifestation on earth. However, there are dangerous people with power in government that want to control our free speech. Which one of the following do you agree with? However,

"I think that some restriction on speech is appropriate." [52] — Dianne Feinstein

Think about this. Just who gets to decide what the restrictions should be? Who decides what words in our vocabulary are illegal. This is complete thought control just as George Orewell published in his book 1984 about a totalitarian government. Diane Feinstein is a TYRANT working directly against the free will of God's children. I cry to think that she has chosen the shortcut to hell.

"If the freedom of speech is taken away then dumb and silent, we may be led, like sheep to the slaughter." [53] — George Washington

"Better a thousand fold abuse of free speech than denial of free speech." — Charles Bradlaugh

(Pay attention snowflakes, grow a set and live with it) [54]

Yes! We all have the legal right to offend each other. It is a distasteful practice for sure, but if we do not allow this, we will quickly turn ourselves into a society that wears straight jackets with duct tape on our mouths.

This first amendment also gives every citizen freedom of religion. It states that congress shall make no law regarding religion or prohibiting the free expression thereof. This no doubt is included as correcting the situation where King George of England kept trying to shove the Church of England, Anglican, down people's throats.

Many people fled Europe for this very reason, to get away from being dominated by the Anglican Church, The Church of England, and similar situations in other European countries as well.

---

[52] https://www.azquotes.com/author/4711-Dianne_Feinstein
[53] https://www.brainyquote.com/topics/freedom_of_speech
[54] https://www.brainyquote.com/topics/free_speech

Amendment II:

A well regulated Militia, being necessary to the security of a free State, the right of the people to keep and bear Arms, shall not be infringed.

The existence of the second amendment regarding the right to have weapons is a further recognition of the ultimate power of the people over their government. Each of us has the right to bear arms. This right is not given to us by the government, it is given to us individually by God himself. Remember, it is the individual who is sovereign in the eyes of God. The second amendment only reaffirms this in the bill of rights.

"In our own country, prior to the Revolutionary War, some colonists did own firearms but in the months before, and directly after, the war began King George's generals implemented gun confiscation policies - a primary driver behind the adoption of the Second Amendment by our founding fathers."[55]

They had lots of guns and most American colonists didn't. It is for this reason and the many lessons of history that we have the right to bear arms. Weapons are NOT just for hunting as democrat Joe Biden is famous for saying. Weapons are for personal protection and are the last resort protection of the sovereign people from their own government.

A question: Are you afraid of our government? Or is our government afraid of you? Be honest with yourself. Are you afraid of our Federal and State governments? If you answered that the government is afraid of you and other citizens, they you live in a democracy. If you are afraid of the government, then you live in a tyranny. It is just that simple. In my view, we now live in a democratic tyranny. We vote for the people we want to control us. We have all the superficial trappings of a democratic republic, but government has grown to an out of control behemoth. This behemoth is demonstrated by California. This state even made plastic straws illegal and you can go to jail if you knowingly distribute these evil tubes of environmental destruction.

---

[55] https://www.naturalnews.com/039264_gun_control_timeline_true_history.html#

Amendment III:

No Soldier shall, in time of peace be quartered in any house, without the consent of the Owner, nor in time of war, but in a manner to be prescribed by law.

It states that no soldier in times of peace shall be quartered in any house without the consent of the owner. This isn't much of a problem these days. But during the colonial days housing was a problem. Basically, this amendment says that the military shall respect the sovereignty of citizens regarding their houses, homes and personal effects. Again, it is our Constitution that recognizes that true and legitimate power originates with God and His sacred children. This is to be respected at all times.

Amendment IV

The right of the people to be secure in their persons, houses, papers, and effects, against unreasonable searches and seizures, shall not be violated, and no Warrants shall issue, but upon probable cause, supported by Oath or affirmation, and particularly describing the place to be searched, and the persons or things to be seized.

It states that the right of the people to be secure in their persons, houses, papers, and effects, against unreasonable searches and seizures, **shall not be violated**. In other words, citizens are protected from the police or other government authorities to enter their homes, confiscate their possessions without due process of law where the government must show good cause to a court to attain limited access and confiscation.

Today this amendment has been completely crushed into oblivion by government and police agencies. This amendment has been ignored by our police state in search of your money in order to fund itself stealing your hard earned money under false pretenses. No criminal charges need to be filed against you to lose everything you have, nope. Not only that, president Trump supports this wreckage of an idea that trashes any form of fairness and due process. All that need happen is for you to be in the wrong place at the wrong time and the police will steal everything you have. The usual imaginary reason is some sort of drug activity. [56] [57]

---

[56]   https://www.nbcnews.com/think/opinion/police-abused-civil-forfeiture-laws-so-long-supreme-court-stepped-ncna974086

[57] https://www.aclu.org/issues/criminal-law-reform/reforming-police-practices/asset-forfeiture-abuse

Simply put, if you are stopped for example for a traffic issue, you can lose all the money or other valuable goods you have with you at the time under so called "civil forfeiture"laws. You do not have to be charged with a crime. The police simply steal your possessions and you will have hell to pay in order to get your rightful possessions returned to you. Why would police do this to normally law abiding citizens? It is because they get to keep what they steal from you and spend it as they please. This footnote is just one example out of many thousands. [58]

In addition to these atrocities against innocent God's children, many people have been purposely killed by police as these thefts are taking place. [59] Remember, dead people cannot tell their side of the story now can they.

In Maryland police killed another citizen. [60] One common thread that runs through all these surprise police raids against law abiding citizens is that they always seem to occur in the morning hours of between 3 AM and 5 AM, when the innocents are sleeping.

One common scenario is getting pulled over in a traffic stop. First DO NOT ROLL DOWN THE WINDOW ALL THE WAY! This gives the cop the opportunity to claim he smells an illegal substance. Roll it down just about one inch, enough to pass through your insurance and license information. He will complain but too bad for him. On this same point, NEVER give a cop permission to search your trunk, "just to see if everything is OK". This is a fishing expedition that leaves you open to whatever he or she wants to do to you. NEVER give any search permission. [61] [62]

This is a very sad commentary on the situation today. Again, all this tyranny we are exposed to today did not exist a mere 50 years ago. Are you afraid of your government? Don't lie to yourself now. If yes they you live in a tyranny.

---

[58] https://ij.org/case/caforfeiture/

[59] https://www.breitbart.com/politics/2018/11/11/maryland-law-enforcement-goes-to-confiscate-guns-kills-gun-owner/

[60] https://www.ammoland.com/2018/11/home-owner-killed-maryland-police-trying-confiscate-guns/#axzz5bmjlqW8g

[61] https://www.expertlaw.com/library/criminal/police_stops.html

[62] https://www.nolo.com/legal-encyclopedia/police-stops-when-pulled-over-30186.html

Amendment V:

No person shall be held to answer for a capital, or otherwise infamous crime, unless on a presentment or indictment of a Grand Jury, except in cases arising in the land or naval forces, or in the Militia, when in actual service in time of War or public danger; nor shall any person be subject for the same offence to be twice put in jeopardy of life or limb; nor shall be compelled in any criminal case to be a witness against himself, nor be deprived of life, liberty, or property, without due process of law; nor shall private property be taken for public use, without just compensation.

Another protection for God's children is this amendment. It recognizes that a person cannot be forced to testify against themselves. In other words, you do NOT have to talk to the police. Keep your mouth shut until you are represented by a competent lawyer. Nor can you be tried in court for the same accusation twice. Also, citizens may not be deprived of life, liberty or property without due process of law. Again, this amendment is designed to protect the citizen recognizing their natural God given rights as a human being limiting government power in the process. This amendment has been mutated and perverted in today's world.

The police can now legally lie to you while it is illegal for you to lie to them. So, shut up! The police can tell you any lie or batch of lies they want to for any purpose they want. All this is completely legal and is a complete abomination to any sense of honesty or fairness.

If you are stopped by the police for any reason whatsoever, keep your mouth shut completely. NEVER TALK TO A COP NO MATTER WHAT PSYCHOLOGICAL PRESSURE THEY PUT ON YOU OR GUILT TRIP. Like, "Why won't you talk to me, what are you hiding?" You are making me suspicious that you have committed a crime, haven't you? Crap like that. They are only trying to entrap you into saying something they can later hang you with.

This amendment protects citizens if they are accused of a crime. They are entitled to a speedy trial and judged by their fellow hopefully impartial peer citizens. The accused has the right to confront their accusers and witnesses against them in a public court and to provide witnesses that are in their favor. The accused has the right to legal counsel.

This amendment also guarantees "We the People" freedom of speech and expression. This is foundational to our way of life.

Amendment VI:

In all criminal prosecutions, the accused shall enjoy the right to a speedy and public trial, by an impartial jury of the State and district wherein the crime shall have been committed, which district shall have been previously ascertained by law, and to be informed of the nature and cause of the accusation; to be confronted with the witnesses against him; to have compulsory process for obtaining witnesses in his favor, and to have the Assistance of Counsel for his defense.

Each defendant has the right to a speedy trial by an impartial jury of his peers. Simple enough. In legal language it is referred to as "habeus corpus".

Amendment VII:

In Suits at common law, where the value in controversy shall exceed twenty dollars, the right of trial by jury shall be preserved, and no fact tried by a jury, shall be otherwise re-examined in any Court of the United States, than according to the rules of the common law.

This gives defendants the right of trial by jury of their peers. Below a certain monetary sum, it is an impartial judge that will decide the matter before the court.

Amendment VIII:

Excessive bail shall not be required, nor excessive fines imposed, nor cruel and unusual punishments inflicted.

Excessive bail shall not be required, nor excessive fines imposed, nor cruel and unusual punishments shall be imposed upon people. To this writer, it depends on which state of the union you are in that determines the severity of punishment, for some things are legal in certain states that would put you in jail in others.

Regarding severe punishments being illegal I remember as a child reading an article in National Geographic magazine about Muslim countries. The article showed a man standing beneath a horizontal piece of wood. Hanging on a string from the wood was a human hand. The string was attached to one of the fingers. The article stated that the man in the picture was convicted of stealing a loaf of bread for his family. They cut off his hand for his punishment and hung it on that string and made him stand there taking his picture.

This is one image that I cannot get out of my head it was so shocking to an 8 year old little boy. It turns out that this is indeed a prescribed punishment within the Sharia Law of the Islamic religion of today. Yes, this still happens TODAY! I will list the countries in the section on Islam. Horrifying but true! We do not hear about this because we want their oil.

Amendment IX:

The enumeration in the Constitution, of certain rights, shall not be construed to deny or disparage others retained by the people.

This is a global statement that basically states that the Constitution shall not purposely be misinterpreted in such a way as to deny or disparage other rights retained by the people. In other words, just because something is not explicitly mentioned either in the Constitution or Bill of Rights does not in any way deny those rights to "We the People". Again, our founding fathers were farsighted enough to understand that they could not anticipate all circumstances that would occur in the future, so this amendment is meant to lay the groundwork for additional rights as changes occurred in the world.

Amendment X:

The powers not delegated to the United States by the Constitution, nor prohibited by it to the States, are reserved to the States respectively, or to the people.

From this it is easy to understand that our founding fathers did not envision a large central federal government. But that is exactly what we have today. They would be shocked to see what we have today where government soaks up about 40% of all the earnings of "We the People".

Bill of Rights Summary:

From the above we can see that the intent of these Constitutional amendments is to ensure global individual rights to each citizen in the United States. This is wildly important to the health and wellbeing to all citizens in our country. These rights are also complete consistent with the will of Almighty God and our purpose for coming to this planet for a time. It is also intended to limit the power of government over citizens. Our founding father's intent was to create a small federal government sufficient enough to protect all American citizen from external attack, to protect our trade routes to ensure that all our states worked together in harmony for the best interest of "We the People".

They NEVER intended nor foresaw the behemoth government we now have today that reaches into every aspect of our lives. Our federal government is a total perversion of what our founding fathers intended for us their descendants. It all started with president Roosevelt a long time ago with his so called "New Deal". This established government as a nanny who will take care of people instead of their families, friends and local charities.

Where does this lead? The California state budget for spending in 2019 is $209 Billion. Revenue is only $202 Billion for an increase in debt for California citizens of $7 Billion. The population of California is 40 million plus all the illegals living there. Therefore, the State of California spends an average of $5,225 per person in the state.

Lastly keep in mind that all 40 million do NOT pay taxes. If US averages hold true for California, 44% of the people do not pay any state tax. This puts the tax burden on 22.4 million people in the state. Each pays direct or indirect, like taxes hidden the price of things, $9,330 each year. This is why your quality of life continues to go down. Gee…thanks President Roosevelt, and a special thanks to Gavin Newsom our new governor. Now a total between 35% to 40% of the productive lives of each of God's children are confiscated by all levels of government.

We need an amendment that limits the total percent of a person's productive life that is confiscated by government. God wants only 10% tithe. Why should the government want so much more? Lastly at what percent confiscation of your life does slavery start?

Additional Amendments:

There are an additional 17 amendments to the Constitution passed over the years. These address more areas of life giving citizens additional protections for their freedoms from government.

State governments were created so as to address the regional differences between different groups of Americans that have settled in different areas of our country. In large part this has been successful. But like the federal government they too have grown into monsters of their own individually taking far more in taxes than was foreseen by our founding fathers. Each state now taxes"We the People"far more than what our founding fathers saw for the total of both federal and state tax burdens.

The last amendments to the constitution include subjects such as:

Amendment XI:

State sovereign immunity. States are protected from suits by citizens living in another state or foreigners that do not reside within the state borders. Ratified: Feb. 7, 1795

Amendment XII: Modifies and clarifies the procedure for electing vice-presidents and presidents.

Amendment XIII:

Except as punishment for criminal offense, forbids forced-slavery and involuntary servitude.

Amendment XIV:

Details Equal Protection Clause, Due Process Clause, Citizenship Clause, and clauses dealing with the Confederacy and its officials.

Amendment XV:

Reserves citizens the suffrage rights regardless of their race, color, or previous slave status.

Amendment XVI:

Reserves the U.S. government the right to tax income.

Amendment XVII:

Establishes popular voting as the process under which senators are elected.

Amendment XVIII:

Denies the sale and consumption of alcohol.

Amendment XIX:

Reserves women's suffrage rights. "On May 21, 1919, U.S. Representative James Mann (R-Ill.) re-introduced the 19th Amendment and it finally passed the House by a vote of 304-89. Ninety-one percent of Republicans voted for women compared to only 59 percent of Democrats. On June 4, 1919, it passed the Senate 56-25. Eighty-two percent of Republicans voted in favor of the amendment while 41 percent of Democrats continued their War on Women. It was then sent to the states for ratification."[63] As you can see, historically Democrats were not happy with giving women the right to vote. Surprise!

Amendment XX:

Also known as the "lame duck amendment," establishes date of term starts for Congress (January 3) & the President (January 20).

Amendment XXI:

Details the repeal of the Eighteenth Amendment. State laws over alcohol are to remain.

Amendment XXII:

Limit the terms that an individual can be elected as president (at most two terms). Individuals who have served over two years of someone else's term may not be elected more than once.

XXIII Amendment:

Reserves the right of citizens residing in the District of Columbia to vote for their own Electors for presidential elections.

Amendment XXV:

Citizens cannot be denied the suffrage rights for not paying a poll tax or any other taxes.

Amendment XXV:

Establishes the procedures for a successor of a President.

---

[63] https://www.theblaze.com/contributions/in-1920-republicans-defeated-democrats-war-on-women

Amendment XXVI:

Reserves the right for citizens 18 and older to vote.

Amendment XXVII:

Denies any laws that vary the salaries of Congress members until the beginning of the next terms of office for Representatives.

Summary:

Taken as a whole the additional Constitutional amendments do the following things:

1. Established the electoral college (The self-serving democratic party wants to abolish this institution because they lost the last election) Never mind that this is an integral part of balanced representation of the states in the federal government.

2. Definition of a citizen of the United States

3. The abolishment of slavery. To all the black people who hate white people. It was white people who ended slavery. It existed thousands of years before the United States. Your leadership are a pack of liars.is not telling you historical truths.

4. Anyone who has participated in insurrection or rebellion against the United States is not eligible for any elected office. Barack Obama should be in jail by now after aiding and abetting Iran (Death to America) by giving them $150,000,000 in cash during his last two weeks in office. This is treason by any measure.

5. The right to vote shall not be denied on account of race, color or previous condition of servitude. But you have to be a citizen. Only citizens have the right to vote. However, Democrats want to give the vote to illegal aliens. [64] [65] [66] I cite three sources. There are many more. Do your own research on this. Disgusting and treasonous.

---

[64] https://www.investors.com/politics/editorials/rasmussen-poll-on-illegals-voting-reveals-political-motivation/

[65] https://www.wnd.com/2017/08/lyin-democrats-use-illegal-immigration-to-destroy-america/

[66] https://menrec.com/democrats-push-legislation-granting-voting-rights-to-illegal-immigrants/

6. Congress shall have the power to tax.

7. Each state shall have two senators with one vote each.

8. Intoxicating liquors are prohibited. Amendment 21 repealed this amendment.

9. The right to vote shall not be denied on account of gender. Democrats voted against this!!!

10. Sets the time fixed for the beginning of the term of the president and successor in case of death.

11. Sets term limits of the president to two terms. Sets rules for succession in case of death for the office of vice-president.

12. Sets the voting age to be 18 years old. (Frankly, my idea is that only people who can produce a legitimate tax return showing taxes paid should be allowed to vote. This would eliminate people voting money out of other people's pockets that they worked hard to earn, God's will is that the earnings of a person is first his or hers, not someone else's like it is today through tax confiscation)

It is this Bill of Rights and the Constitution that has created the framework for our culture and society that we live in today. Over the years since these documents were first written there have been many dangers against our way of life and the fundamental structure of our society. The last amendment to the Constitution was proposed in 1789 and ratified in 1992.

One thing everyone needs to remember, the Constitution and the Bill of Rights codify the rights of "We the People" consistent with the will of God as I have previously documented.

Beware of those politicians who demonize one group of God's children while saying another group is being victimized by them. It is these political people who calculate and divide God's children against each other for superficial and temporary political gain to satisfy their lust for earthly power. Barack Obama was a master at this. It is these people who will find hell as their eternal reward. Always remember that there is nothing in the universe that is hidden. Everything is known, everything! Biblical speaking, God knows the number of hairs on your head. Think of this. I have personal divine mystical experiences that testify to the truth of this. Nothing can be hidden in God's creation...nothing.

PART 3

The Misguided and Unholy Mess We Are in Today

Our Terribly Perverted Government

I have to say that I have been dreading the thought that one day while writing this book, I would come face to face with this awful chapter. I consciously, willfully and actively pursue the truth of our objective reality that we all live in. To survive, to prosper and protect all loved ones a person must understand his or her entire reality. This means physical, emotional, governmental, security factors and sources of income for food and shelter. This also means the rules for living a Godly life and leaving this earth in better shape than when we came here.

To view this physical life successfully everyone needs to view it within its larger, much larger, spiritual context. You must always remember that your personal world is but a microscopic dot on an infinitely larger creation that you are a very important part of. Don't let size fool you. When one part is missing, the entire whole is not whole any more. You are that important, irreplaceable and one of a kind never to be replicated...ever. Our physical world was put here for us by those in the spiritual realm. Thus, not much will make any sense if you ignore the spiritual world. Your limitations will remain too great.

We Have Gone Astray from God's Will for Us:

Terribly so we as a nation have wandered far away from our Judeo-Christian foundational values and constitutional rights. It is this that is the fundamental cause of all the problems we have in the United States today. It is because we have drifted into the mentality that we are entitled for whatever reason to someone else's money and support. We also now feel that each of us has our own version of reality. This wretch of an idea is promoted by the Democrat party. This goes completely and directly against the created objective reality that Almighty God has made for us to learn, to grow and to fulfill our purposes here so that doors will be opened to us with wonderment and joy after we leave this physical world.

It is my belief that the United States of America peaked during the late 1960's and very early 1970's. It was the time of the Apollo program taking astronauts to the moon and back. It was a time of far more personal freedom then than we have today. Young people today have no idea what real freedom feels like. They have grown up in an ever increasing socialist welfare state with monster increases in regulations, laws, horrific taxes, degradation of moral values resulting in terrible crimes of all kinds. The young people of today think all this horror is normal. It is NOT! Yet it is the situation today.

When I was in elementary school in Chicago, I walked to school and back home every day without fear of crime. Everyone did the same thing. Children were safe walking the streets. The basic morality of people was far higher than it is today. No home security systems and felt no need for them. Nobody feels safe anymore.

The second thought is that there was no monster government making rules for every itty bitty thing like driving your kids to school or drinking straws in California. No "Department of Education". There is really no need. My daughter is a fifth grade teacher and the rules and regulations our gargantuan government forces on schools is horrific. She represents the consensus. Common Core should be renamed "Rotten to the Core".

Other examples abound. Enough said.

The Morality of Taxes

After I write this following section, I am going to have a large glass of wine, pet my two doggies, eat a small dinner and wonder how in the hell does the United States still exist considering what I am about to tell you. This is a morbid and ugly story perpetrated upon American citizens by their very own government. It started back in 1913 on October 3 when the states ratified the 16th amendment creating the federal income tax. It was a whopping 1% after deducting loads of deductions from your income. You could deduct lots of stuff that you could never think of deducting today. People back then rightly realized we did need a central government to keep the states glued together and provide for a common defense and to negotiate treaties with foreign countries along with trade agreements. That's what the federal government was invented to do and nothing more. It was never intended to get involved in such things as social policy or education or minority rights or any other such modern day politics that we all get worked up about.

The Government is Confiscating Way Too Much of Our Productive Lives:

Fast forward to today. The top tax rate for individuals to the federal government is 40.8%, up from that awful 1%. I live in the state of California, the leftist lunatic fringe. The state that invites the rest of the entire world to come on in and flood to our sanctuary cities and we will take care of you lock stock and barrel, the American taxpayer will pay for it. As Gavin Newsom said, our new governor, in early 2019, "I will not be afraid to make glorious mistakes". This is frightening because I believe him, and he will end up being extremely glorious.

In addition to our federal friends, the California state income tax tops out at 13.3%. Now if you wish to go out and buy something like food or other household goods, you get to pay an additional 7.25% to 9.5% sales tax. Now understand that this last tax is paid with money that is what the pros called after tax money which means you already paid income tax to get the money in your pocket to pay sales tax. So, in effect you had to earn an additional 15% to 18% more money to pay the California state and county sales tax.

Where does all the money go? Good question. It goes to a blizzard of government agencies you never heard of. California is a great example of this. There are 519 separate State agencies in California. Disgusting. I do not know where to begin to list all the federal government agencies.

We must have a government for many good reasons. We need to pay to support our government both state and federal. But what is happening is our government is confiscating all too much of our productive lives in taxes. Taxes vary widely depending on income.

How Much Does the Average American Pay?

Taxes..."are highly variable from person to person, if you add the four income-based tax rates together you get a total tax rate of 31.85%. Multiply that rate by the average gross income per return and you get a grand total of $20,944. Of course, you are likely aware that this figure still doesn't tell the whole story. We haven't even discussed a number of taxes that millions of Americans are subject to such as property tax, vehicle tax, sales tax, and more. Still, if you are looking for what the average American pays in taxes, I'd argue that figure is about $20,944 minimum, give or take."[67]

The real figure is probably higher than the 32% stated above because you pay sales tax with income you already paid taxes on. This does not count things like licenses and other government charges. My feeling is that the average American pays about 35% to 40% of their income to the government one way or another.

It is right and good that each of us contribute to the benefit and well-being for the larger community that we all participate in. But for all this to work, taxes have to keep going up and up. And so, they certainly did for the last 90 years. Women had to enter the workforce to make ends meet where before one salary could raise a family and send the kids to college. Not anymore. Why. People discovered they could vote money out of other people's pockets. That demonic scheme is doomed to fail in the very near future dear friends. It violates the second of the two great commandments.

Where does the money go? Here is only one example from the Democratic 2016 Platform, "We will work to ensure that all Americans—**regardless of immigration status**—have access to quality health care."First off, these are illegal aliens. They should not be here. We cannot pay for everybody. They are NOT Americans. YOU pay for their health care at the expense of your family.

Lastly, I pose the question, how much of a person's income should be given to the common good. The best answer is in the Bible. It is the tithe amount, 10%. That is what God thinks is appropriate. The US government is entitled to no more than that. But they burden us with 35% to 40%. That is slavery to me.

We got here incrementally by voting for things that sound good but are poison for us when we add them up all together over time. Our tax burden has become onerous and is seriously interfering with family life in our country. Our earnings have become big political footballs that lobbyists and politicians play with. I will never forget watching a video of former governor of California Jerry Brown. He said, "money is what runs politics". This goes against the will of God and why we are here to begin with. So, how do we extract ourselves from the mess we have gotten into?

---

[67] https://www.fool.com/taxes/2017/03/14/how-much-does-the-average-american-pay-in-taxes.aspx

Fascist Tax Tactics:

It is well known that during the Obama presidency the IRS was used to target conservative political groups called the tea party. It is also well known that Obama used multiple federal agencies against political foes to conquer them.

"The American Center for Law and Justice (ACLJ) has won a years-long legal battle against the Internal Revenue Service in which the agency admitted that it wrongfully targeted Tea Party conservatives, during the Obama Administration, specifically because of their political viewpoints."[68]

This is one disgusting example of his war against the American people, children of God. There are many others. This is the same tactic Hitler used with his Gestapo. Obama was the worst president in American history.

Democrat Party is currently holding up the confirmation of hundreds of judicial nominees because they fear the Christian blood in them. Look what Feinstein and Sanders did with their anti-Christian litmus tests to two judicial nominees documented elsewhere in this book. Satan runs wild within the minds of these people. We need to recognize evil when we see it.

For more research into the many scandals of Barack Obama not reported by our mainstream media start by going to the website in the following footnote. [69]

Other Forms of Slavery in The United States:

Another form of slavery to our masters in government is our time spent complying with government regulations that are not productive for us. One shining example is standing in line at the DMV even if you have an appointment made a month in advance. I spent three hours there last time. Or, according to the IRS it takes an average of almost three working days (22 hours) to fill out our 1040 tax form and send it in. Compliance with carpool lanes during the time we need the extra freeway lanes the most in commute hours, the government decided to restrict the number of lanes the children of God can

---

[68] https://www.zerohedge.com/news/2017-10-28/obamas-irs-admits-specifically-targeting-tea-party-conservatives

[69] https://www.nationalreview.com/2017/01/obamas-many-scandals-abuse-government-power-worse-sex-scandals/

use to get to work and back. In California they are called "diamond lanes". Gee what a nice misleading term for government restriction.

This is not to mention the billions of tax dollars spend just in California alone constructing the extra freeway bridges to accommodate these commuter diamond lanes, your tax dollars at work to slow you down. This slows the rest of us down and burn more gas increasing our expenses to favor a few the government likes more than you or me. Speed bumps…these hated things were imported from Europe (the Netherlands) to slow us down when we already were going slow. Interestingly in everything I have read in the literature never mentions any problem statistics. Speed bumps take the appearance of a government forced nuisance solution to a non-existent problem. They spent your money for a non-existent problem.

The Federal Register is the document that summarizes all the rules and regulations that people must comply with. This does NOT include state and local governments. As of 2016, there were 97 thousand pages courtesy of Barack Obama and those before him. As of 2017 that decreased to 67 thousand courtesy of Donald Trump. Barack built that, Trump tore it down. That is a monster burden decrease off the backs of the American people. Thank you. Bet you never heard this on the mainstream news huh.

Our entire economy bears the direct cost of complying with these rules and regulations. It ends up in the prices and availability of the goods and services we all need to live. Intuitively we all know that adding lots more regulations on the production of goods and services slows everything down and adds cost. It also increases taxes. In 2010 our federal government spent more than $55 billion to enforce the regulations it has. No word on what it increased to in the latest year.

Now I will end the discussion on other forms of slavery in the United States with this gem. According to an article by Jennifer Harper in the Washington Times:

"Regulations cost more than the federal income tax," stated a study released Wednesday by the nonprofit Competitive Enterprise Institute which reveals that the costs of complying with stifling new federal regulations hit $1.885 trillion — higher than the individual and corporate income tax burden of $1.82 trillion"[70]

She goes on to say:

---

[70] https://www.washingtontimes.com/news/2016/may/4/compliance-with-federal-regulations-now-cost-19-tr/

"It's a huge hidden tax that amounts to about $15,000 per U.S. household each year," the study noted."

Put all this together and we have become slaves to our government. The reason we are not rebelling with pitchforks and torches marching in front of the capital building is that enough of us have already been bought off by the leftists among us that get a government check each month and they do not want to rock the boat feeling entitled for whatever reason to whatever they get. Remember, about 44% of the individuals in the United States do not pay any income tax at all.

This whole thing is a scam from one end to the other. There are simple ways to fix things. Yes, there are simple fixes to these problems but at least 44% of our population will scream bloody murder. Yet God will smile because it will be very consistent with His laws and the Judeo Christian morality and ethics that this country is founded on.

But I can hear the screaming, the wailing and the gnashing of teeth if what I said ever gets implemented. If we do implement the above the result will be a return to a society that built this great nation. It will be a return to a far healthier society than what we have today. It will be a return to a far more responsible and moral society than we have today. We will be healthier physically, emotionally and morally.

The Moral Failure of Our Political Class (Politicians)

So, we have learned that being moral, honest and a loving person is simple. I did not say that it is easy. It is not. But the principles of moral and Christian life are indeed simple. It is the two great commandments. There are so many ways to get tripped up on the "morally and spiritually good person" road. One good Jesuit friend of mine says that "I get up in the morning, do my best, go to sleep, get up the next day and try again". That is a true mark of a Christian.

Our politicians have decided to go on another road entirely, they are on the road to hell. This is a wide freeway actually. Most of our population are on that same road in my humble opinion for a zillion reasons. There is a road to hell but only a stairway to heaven. Remember this.

The previous section outlines the simplicity of sacred loving behavior. But life is complex. If you goof up will God zap your butt? It depends. Depends on what? It depends on your INTENTIONS! Yes, intentions dear child of God. If you intend good things and mess up and somehow it hurts someone in some way, you will not get a cosmic spanking. You of course must make amends in any way you can with a humble heart. But we all make mistakes trying to do our moral best. And please do not believe that stupid saying that "the road to hell is made of good intentions". Absurd.

One Example of Politicians:

As I write this, it is February 5, 2019. In a few hours President Trump will deliver his "State of The Union" speech to the nation. It is already being reported that Senator and minority leader of the Senate Chuck Schumer has issued statements condemning the president's address. Now lets just think for a moment. Usually we just don't pay attention to stuff like this.

Here is an adult male human being complaining on the national news networks about something that he has not yet seen or heard. First, do sane rational people do this? Reported by Matthew Choi at Politico today:

Speaking on the Senate floor Tuesday morning, Schumer (D-N.Y.) forecasted that Trump would exaggerate — if not lie about — his administration's achievements and offer a litany of empty promises. [71]

Now this is sinful frankly. It is dishonest and deceitful. The fact that most of us will just glide by the above statement shows just how badly we as a nation have become corrupted away from what we are supposed to be and where we are headed with Schumer being our band leader down the freeway to hell. Next...

Schumer listed a number of promises Trump made during his last State of the Union, from defeating ISIS to opening more manufacturing plants in the country, that the minority leader said the president has failed to keep in the months since. [72]

This is also reported today by Matthew Choi at Politico. Both these "Schumer facts" are completely untrue. They are "lie to your face untrue". Our Military has reported months ago we regained 95% of formerly held ISIS territory. Also, a flood of manufacturing jobs and plants are indeed returning to our nation. Look it up. We do live in an age of lies and deceit. Especially when things are said out of Washington D.C.

---

[71] https://www.politico.com/story/2019/02/05/state-of-the-union-2019-schumer-1147207
[72] https://www.politico.com/story/2019/02/05/state-of-the-union-2019-schumer-1147207

Remember the psychopaths in Washington DC. Chuck Schumer's behavior points him out as one.

I listed a Democrat here. It is because he shot off his mouth with lies and deceit to the entire nation today the day of the State of The Union Presidential Address to our nation. Do NOT think Republicans are any better. They lied about their wars in Iraq and the mideast and even 911. Does anyone believe their investigation? Objective forensic evidence from the towers clearly demonstrate that they are lying to our faces about 911. [73]

But just think of what kind of person does it take and what kind of moral bearing is needed to do this in front of millions of people and for what purpose. Well the purpose is ultimately to get votes. Votes means retaining political power over people. This lastly means dominion over others of God's children, just exactly what Lucifer did so very long ago and wound up in hell for eternity. You now know understand the spiritual destination for Chuck Schumer, the Bushes and people like them in my opinion Wash the feet of others of God's children, do NOT try to dominate them. Raise them up instead. Enough said.

Politicians Cannot Think Like Normal Humans:

Politicians are a special lower form of humanity. They live in a fantasy world of regulations, the law, confiscating money like there is an infinite supply, create false immoral the Democrat entitlements, feel great with the societal power they have and generally not understand the population they want to control.

Their statements reflect a complete absence of proper analytical and objective thinking. For example:

1. Statistics say that 11 million people still have Obama care. Democrats claim that 24 million would die if Obamacare is repealed. Where will the additional 13 million come from? Of course, that assumes that all 11 million would also die.

2. Democrats always complain about wage inequality between men and women. If women are indeed doing the same job for less, they why do companies willfully hire men for more money?

3. Years ago, during the Obama administration attacks from ISIS were caused by climate change, and a plea for jobs the Democrat party said. Yes, they said this. Now with President Trump in office, ISIS attacks are now due to his presidency.

---

[73] Where Did The Towers Go? The New Investigation, Judy Wood, B.S. M.S. PhD

Where did climate change go if we are all going to die in the next 12 years according to Constantina Ocasio Cortez.

4. Liberal Democrats now say that gender is not binary, but it is fluid between them. Boys can be girls and girls can be boys. They say that there is really no difference and genitals do not cause gender. Well, if all that is true then why to Democrats constantly harp on women's rights? Are they just part of a gender continuum? They could be men!

5. Why do Democrats think superdelegates are just fine, then why to want to destroy the electoral college? Both are much the same thing.

6. If Democrats don't want foreigners influencing our elections, then why do they want to give the vote to illegal aliens?

7. The Democrat party says that we are in an existential crisis regarding our climate. We will pass the "tipping point" and life on earth will perish. So, everyone in the United States MUST adopt all the draconian rules outlined in the New Green Deal. Problem: the US makes only 13% of worldwide carbon pollutants. China and India make 33%. The rest of the world makes the rest. If the US were to completely shut down, the world would still produce 87% of what they say is killing us all. And that is increasing. Make any sense to you? The complete lack of any thinking is stunningly absent.

Summary of Hoaxes and Big Lies Perpetrated Against the American People

The following is just a partial summary of all the lies and deceit committed against us the American people by different president of the United States. Each monster act of dishonesty has led to pain, suffering and death to many people both here in American and in other countries.

This list is in no way complete. It is only to give you a taste of what miserable rotten things different presidents have done while in office that we know of. God only knows about the things we have not discovered. Power corrupts, big power corrupts big time.

1. The Gulf of Tonkin incident by President Lyndon Baines Johnson to get the United States involved in the Viet Nam war.

2. Watergate by President Richard Nixon to obtain illegally obtained information of the Democrat Party by breaking into their party headquarters in the Watergate hotel, and Nixon's famous words, "I am not a crook".

3. The Iran-Contra arms smuggling deal by President Ronald Reagan

4. Multiple sexual misconduct episodes by President William Clinton. "I did not have sex with that woman."

5. "Read my lips, no new taxes"by George Bush our 41st president

6. Saddam Hussain has weapons of mass destruction by George Bush our 43rd president

7. Barack Hussain Obama is a Muslim and an illegal alien from Kenya with a forged birth certificate posted on the White House website. It had nine layers of falsification to it when it should have had none.

8. The IRS Tea Party scandal using government resources directed by Barack Obama to harass political opposition

9. The "Russian collusion"scandal against President Trump created by the Hillary Clinton campaign with help from the Barack Obama administration to damage Trump's political campaign then to serve as false grounds for impeachment

10. The Uranium One scandal selling 20% of America's uranium reserves to Russia authorized by Secretary of State Hillary Clinton in exchange for a $145 million dollar contribution to the Clinton foundation two months later.

11. The Benghazi scandal and coverup where Secretary of State Hillary Clinton refused to send military support to our consulate under siege resulting in the deaths of four people including our ambassador.

Operation Fast and Furious where Barack Obama and his Attorney General Eric Holder armed Mexican drug dealers with automatic weapons. This resulted in the deaths of many people including a border agent.

12. Lies told by Barack Obama:
    a. If you like your health car plan you can keep it

    b. All but 10% of the whopping budget deficit is George Bush's fault

    c. Constant use of general terms describing Islamic terror as such things as"workplace violence"or blaming YouTube etc

d. "over the past eight years, no foreign terrorist organization has successfully executed an attack on our homeland…"A lie. Fort Hood just one example

e. "We have not had a major scandal in my administration" A real whopper!

PART 4

Clear and Present Dangers Inside Our Country

The Anti-Christian Politics of The Democratic Party

The Democrat party poses a real and present danger to the health and well-being of our beloved United States of America and everyone living here especially Christians. In my research I have found terribly disturbing facts about the history of Democrats and recent quotes from Democrat politicians. These Democrats are anti-Christian because Christian principles get in their way. They are very divisive in separating God's children into different groups and then trying to pit those groups against each other.

They promote the murder of developing fetal human beings in the name of women's rights. And when they lose a presidential election they work and scheme in every possible way using every possible excuse to circumvent the will of "We the People"perverting our legal processes to remove our duly elected president. Our first president George Washington warned us about people like the Democrats. He said:

The propitious smiles of Heaven can never be expected on a nation that disregards the eternal rules of order and right, which Heaven itself has ordained.

George Washington, First Inaugural Address, April 30, 1789 [74]

These people have no moral foundation at all with the things they say and do. Therefore, I believe the Democrat party is the single largest threat to the health and well-being of our country and everyone living here.

The drumbeat of hatred toward Christians is getting louder and louder and we must address this before it gets so loud our songs of love for God cannot be heard. I discovered that Democrats have always been this way. Their current hateful behavior did not just start recently. They have a disturbing historical history of being antagonistic. They give every appearance of having no conscience. To this James Madison said:

---

[74] http://www.marksquotes.com/Founding-Fathers/Washington/index5.htm

Conscience is the most sacred of all property. — James Madison, Essay on Property, March 29, 1792

Compare this loving thought with the following:

"Candidates with deeply held Christian beliefs are unfit and disqualified from serving as a federal judge." – Charles (Chuck) Schumer (D) minority leader of the US Senate.

What more proof do us Christians need to understand the hate Democrats hold against Christianity?

A Simple Christian Prayer in Pennsylvania:

In Pennsylvania March 2019, Democrats attacked Representative Stephanie Borowicz for invoking the name of Jesus Christ in her opening prayers in the assembly.

"State Rep. Stephanie Borowicz, a Republican and associate pastor's wife who was elected to the state House in November, was accused of bigotry after she invoked the name of Jesus at least 13 times just before the Legislature swore in its first Muslim woman at the Statehouse in Harrisburg."

"I claim all these things in the powerful, mighty name of Jesus, the one who, at the name of Jesus, every knee will bow, and every tongue will confess, Jesus, that you are Lord, in Jesus' name,"Borowicz said.

Democrats responded to the Christian invocation as follows:
1. Democratic state Leader Frank Dermody said Borowicz's speech was "beneath the dignity of this House". My opinion is that you could not find a shovel big enough to dig that deep to find its dignity.

2. State Rep. Jason Dawkins, another Muslim lawmaker, opened the session Tuesday by reading from the Quran, prompting applause in the chamber. Do these morons realize they are clapping for Allah who wants all Christians dead? It's in the Koran you idiots!

3. Some Dems claiming to be "horrified"by the remarks and accusing the female lawmaker of Islamophobia. Nobody is afraid of Islam. We are opposed to it. Get the difference?

Democrats Hate American Freedom and Judeo Christian Principles:

The Democratic Party has been completely overtaken by their own creation, political correctness. This necessitates attacks on people of faith, especially Christians. It is very dangerous and sinister about having to attack people of faith or any expression of faith. In doing so, they are attacking a full 70% of all American citizens.

I think that very few people can forget the awful display at the Democrat National Convention in 2012 when they actually booed God. The video is on line. Democrats are anti-Israel opposing them moving their nation's capital to Jerusalem. They also removed God from their party platform. What kind of morality does it take to do things like this? Who is influencing them to do this? My answer is Satan. Who else?

It is fair to say that Democrats want to take God out of our daily lives, out of our children's lives and everybody else. They want to take our country down a very self destructive path. Democrat state Sen. John Marty said: "The money in my wallet has to say, 'In God We Trust.' I think that's offensive." So Almighty God is offensive to the wretched democrat human being. And to add insult to injury, we Christians are forced to pay for the salary of this pile of water, protein, fat and bone.

Democrats are responsible for removing God out of our schools. He has been replaced by the extreme indoctrination of our kids with leftist liberal propaganda and programs that oppose the values and principles that parents teach their children at home. The schools do not seem to care about this and fight with parents who complain. Democrat political correctness has infested our schools to such an extent that common sense cannot be detected.

As the Democrats'attacks on God and people of Christian faith continues on, we as a nation suffer from the weight of it all. And there will be damage to the minds of our children who become so confused as to which way to turn. Remember that Satan works through the minds of vulnerable and weak people. This is the foundational dynamic of what is happening to our children.

Democrats treat God as a big problem for them. Well, Satan says the same thing. And so too do the democrats. To be a democrat these days you must hate Christianity! This is because the Democratic platform promotes so many so called "rights" that completely go against the Godly principles this nation was founded on and Biblical Christianity. It is just that simple. We all know who the premier God hater in all creation is.... Satan. And yes, he does exist. His influence in the minds of Democrats is so very apparent to me.

Evolution:

Democrats must believe in evolution. This is because they cannot believe in God. If they believed in God, they would have to behave according to all of God's commandments like "thou shalt not murder babies in the womb". They cannot believe that God created all of us. So, they must believe that we are all evolved from a bunch of primordial slime in a bog somewhere. The problem is that in order to assemble just one molecule of a simple protein in the random fashion that evolution says, it would take 1×10^{164} seconds. [75] That is longer than the universe has been in existence, just for one protein molecule.

Forget one complete cell and forget believing a Democrat when they start talking about evolution. Democrats refuse to hear, see or speak the truth about what science says about creation. Here is what they remind me of:

Anti-Christian Litmus Test by Democrats for Nominees:

Questions posed to Brian Buesc nominee for District Court in Nebrask; Kamala Harris. "Have you ever, in any \ assisted with or contributed to advoc against women's reproductive righ Since 1993, you have been a member of Knights of Columbus, an all-male soc comprised primarily of Catholic men. V you aware that the Knights of Columbus opposed a woman's right to choose?

"Have you ever, in any way, assisted with or contributed to advocacy against women's reproductive rights?" [76] Kamala Harris

She cannot stand the Christian belief that a pregnant woman is carrying a developing fetal human being in her womb. No female has the "right" to kill another human being no matter what vocabulary you choose to use to cover the truth that abortion is killing a developing fetal human being.

Russell Vought, now acting director of the Office of Management and Budget said, "I'm a Christian, and I believe in a Christian set of principles based on my faith". By the end of the exchange, Bernie Sanders said, "I would simply say, Mr. Chairman, that this

---

[75] https://www.youtube.com/watch?v=W1_KEVaCyaA
[76] https://freebeacon.com/columns/the-outrageous-assault-on-the-knights-of-columbus/

nominee is really not someone who is what this country is supposed to be about." [77] In saying this Sanders is rejecting the very foundations of our country and God Himself, and Sanders represents the Democratic party.

The Federalist reports the following. *Texas Democrats Seek to Ban Christianity Using So-Called Anti-Discrimination Laws. By James Wesolek, January 28, 2019.* New bills are "going to the legislature. They would create new government powers and "protections" that ban the free expression of biblically grounded beliefs, especially teaching on marriage and sexuality. Numerous bills seek to force people of faith to conform to others' personal and political activities, while setting aside their own sincerely held religious beliefs. Those who do not comply will face fines, possible jail time, or other criminal charges." [78]

When Mike Pompeo was the nominee for Secretary of State he needed to be confirmed by the Senate. Here is part of a news report from 04-23-2018 by Jennifer Wishon. "**All Democrats on the committee say they'll vote 'no,' citing Pompeo's conservative Christian values on matters** like same-sex marriage.""During his confirmation hearing, Sen. Cory Booker (D-NJ) told Pompeo he wouldn't vote for him because of his Biblical opposition to gay marriage, applying a religious litmus test for the job."[79]

Consider the Democrats on the Senate Judiciary Committee to Amy Coney Barrett, a law professor at Notre Dame Law School and a professed Catholic Christian who was being considered for the U.S. Court of Appeals in the 7th Circuit. Democrat Diane Feinstein from California said to her, "I think whatever a religion is, it has its own dogma. The law is totally different.... When you read your speeches, the conclusion one draws is that the dogma lives loudly within you. And that's of concern when you come to big issues..."[80]

What Feinstein said was completely unconstitutional and anti-Christian. Religious tests are prohibited. That did not stop this or any other Democrat. Lastly, note she said, "whatever a religion is". This human being is purely secular with no faith at all, so very sad.

---

[77] IBID

[78]   http://thefederalist.com/2019/01/28/texas-democrats-seek-ban-christianity-using-called-anti-discrimination-laws/

[79]   http://www1.cbn.com/cbnnews/politics/2018/april/senate-snub-will-pompeos-faith-sink-his-chances-at-becoming-americas-next-top-diplomat-nbsp

[80]   https://www.washingtonpost.com/opinions/senate-democrats-show-off-their-anti-religious-bigotry/2017/09/14/30f11e5e-9970-11e7-82e4-f1076f6d6152_story.html?utm_term=.1fc3d41c32f8

Sixty-eight percent of Democrats say employers should grant a request for prayer space by Muslims — but only 45 percent say employers should grant a similar request by Christian employees, says a survey by Grinnell College. [81] Keep in mind that Muslims kill many thousands of Christians every year. I send a good amount of money to a Christian relief fund that helps Christian families reconstruct their lives after attacks from ISIS and other Muslim terrorists. Just imagine the personal horror these people endured. Thank you, Democrats. You are evil in my opinion.

Democrat hatred for Christianity and the faith of God's children is reason enough for Christians to never vote Democrat in 2020 or any other election. Why vote against your own wellbeing?

Democrats Want Total Control Over People's Lives

Contrary to the Christian principle of personal responsibility over your own life, Ugo Okere, a Democratic candidate for Chicago city council wants government control over every single facet of our lives. This guy is mainline Democrat in his thinking. He wants government to control his entire life and the lives of all other people too. He said,

"Democratic socialism, to me, is about democratic control of every single facet of our life," he said. "Government is led by the people, not by big corporations, not by multibillionaires, the world through a socialist-feminist lens... and working people actually have control over who we elect to be our politicians, over how elections work, and over how our government is structured. People have the power." [82]

This guy must miss his mommy or still lives in her basement, not sure. He must miss his security blanket and hobby horse and winky to play with.

Has he read anything on socialist history? Their intent is to force "sameness" and "one size fits all" upon all of God's children that live here in the United States of America. This alone is a heinous crime of monster evil against both God's children and "I Am" Himself. This is precisely what Satan wants on his road to destruction of the United States and the children of God. Necessarily so the Democrat party MUST hate all Christians for they rebel against God in their politics in abortion, killing developing fetal human beings,

[81] https://godfatherpolitics.com/national-poll-shows-democrats-vastly-favor-muslims-over-christians/

[82] https://freebeacon.com/politics/chicago-dem-wants-socialism-to-have-control-of-every-single-facet-of-our-life/

opposing the southern wall to protect God's children from the evils we know live there that Satan has made manifest in this world.

President John Adams: *"righteousness exalteth a nation but sin is a reproach to any people."*

"You be you. Live your truth. And know that New York City will have your back,"[83] Mayor Bill de Blasio said these words. This plainly states that there are no Godly rules, there are no divine commandments and you may indulge in any kind of perversion or action against others of God's children as you wish. This is Satan talking through the mouth of Democrat Mayor Bill de Blasio just like he did in the garden of Eden promising that knowing both good and evil will make the metaphorical Adam and Eve into Gods. We Christians know what happened after that. I feel that this Democrat Mayor has a snake in his mouth.

The above is just the start.

Women:

The big lie at work. Going to the 2016 Democratic Party platform under the title "Guaranteeing Women's Rights", I found the following sentence, "We are committed to ensuring full equality for women." But then in huge blue letters I saw the emphasis on, GUARANTEEING LESBIAN, GAY, BISEXUAL, AND TRANSGENDER RIGHTS". Yes, it was in capital letters. With a huge paragraph following. So, we know where the Democratic Party is headed with their guarantee. Yes, they guarantee it in their platform. Look it up at Democrats.org.

Democrats urge all women to be "sexually free to be themselves and do what they want." If you get pregnant do not worry, we will call murdering the developing fetal human being in your womb a case of "women's reproductive rights" and "women's reproductive health care."

We will also attack all the males in our society using the term "male toxicity." They think this will help women deal with the men in their lives by attempting to turn men into some form of woman. This is why they celebrate transgender and other forms of sexual deviance of all kinds.

---

[83] https://www.nationalreview.com/2019/01/transgender-birth-certificate-law-gender-identity-legal-concept-weak/

Democrats and Slavery:

Did the Democrats support slavery? Yes. Yes, very actively before and during the Civil War. After the war of course there was no slavery to support, but the Dixiecrats were solidly against equal rights for former slaves. It wasn't until John Kennedy and the 1960s that the Democrats began supporting racial integration and equality."[84] That is the short answer. Investigate further if you wish.

Getting the Black Vote:

More Democrat truth, Lyndon Johnson said, "I'll have those nig**rs voting Democratic for 200 years." [85] According to Ronald M. MacMillan, former Air Force One steward who was present when Lyndon Johnson expressed those words. "That was the reason he was pushing the bill," said MacMillan, who was present during the conversation. "Not because he wanted equality for everyone. It was strictly a political ploy for the Democratic party to get more votes and retain political power. He was phony from the word go."[86] All this is from Snopes, a liberal leaning truth seeking website. Is it true? I have lived through the Johnson administration and personally known people just like Democrat Johnson from the south in my family, their attitudes toward blacks and the language they use is awful. It is reasonable to believe this quote to be true. But in openness will leave it up to you.

Booker T. Washington was a great educator and a black man. He was very wise, and the following is a quote from him that summarizes very well the situation back then and we still have today. Bottom line, no progress regardless of all the money we have spent to lift up black people from their poverty and education, material well-being and in spirit. Booker also refers to the kind of people that we see in Jesse Jackson and Al Sharpton. They make a great amount of money by sporting all the black grievances but really do nothing about it but complain and go to the bank.

"There is another class of coloured people who make a business of keeping the troubles, the wrongs, and the hardships of the Negro race before the public. Having learned that they are able to make a living out of their troubles, they have grown into the settled habit of advertising their wrongs — partly because they want sympathy and partly because it pays.

---

[84] http://www.answers.com/Q/Did_democrats_support_slavery

[85] Inside the White House: The Hidden Lives of the Modern Presidents and the Secrets of the World's Most Powerful Institution, pg33,Ronald Kessler, 1995

[86] https://www.snopes.com/fact-check/lbj-voting-democratic/

Some of these people do not want the Negro to lose his grievances, because they do not want to lose their jobs."[87]

The bottom line is that the civil rights legislation led by the Democrats in the 1960s was designed to capture the black vote so the Democrats could stay in power. It was nothing else. In the ensuing years they refined their hold on the black community with ever increasing giveaway programs that did not really help anybody escape poverty. I observed this as it happened. I went to the south side of Chicago when I was a small boy to visit my aunt with my parents. I remember the tenement buildings, awful. Toughest gun laws, highest murder rate, both in Chicago. Democrat Rob Emmanuel is an evil snake in my opinion. Look at his eyes.

If the black children of God ever rose into the middle class, then the Democrats would lose their control over them. Don't believe me? Ask why Democrats are against school vouchers. That would free kids from lousy schools. Booker T. Washington was right. "If you can't read, it's going to be hard to realize dreams."

It is also my opinion this is the way Satan works with drug addiction but in this case, it is money from government programs that is the addiction. Again, my personal opinion. Think about it. All the money spent over in the last 50 years has done nothing. And it will do nothing in the coming 50 years, except get worse. And the poor people will continue to vote Democrat. They think it is sacrilegious not to.

The Scandal of Barack Obama:

Would any political party in the United States accept a candidate for high office without knowing everything about that person? The American answer is no. But that is not what the Democrat party did in 2008 when they chose Barack Obama. At the time we had proper suspicions that he was not a real American citizen and that he was a Muslim. Islam is a religion/political movement hostile to Christian principles and values. All this was chosen to be ignored.

We now live in a country where 90% of journalists are liberals. This does indeed bias all that is said in our media. It is so easy when you are in power to just ignore things that might put liberalism or the Democrat party in a bad light.

Here is a list of things that the Democrat party hid from us and the liberal media aided and abetted.

---

[87] https://www.azquotes.com/author/15322-Booker_T_Washington

1. When a major political party investigates a candidate to be a candidate, why did the Democrats choose to overlook these missing items from Obama's hidden history:

   a. birth certificate (Proven to be a forgery). I have videos showing Obama saying that he was the first person born in Kenya to be the president of the United States.

   b. kindergarten records

   c. SAT score

   d. L SAT score

   e. Occidental College records

   f. Columbia College records

   g. Columbia college thesis

   h. Harvard College records

   i. medical records

   j. law practice client list

   k. scholarly articles

   l. baptism certificate

   m. Senate records

   n. Passport

2. Barack Obama is a Muslim. There are online videos that show him referring to his Islamic faith. Pictures of him wearing Islamic clothes as a young boy etc.

3. Some quotes from Obama regarding his Muslim faith. He claimed to be a Christian. The Democrat party had to know he is a Muslim from Kenya. No one is that dumb.

   a. *"The future must not belong to those who slander the Prophet of Islam"* [88]

---

[88] Obama U.N. Speech: A New Religion Doctrine, Lauren Markoe, www.huffingtonpost.com. September 27, 2012.

b. *"The sweetest sound I know is the Muslim call to prayer."*[89]

c. *"I look forward to hosting an Iftar dinner celebrating Ramadan here at the White House later this week."*[90]

d. *"I consider it part of my responsibility as President of the United States to fight against negative stereotypes of Islam wherever they appear"*[91]

e. *"Islam has a proud tradition of tolerance."*[92]

f. *"We do not consider ourselves a Christian nation "*[93]

g. *"Islam is not part of the problem in combating violent extremism - it is an important part of promoting peace "*[94]

h. *"Throughout history, Islam has demonstrated through words and deeds the possibilities of religious tolerance and racial equality"*[95]

My search for objective truth led me to the above horrific information. The above points to awful lies and deceit committed against the American people by the Democrat party and against our Judeo-Christian foundations. Think about just how many people it took to hide all of Obama's history. Think about how many people it took to hide all the previously existing birth records and create a forged birth certificate on the White House website. The tragedy about Obama's birth is it makes everything he did as president becomes null and void.

If this were not enough, Barack Obama when he was in Kasarani, Kenya, he said, "I am the first Kenyan American to be the President of the United States". From this we can see he identifies himself as not an African-American but a Kenyan-American. He stops just short of admitting he was born there. [96]

This was eight years of dishonesty and corruption in the highest places in our government. Democrats cheered. Their true character has surfaced from the

[89] www.huffingtonpost.com. February 4, 2016

[90] obamawhitehouse.archives.gov. August 11, 2010.

[91] A New Beginning: Speech at Cairo University, delivered 4 June 2009, Cairo, Egypt

[92] IBID

[93] The President's News Conference With President Abdullah Gul of Turkey in Ankara, Turkey, April 6, 2009

[94] A New Beginning: Speech at Cairo University, delivered 4 June 2009, Cairo, Egypt

[95] IBID

[96] https://www.youtube.com/watch?v=ROSKprLNqb4

dark into the light where we can see who they really are since President Trump took office. It is ugly and very sad.

Obama Era Scandals:

Now, former vice-president Joe Biden under Barack Obama wants to run for President in 2020. That ought to be entertaining considering all the Obama era scandals that were covered up during that time. Joe Biden has his fingerprints on all of this stuff I believe. He can't help but know all of this. Here are a few:

1. Fast and Furious: A plan devised by numbskull Eric Holder to give automatic military assault weapons to drug lords in Mexico. Gee what could go wrong with that? This resulted in many deaths including one of our precious border agents killed by a gun Obama gave to the drug lords.

2. Obama Care: Everything about Obama Care was a scandal. From the President's incessant lies about keeping your old plan if you liked it, keeping your doctor, to Rep. Nancy Pelosi's "we need to pass it to find out what's in it" dereliction of Congressional duty, to forcing mandate payments on people who do want insurance.

3. The IRS Scandal: Where legitimate political groups were denied appropriate statue due to their political convictions, like the Tea Party and Pro-life groups. The IRS became a political weapon by the Obama Administration

4. The Benghazi scandal: It was a disaster after Obama's unlawful military operation in Libya and they needed to cover their tracks during election season. So they blamed a YouTube videotape to cover the death of US Ambassador Christopher Stevens.

5. Hillary Clinton's email server scandal: She perpetrated her email offenses as Secretary of State of the United States of America. Obama knew about it. This is coming under investigation again.

6. The Iran Nuclear Deal: The best symbol of this deal is the $150 BILLION in cash flown into Iran by the Obama administration during his last two weeks in office.

There are more but this is enough so as to paint a real picture.

Reasons Why Thinking Christians Cannot Be Leftist Liberals

Case 1: Liberals look to government secular solutions for all problems. They never ever look to God their creator.

"Here's the truth: infrastructure spending isn't a transportation issue for most Americans — it's a human rights issue."Twitter Kamala Harris 6:23 PM - Jan 24, 2017

The problem with her comment is the extra tax burden this will mean to already heavily taxed working people slaving to make ends meet. The tradeoff is enslave someone to give someone else a goodie by labeling it a "right". Classic secular government thinking throwing someone else's money at it.

Case 2: Everyone has a sacred right to life, the life that God has bestowed to each of us as individuals. Christians believe this in their hearts. Liberals vehemently disagree with this. You can see this in their rhetoric and actions each and every day of the week.

Abortion: Sacred human life begins at conception. This is a scientific fact. When the egg gets fertilized the result now fits the scientific definition of life. It is human life. Period. From then on it is called a developing fetal human being. If liberals are so willing to make transportation a human right, why don't they give the same rights to a developing fetal human being?

Actually, they give the fetal human being a lower standing than getting from here to there because they do NOT give the fetal human being any rights at all. Only the voting mother has any rights. They call it, women's reproductive rights, or women's reproductive health care. NO! Killing sacred fetal human beings does not advance a woman's health. This is an established medical fact. Democrats willfully ignore this. Why? There is an answer. Read the details about this in the section on abortion. It is horrifying. No believing Christian would ever support the Democrat position on abortion no matter what they call it. It is murder of a developing sacred fetal human being. All human life is made in the image of God and therefore sacred and must be protected.

Case 3: Liberals always use the term gun violence. This is because they want to remove all weapons like guns from private hands so the government will be the only ones to possess them. History shows when this happens governments always turn tyrannical toward their citizens no matter what form of government there was before. The possession of weapons by citizens is what prevented Japan from invading the West Coast during World War II.

General Isoroku Yamamoto famously said, "There would be a rifle behind every blade of grass". Our founding fathers were wisely very worried about government domination over the children of God and rightly so. They were students of history and saw the ravages of the kingly system of government and what it could do to people and their lives. This was especially true with Thomas Payne. This is why we have the second amendment right behind the first for freedom of speech. It is that important.

If anyone cares to really think about it, guns are actually a completely inanimate object capable of doing nothing by themselves. Like every other inanimate object, they have the potential to do good or bad things depending on how they are used by the human being. They are exactly like a car, a hammer, a saw, a knife, an airplane, or any other object, chemical, and so on. It takes a human being with a mind and intentions and a will with motivation to put these inanimate objects into motion.

Everything that occurs in the physical world always, happens first in the mind of a human being. A decision is then made in the mind of that human being either to do an action or not depending upon that person's morality, ethics and sense of responsibility. Nothing happens until all of this occurs within the human mind. It is the human mind where Satan plays his games. It is the human mind were good and evil battle each other. So, in a very real sense guns have nothing to do with violence. Guns are a "method of violence"not a cause.

In London they banned all guns because they said there is too much gun violence, the favorite term of our Democrats. Here is a headline from the New York Times. [97] London Confronts a Spate of Murders, With Most Victims Killed by Knives. London's Muslim mayor Khan is embarrassed and now wants to ban knives. "No excuses: there is never a reason to carry a knife. Anyone who does will be caught, and they will feel the full force of the law." [98] These are two cities with the most draconian gun control in the world. People just get murdered a different way.

On September 1, 2001 airplanes had everything to do with violence. Then why do Democrats pound the drum about banning guns from citizens, taking them from God's children? It is a matter of control over our lives. They want complete control over our lives. If you cannot believe this well.

Case 4: 22 Year old Ugo Okere, a Democratic candidate for Chicago city council wants government control over every single facet of our lives. He said, "Democratic

---

[97] www.nytimes.com/2018/04/07/world/europe/london-murders-knife-attacks-stabbing.html
[98] https://madworldnews.com/london-muslim-mayor-gun-ban/

socialism, to me, is about democratic control of every single facet of our life," he said. "Government is led by the people, not by big corporations, not by multibillionaires, the world through a socialist-feminist lens... and working people actually have control over who we elect to be our politicians, over how elections work, and over how our government is structured. People have the power." [99] No! They will not! That is an illusion bought by millions in history paid by the deaths of many tens of millions in history. Just read the history books.

Ugo's quote above represents mainstream thinking within the Democratic Party. This is completely opposite of what God intended for all of his children here on planet Earth. This is completely opposite of what he intended for you and me. We were intended to have freedom of mind and action so we could work out our spiritual direction in learning, gathering knowledge and experience, understanding more deeply the workings of God's creation and in doing so growing closer to Him in more exciting ways. These are parts of the reasons we came here to begin with.

Anything that interferes with this, destroys or stops this can only have one source. And it is from the one that has sworn to fight God in every way he possibly can because he hates God now that he has been thrown out of the heavenly kingdom. You know who he is. And he has one third of the angelic host with him now called demons. Always remember they are extremely intelligent, more intelligent than most of us. But there are always telltale signs of their workings in our minds because, again, they have to fit a certain pattern either by deception or lack of love and peace.

Case 5: There is a concerted and constant campaign against Christian representation in government by the left called the Democrat Party. They grill nominees for appointed office about their religious beliefs during their confirmation hearings. This is strictly prohibited by the constitution of the United States. They ignore that and do it anyway. Here are a few examples.

"Do you consider yourself an orthodox Catholic?" The Constitution forbids this question completely, but Democratic Senator Dick Durbin from Illinois asked it anyway to a judicial nominee. [100]

---

[99]   https://iotwreport.com/ugo-okere-a-dem-candidate-for-chicago-alderman-wants-socialism-in-control-of-every-facet-of-our-lives/

[100]   https://www.dailysignal.com/2017/09/06/two-democrat-senators-show-hostility-to-religion-in-questions-for-judicial-nominee/

Sen. Dianne Feinstein. D-Calif., chided a judicial nominee for being a practicing Catholic, proclaiming, *"The dogma lives loudly within you, and that's of concern."* [101] *Feinstein was addressing Amy Coney Barrett an appellate court nominee. Feinstein was worried that she would not agree that developing human beings under the banner of women's reproductive health was a right.*

Bernie Sanders chimed in with his version of hating Christianity during a confirmation hearing for a nominee in the Office of Management and Budget. Bernie said, "You wrote, 'Muslims do simply have a deficient theology; they do not know God because they've rejected Jesus Christ His Son, and they stand condemned,'" Sanders said, reading a quote from Vought's writings. "Do you believe that that statement is Islamophobic?"

"Absolutely not, Senator," Vought answered. "I'm a Christian, and I believe in a Christian set of principles based on my faith."

After more heated questioning specifically directed to Vought's Christian beliefs, Sanders concluded, "I would simply say, Mr. Chairman, that this nominee is really not someone with what this country is supposed to be about." [102]

Kamala Harris grilled Brian Buescher nominee for United States District Court of Nebraska on December 5 2018. [103]

Do you believe that Roe v. Wade was correctly decided?

What did you mean when you said that you would refuse to "compromise" on your anti-choice views?

During your nominations hearing before the Judiciary Committee, you emphasized that you took these anti-choice positions as a candidate running for office, yet as noted above, you also said that your anti-choice views were part of your "moral fabric."

If confirmed, would you set aside the entirety of your "moral fabric" when issuing rulings?

There were more questions from Democrat Sen. Kamala Harris on his Christian beliefs. These questions are entirely illegal and unconstitutional. But this did not stop the senator from asking them anyway. It is clear that Democrat Harris is anti-Christian. She does represent the vast majority of the Democrat party power structure in both Washington and the 50 states.

---

[101] IBID

[102] https://www.churchmilitant.com/news/article/senate-bias-against-catholic-nominees

[103] https://www.judiciary.senate.gov/imo/media/doc/Buescher%20Responses%20to%20QFRs.pdf

The summary of all of this is that the liberal left Democrats have replaced God in their minds with man-made secular government funded by God's children. They look to government rules and regulations for guidance. They look to government for support, to take care of them. They look to government to be their nanny. They look to government to be their counselor, and their medical provider. And all they have to do in return is send most of their money to the government in taxes. The rest will be taken care of. This is basically their view of life. Frankly, all of this is nothing more than another Tower of Babel.

Lastly the above does not include:

1. Knowingly inviting, making possible deadly drugs that kill thousands of Americans each year, human (sex) trafficking with its horrors and dangerous criminals to prey on our citizens every day, into our country from our border with Mexico to do what LBJ did in 1968 with black voters to vote Democratic. It is all about power.

2. Democrats complain bitterly about a wall on our southern border to protect our citizens from evils that we certainly know exist and have measured. They also complain about ICE having to separate children from the adults they are with to ensure the adults are indeed the children's parents and not human traffickers. Democrats repeatedly say this is inhuman to treat children this way. Yet they promote killing fetal human beings and call it a woman's right to do so. Recently, they have proposed the heinous thought of killing children already born or in the process of being born, calling it abortions and woman's reproductive health. As this is written legislation is already proposed in New York by Democrats to do just this.

These two completely opposite positions indicate without doubt that the Democrat party of today has no moral foundation at all. This is evil at its root. In these two political positions they have taken they expose themselves as not giving a damn for the health and wellbeing of American citizens while they try to rephrase killing developing fetal human beings into woman's reproductive rights. They lack any real sense of morality, respect for human life and Godly love for their fellow human beings. A love that Jesus said we all must have when we love God first and love our neighbors as ourselves.

No Christian in their right mind would ever vote for this. Voting Democrat would be doing exactly that.

4. Giving $150 billion to Iran, a hostile Islamic country, that has repeatedly called us the great Satan and wants to destroy us. Thank you, Barak Obama. Their goal is to dominate and kill Christians and Jews because Mohammad said so 1,400 years ago.

5. Supporting the violence of Antifa against Christians and those who disagree with Democratic socialism. Thank you, George Soros. Democrats have never spoken out against this violent group of thugs that attack people who they disagree with.

Just how dismal can you get? Just how short of the sparkling wonderment that God put before us in sending us here to create a future for us and our children. Remember, it all turned bad when Lucifer committed the ultimate sin by attempting to raise himself higher then Almighty God and now, he is working through anyone he can to destroy all of God's children. Right now, this means the liberal left and the creeping socialism preached by the Democratic party. If you vote Democrat, the above is what you are voting for. Do not vote Democrat in 2020! Doing so will be a huge refutation of your professed Christianity.

Why Christians Must Not Vote Democrat in 2020 [104]

We have already seen ample reasons why Christians should never vote Democrat. Simply put, it is because the Democrat party political platform goes completely against Christian teachings, the 10 Commandments, what Jesus Christ taught us and our Judeo-Christian foundational values and ethics. It is these foundational Christian values that formed and created our country and allowed us to prosper far beyond any other country in the world.

Since losing the election in 2016 Democrats now want to change the rules for elections and change the very structure of our government. These changes are designed to wildly favor a leftist liberal point of view. If this is allowed to happen, we will see malignant increasing attacks against Christians and Christianity throughout our country. They will turn the United States of America into a hellhole where anybody in the world can come here and take advantage of the American taxpayer. As I have said before, democrats would rather control and rule over a dung heap than participate in a sparkling society.

As of this writing here are some of the major proposals the Democrat party will be trying to sell to the American people for the 2020 election.

---

[104] https://www.foxnews.com/politics/15-far-out-ideas-from-the-democratic-2020-field

1. Because Pres. Trump succeeded in placing two constitutional Supreme Court justices, Democrats now want to pack the Supreme Court with more leftist justices that if elected they will appoint to reverse the constitutional favor that now exists. In other words, since they lost, they want to change the rules in their favor. They want to destroy that institution which has served the American citizens so very well since the founding of our country. This is adolescent behavior on a very large destructive scale.

2. Democrats want reparations to black people in cash for slavery. In other words, because if you are white and your great great great grandfather may have owned slaves in the South you will be required to pay substantial amounts of money to the government. Never mind that my ancestors did not arrive in this country until 1907 after slavery ended. The government then would give this money to black people. I cannot think of a more racist and destructive and hate filled idea. This goes completely against Judeo-Christian values where all of God's children are created equal. Also, one of God's children must not be forced to pay for someone else's sin. Only vast amounts of hatred will result from this. This proposal bubbles and foams with hate in every direction.

3. Elsewhere in this literary work I discussed in detail Constantina Ocasio Cortez's green new deal. It has many provisions in it that are completely anti-Christian within its foundational understanding of reality. This woman is a complete adolescent that lives in fantasy land with no connection with objective reality.

4. Democrats want Medicare for everybody. This includes all illegal aliens in our country. If elected Democrats will make illegal any private medical insurance you may have. They will force you just like Obamacare into one big boiling cauldron of government controlled health care. If you like the DMV, you will love this. This proposal goes completely against Christian values because it treats everybody the same. God created us all as unique individuals, one-of-a-kind. Force fitting everybody into one shoe size would be catastrophic for everybody. Everybody is not size 10.

5. Democrats want to lower the voting age. This is simply a lust for power on their part. 16-year-olds know nothing about how the world works and are the most gullible to political propaganda. Democrats know this. This is why they want to lower the voting age because they know teenagers will most likely vote for the shiny paint job of falsified political rhetoric. There are some things in this life

you must earn. You earn the right to vote through sufficient life experience that teaches you how the world works. Do you want 16-year-old teenagers to be in control of your financial plan and your security as a nation?

6. Democrats want to abolish the death penalty. Good! I agree with this. I believe it is a foundational Christian value that no child of God has a right to take the life of another human being, abortion included. The alternative? Just lock them up for the rest of their lives away from society where they can do no harm. But do not turn the prison into a resort with cable TV and all the other niceties.

7. Democrats want to provide Social Security for all illegal aliens. They call it" comprehensive immigration reform". American taxpayers have paid into Social Security to provide for their retirement. It was a separate trust fund with money in it to be paid out to taxpayers when they retired. No more. Now Democrats want to give your money away to all illegal aliens. This goes completely against Judeo-Christian values and ethics. The government forcibly confiscates through taxation an increasing amount of your productive life as measured in dollars and now wants to give it away to illegal aliens who have broken our laws by being here.

8. Democrats want a wealth tax. The concept is simple. If your assets are more than what the government thinks you should have, then they will tax that not based on income but on the value of the asset. This is simply government confiscation of what you worked hard to earn. This also goes completely against Judeo-Christian values because it is basically legal robbery of what you own.

9. If you have chronic and serious pain which a lot of people have, Democrats want to make it illegal for your doctor to prescribe more than seven days of opiate painkillers. Again, this is like force fitting everybody into the same shoe size. The government denies the fact that God made us all unique one-of-a-kind individuals with unique one-of-a-kind medical issues including pain. Not only is this anti-Christian in its foundational value but it will also do nothing to address the opiate crisis because that is due to all the illegal drugs flowing into this country from Mexico. This is a proven fact. But Democrats want open borders.

10. Democrats want to remove all border security with Mexico. This goes directly against the very first and foremost function of government which is to protect

its citizens from outside criminality. Why do Democrats want to do this? Because it will gain them more votes. Remember Democrats want power above all else including you. It matters not what pain and agony they inflict to American citizens in the process. You and I are just collateral damage to be ignored.

After understanding the facts presented above, I cannot fathom how any Christian would ever vote Democrat in 2020.

Democrats Love Socialism

The Democratic Party is in love with anything that is a government program. This is the main thrust of all their policies and political platform. This kind of posture and role of government in our society goes completely against the foundational and constitutional values that are country was founded on. It is also the handmaiden of socialism.

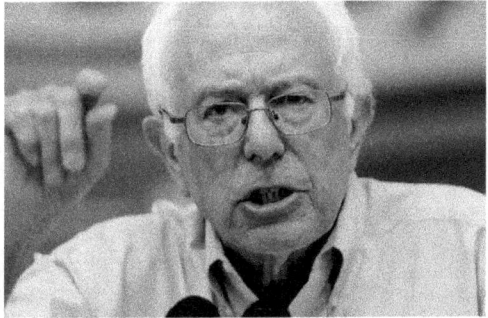

"Several recent polls, plus the popularity of Sen. Bernie Sanders, demonstrate that young people prefer socialism to free market capitalism. That, I believe, is a result of their ignorance and indoctrination during their school years, from kindergarten through college. For the most part, neither they nor many of their teachers and professors know what free market capitalism is."[105]

Our country is founded upon free markets and capitalism. It is this economic system that has allowed us to do two things. The first is that free market capitalism is completely consistent with Judeo-Christian principles of freedom, individual enterprise, the free exchange of goods, services and ideas between God's children. This is completely opposite to socialism where every aspect of your lives is controlled by the government.

Remember the following:

---

[105] By Walter E. Williams Professor economics George Mason University June 2, 2018 www.creators.com

'What are you worrying about? Capitalism as a whole will now be destroyed, the whole people will now be free. We are not fighting Jewish or Christian capitalism; we are fighting every capitalism: we are making the people completely free.' — Hitler speech 1922

"My object in life is to dethrone God and destroy capitalism." — Karl Marx

Many tens of millions of innocent people murdered, executed, death by starvation, and killed by troops all because these two wretched human beings had socialism or communism stuck in their heads. No right minded person would ever consent to that, so they had to force it down their throats with guns and death.

60 years ago, Venezuela was 4th on the world economic freedom index. Today they are 179th and their citizens are dying of starvation. In only 10 years, Venezuela was destroyed by democratic socialism. You will never hear this from crazy Bernie Sanders who idolizes Fidel Castro and Carl Marx, two people responsible for the deaths of millions of people. At age 74 you would think Bernie would have learned better, but he still is an adolescent.

Socialism Kills the Human Spirit:

Socialism is doomed from the start. Because it attempts to take unequal human beings, each born with different God given talents in different amounts and born into different circumstances and then forcing all that into equal results. This necessarily means pounding down successful people to rise up the unsuccessful. Doing this requires tremendous and costly force against productive people and a large distribution network.

Aristotle knew this ever so long ago when he said:

"The worst form of inequality is to try to make unequal things equal." Aristotle

Free market capitalism is proven to be consistent with Judeo-Christian principles and the will of God. Socialism is NOT and kills the human spirit. It does this by spreading poverty equally among the people. It robs people of any incentive to better themselves and grow as God intended. Want proof? One unavoidable result of socialism is homelessness. San Francisco has been run by socialist mayors and city council for many years now. San Francisco is the ONLY city in the Bay Area with serious human public pooping problems. See this map and cringe. [106]

---

[106] https://www.openthebooks.com/map/?Map=32504&MapType=Pin&Zip=94103

This is a pin map showing poop complaints by residents. In the 1960's San Francisco was a wonderful place to visit. But socialism came. Now it isn't for so many reasons. "We see poop, we see pee, we see needles, and we see trash," said one local resident who spoke to NBC. Cleaning it up has become an expensive problem. Of the City of San Francisco's public works budget for "street environmental services" — around $60 million — more than half has gone to cleaning up the poop. [107]

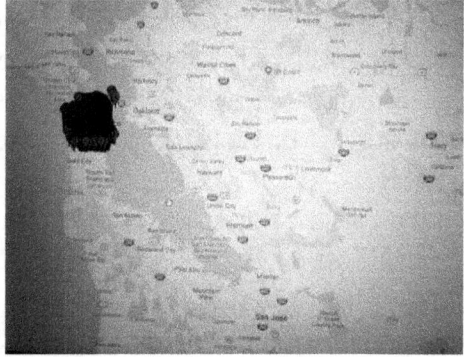

Poop on the streets is just one. Cuba is a hell hole, another example. Notice no other city has any problems at all. San Francisco is also a sanctuary city for illegal aliens to frolic as they want. Nancy Pelosi lives in San Francisco. She likes all this I guess.

San Francisco is not the only national embarrassment. Every city that has been run by Democrat socialists for any significant length of time have ruined what they governed. Seattle Washington is another shining city that has been turned into garbage by socialism and its bankrupt social policies of high taxes, sanctuary laws, limits on protecting citizens. Here is a very good documentary on Seattle in this footnote. [108] The last time I personally saw sights like this I was in poor sections of the Philippines, a third world country watching very little children with no shoes picking through the garbage dump looking for scraps of metal to sell to feed their family living in nearby tents. This is what socialism has done to Seattle Washington. Bernie, want to join me on a trip to the Philippines and get a big dose of truth you bastard idiot?

Huge Government:

Socialism requires a monster sized government that controls every aspect of life. This goes completely against the will of God for his children anywhere they are. Socialists talk about equality. But socialism provides no incentive for people to produce goods and services that will result in the betterment of both themselves and their families.

Therefore, the only equality that exists in socialism is that of spreading poverty, suffering, pain and death equally among the people. History has shown this to be 100%

---

[107] San Francisco's local NBC affiliate, Emily Zanotti, May 17, 2018
[108] https://www.youtube.com/watch?v=bpAi70WWBlw

true. 30 years ago Venezuela was a prosperous country exporting oil. Now since they voted for socialism, the country has completely failed with horrible social unrest. Food is now hard to get and the government makes small food handouts to people. The average adult in Venezuela has lost 19 pounds in the last year alone. Socialism caused a human tragedy.

Prof. Walter Williams has this to say about socialism:

"Free market capitalism, wherein there is peaceful voluntary exchange, is morally superior to any other economic system. Why? Let's start with my initial premise. All of us own ourselves. I am my private property, and you are yours. Murder, rape, theft and the initiation of violence are immoral because they violate self-ownership. Similarly, the forcible use of one person to serve the purposes of another person, for any reason, is immoral because it violates self-ownership.

Tragically, two-thirds to three-quarters of the federal budget can be described as Congress taking the rightful earnings of one American to give to another American — using one American to serve another. Such acts include farm subsidies, business bailouts, Social Security, Medicare, Medicaid, food stamps, welfare and many other programs.

Let's compare capitalism with socialism by answering the following questions: In which areas of our lives do we find the greatest satisfaction, and in which do we find the greatest dissatisfaction? It turns out that we seldom find people upset with and in conflict with computer and clothing stores, supermarkets, and hardware stores. We do see people highly dissatisfied with and often in conflict with boards of education, motor vehicles departments, police and city sanitation services.

What are the differences? For one, the motivation for the provision of services of computer and clothing stores, supermarkets, and hardware stores is profit. Also, if you're dissatisfied with their services, you can instantaneously fire them by taking your business elsewhere. It's a different matter with public education, motor vehicles departments, police and city sanitation services. They are not motivated by profit at all. Plus, if you're dissatisfied with their service, it is costly and, in many cases, even impossible to fire them."[109]

Socialism also creates "false entitlements". No one on this earth is "entitled" to anyone else's money...no one! The idea of entitlements grossly violates what Professor Walter Williams said above. You are indeed you and I am me. We own ourselves, not the government. The government has no friggen right to confiscate 35% to 40% of our

---

[109] IBID

productive sacred lives through monster taxes and then calling taxpayer funded handouts entitlements.

From a Christian perspective each individual is entitled to his or her products of their labor. This is consistent with Biblical literature. Yes, we are to always love our neighbors and help them if we can. This is the second of the two greatest commandments. But under this guise, the government has seized our productive lives which gives the government more power over us. It also stimulates laziness from those people who voted themselves more "benefits"and "entitlements". Each person who comes to this planet has the God given responsibility to work as hard as they can to provide for themselves. We are to help others if they need it as the child of God determines its necessity. By the government taking a monster portion of our productive lives, children of God are now seriously hampered to help other children of God because they do not anymore have the resources to do so. Person to person relationships including charity are the foundational principle of forming loving bonds between people. This is one of the reasons we came to this planet to begin with. But our government wants to continue its confiscation of this.

If you like the DMV, the IRS and the Veterans Administration taking care of all your other needs and controlling every aspect of your life then you will like socialism. It really is that simple. Socialism can be your eternal mommy taking care of you in your perpetual childhood. Just like mommy, the government will make all your decisions for you whether you like it or not. It takes a lot of ignorance and lack of life experience to be fooled into the shiny paint job of a rusted out car like socialism without understanding the rusted and crumbling fenders underneath.

God put us here on earth for many reasons within our individual spiritual growth. God expects us to work hard and make the effort to accomplish the goals he has set forth for all of us. The decision to remain a child and have mommy government take care of you is an insult to your divine birthright and the will of your father Almighty God.

"Beware the left side of most all things, especially in human thought and action"
— Anonymous

Democrats Want Huge Government That Replaces the Will of God

In my lifetime I have observed government grow each year bigger and bigger and bigger. The growth of spending at the federal lever will spin your head. For example, back in 1956 the total federal government spending was $68B dollars. This is compared to the projected federal spending in 2020 to be at $4.75T dollars or $4,750B dollars to compare with the 1956 amount. So, we went from $68B to $4,750B. Unbelievable.

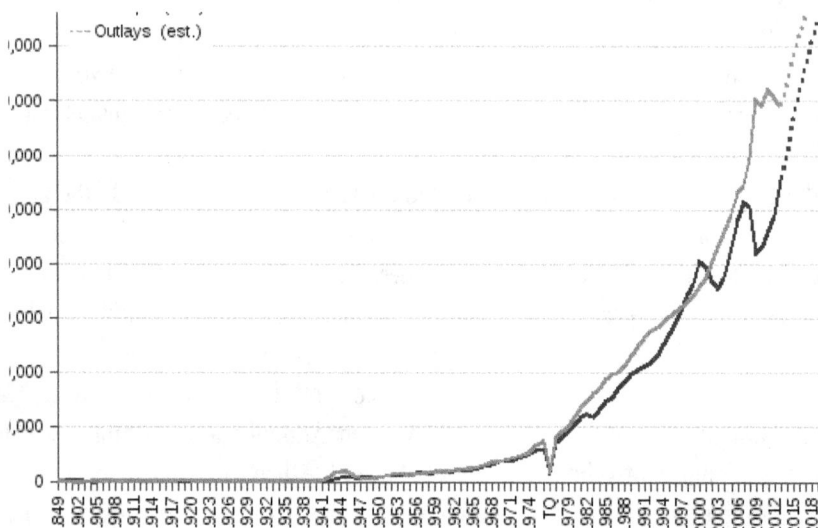

Government will say they are "taking care of us." Our founding fathers would violently disagree.

"I predict future happiness for Americans, if they can prevent the government from wasting the labors of the people under the pretense of taking care of them."[110] — Thomas Jefferson

It is already taking monstrous amounts of money to support our socialist programs in our country. What will it be if the democrats get their way in 2020 and take our country deeper into the socialist rathole? In the process we lose more and more of our freedoms.

Arbitrary power is most easily established on the ruins of liberty abused to licentiousness.[111] — George Washington, Circular to the States, May 9, 1753

---

[110] https://www.goodreads.com/quotes/tag/government
[111] http://www.marksquotes.com/Founding-Fathers/Washington/

Yet, sadly enough, some of our current politicians cannot or will not grasp this Christian truth that all sovereign power starts with the individual sacred human being. No government can call itself legitimate unless it exists only to serve the health and wellbeing of all its individual citizens, not control them. This means individual freedom and not socialist nanny state programs that are already bankrupting our country. It is an attitude of public service based on individual sovereignty and NOT government control. It is dangerous to our culture and society to have politicians say the following quote. It is talk like this that defines the beginning of socialism and class warfare in our nation.

"We must stop thinking of the individual and start thinking about what is best for society."[112] — Hillary Clinton

Individuals ARE society. Just add them up Hillary. This statement is pure poison to the health and wellbeing of our democratic Constitutional republic. Clinton has forgotten that it is the individual sovereign person that IS society. She has it backwards much to the horrific danger to all of us citizens. Perhaps this woman is so deluded that she does not have the faintest idea what Christianity really is. Here is another notable quote.

"I have to confess that it's crossed my mind that you could not be a Republican and a Christian."[113] — Hillary Clinton

In other words, taking almost half of people's productive lives who work and give to those political constituents that vote for her is the real Christian way according to Hillary. Only a rabid socialist or a communist could say those words and mean it. She says these things knowing full well that socialism and communism has always 100% led to mass starvation and death to hundreds of millions of people in the last 100 years of human history.

"The state is that great fiction by which everyone tries to live at the expense of everyone else." — Frederic Bastiat

---

[112] https://www.azquotes.com/author/2997-Hillary_Clinton
[113] https://www.azquotes.com/author/2997-Hillary_Clinton

Mr. Bastiat's description of socialism promoted by the Democratic National party is accurate. The Bernie Sanders, Hillary Clintons, Ocasio Cortez's, the Corey Bookers and on and on ad nauseum of our country destructively insist on a society that can be described as a snake eating its own tail. At first the snake thinks it found an easy lunch. Only later will it realize that it is devouring itself but by then it is too late. I would love to debate her on national TV. Hillary, if you are reading this, thank you. Now I invite you to debate me at a mutually agreeable place and time. If you want more and more of your sacred existence confiscated by our government, then vote for her, Bernie Sanders or Ocasio Cortez.

Our Constitution Gets in The Way of Democrat Socialism:

The philosophy of our Constitution is really quite simple. Government should be limited in size to only take care of protecting the people, protecting all their freedoms, protecting our trade routes with other nations and coordinating the activities of all of our individual states.

Our government is not to be a nanny or welfare state or to provide so much of this and that or the other thing to people that want to rely on government for their support. This is not the role of government that our founding fathers designed nor is it consisted with the will of God and why he put us here to learn the lessons we need to learn for our eternal spiritual growth. Big government means draconian limitations on the freedoms that we as God's children should have in all of our lives.

Look at what Bill Clinton said:

"If the personal freedoms guaranteed by the Constitution inhibit the government's ability to govern the people, we should look to limit those guarantees." — President Bill Clinton, August 12, 1993

"When we got organized as a country, [and] wrote a fairly radical Constitution, with a radical Bill of Rights, giving radical amounts of freedom to Americans, it was assumed that Americans who had that freedom would use it responsibly...When personal freedom is being abused, you have to move to limit it."(Radical??? Really! You just called God a radical in a demeaning manner.)

"The Constitution is a radical document... it is the job of the government to rein in people's rights."— Bill Clinton

God gave us the "radical" freedom you demean Bill, while indicating that you appoint yourself judge and jury to determine if we are "abusing" our sacred freedoms. These freedoms have been at least 6,000 years in the making starting with the Sumerians and the Code of Hammurabi. Our founding fathers took history, the Judeo-Christian morality and created the best country mankind has ever seen. And you suggest that you and people like you "need to control those freedoms".

Two things dear Mr. impeached and disgraced president, in saying what you just did, you are doing EXACTLY what Lucifer did that got him thrown out of Heaven and down to earth. You put your desires ahead of God's will for His children and above the needs of His Children when saying this. Every time you forced yourself on women, you attacked one of God's sacred children and you will have hell to pay for all of it, yes, all of it.

A few more quotes from you and people like you:

"Candidates with Deeply Held Christian Beliefs Are Unfit and Disqualified From Serving As A Federal Judge." — Charles (Chuck) Schumer

"This is government's primary function - to keep us safe" "Walls Do Not Work!" — Charles (Chuck) Schumer

Yet another reason to never vote for a Democrat in 2020. Unless you want ALL your freedoms taken away from you, at least the few we have left.

The New Green Deal... Is socialism:

I have already established that Democrats will radically increase huge government programs that will necessitate government controlling every aspect of our lives. You the American taxpayer will be forced into paying for all this at the expense of paying for the needs of their family, their well-being and their future.

A new shining star in the Democrat party is Constantina Ocasio Cortez. The newly proposed Green New Deal is her big idea and will indeed insert government rules, regulations and controls on all of your freedoms and every aspect of your life. The green new deal in order to be implemented demands this. And this Green new deal is based upon scientific hoaxes, misrepresentations of data and outright lies and propaganda. In seeing OAC on TV I am reminded of a quote:

In politics stupidity is not a handicap - Napoleon Bonaparte [114]

Everything here is taken directly from the full language text released by the Democratic Party. Simply put this Green New Deal is a hydrogen bomb of a program which will completely destroy this nation and our society. It creates a monster government that will control every aspect of your life. Democrats are using bold lies to justify this octopus of 10,000 tentacles reaching into every corner of our existence. How can any Christian voter support this?

1. *The green new deal will eliminate our fossil fuel economy in 10 years.*

2. *No nuclear power, no more fossil fuels, no more natural gas and related infrastructure by the year 2030, about 10 years from now.*

3. *The government will become the employer of last resort and guarantee zero unemployment.*

4. *20 million new jobs with a much needed major public jobs program.*

5. *People will be paid even if they choose not to work.*

6. *All cars, buses and trucks that use fossil fuel will be eliminated within 10 years.*

7. *All electricity and power will be produced by renewable energy sources such as wind and solar.*

8. *We will take all steps necessary to eliminate climate change.*

9. *We face a "perfect storm" of economic and environmental crisis.*

10. *The fate of humanity is in our hands. It is not just a question of what kind of world we want, but whether we will have a world at all.*

11. *The climate crisis is a serious threat to the survival of humanity ...turn the tide on climate change and make wars for oil obsolete – allowing us to cut our bloated, dangerous military budget in half*

Source: Green New Deal proposal from Democrat website.

Here are some of the statistics:

1. *Will cost every American family $65,000 to implement*

---

[114] https://www.brainyquote.com/topics/politics

2. *Goal is 100% renewable energy in 10 years*

3. *You will be forced to buy all new all electric cars, perhaps $25,000 per vehicle*

4. *AFL-CIO represents 13 million workers and says this is a $$ disaster for workers*

5. *This will NOT HELP THE CLIMATE. USA only produces worlds 13% of global carbon, China and India produce 33%. The rest from all other countries.*

6. *This will destroy our military for they need and require fossil fuels to protect us. Democrats want gargantuan budget reductions in our military on top of no fossil fuels in 10 years*

Source: Fox News 7:40 AM March 15, 2019 Interview with analyst & congressman John Barrasso (R-WY)

A Rebuttal with Truth:

This will completely destroy the American economy. Unemployment will skyrocket. This program will eliminate 99% of our electricity. It cannot be replaced within 10 years or so. Being employer of last resort will necessitate the government to print gargantuan amounts of money destroying the value of our dollar. Besides, who would want to work? Then government income taxes would plummet to near zero.

There will be next to no transportation. With no electricity America will be plunged back into the 1800's and have no medicine too. Distribution of critical goods will flounder costing lives. Climate change is a malignant hoax with no legitimate science behind it. Here are some resources: [115] [116] [117]

Who could think that our military is dangerous to us? Our military is NOT dangerous to America, only to our enemies. Humanity will thrive as long as we never elect another disastrous Democrat.

If we implemented everything in the this so called Green New Deal, it would not make a dent in global warming. Why? Because the United States produces only 13% of total earth carbon dioxide and pollution. India and China are the biggest polluters on the planet. They produce three times the amount we do. They are doing nothing to change this. The rest of the world produces the rest. Democrats want us to destroy our economy, our well being as a people only to not make any real change for the earth.

---

[115] https://www.youtube.com/watch?v=Uh5_mJw6B3Q
[116] https://www.youtube.com/watch?v=RZlICdawHRA
[117] https://www.youtube.com/watch?v=RkdbSxyXftc

Remember earlier I said that almost all Democrats are really psychologically adolescents. This is complete proof. Most of the 2020 Democrats who want to run for president in 2020 have announced support of this American self-inflicted disaster.

Climate Change Hoax to Justify This:

Democrats rely on politically based science which uses only modified data that fits with their political ideology. Thus, it is not science at all. Example, climate models they use do not consider our sun and the cyclical variations of its energy output. Our earth wobbles in its orbit around the sun. This affects climate too. This is not considered either. Also, they ignore that the earth was hotter 100,000 and 400,000 years ago than it is today. Then the earth cooled down...twice!

There was an ice age around the earth 20,000 years ago. Then the earth heated up. CO2 did not do that. What caused the earth to heat up? Democrats avoid this. They would rather talk about the Antarctic and the ice sheets melting. Well, guess what. NASA found out that the reason the ice is melting is NOT due to global warming. Rather it is due to geothermal action under the ice cap. There are multiple geothermal vents and volcanos under Antarctica causing increased heat much like Yellowstone. Facts can be so incentive and politically incorrect. [118]

What caused the earth to heat up and cool down? It certainly was NOT CO2 going from 200 parts per million to 400 parts per million as they claim. Also, there was a mini ice age in the 1800's that seems to have been caused by a combination of low energy output from the sun and volcanic activity. Then things warmed back up without human made CO2. All this is false fear mongering with no real objective scientific basis. But they will use any excuse to control people's lives. Satan likes this very much, to control people's lives from lies and false information.

Lastly many climatologists are predicting a cooling trend. I urge everyone to research all this for yourself. Please do your own research from sources that use objective scientific data. Controlling climate change is like herding box full of cats and telling them to give a military salute. Just way too many variables that we cannot control, not to mention that the rest of the nations continue to pollute like crazy. Remember the USA is only 13% of global pollution.

---

[118] https://www.youtube.com/watch?v=NhwqJcFIxe0

Other Lies and False Claims:

Regarding their full employment goals, they failed to mention that unemployment is at the lowest levels it has been in decades, our air is never been cleaner and so too our water. We are not perfect but a lot better than it has been. We have more people working today than any time in our nation's history. But you will never hear this truth from the Democrats. It does not fit their ideology.

There are no wars for oil as <u>the United States is oil independent and an oil exporter</u>. This is a first in my lifetime. There is no crisis ridden economic system. All Democrat lies of monster proportion. Remember Democrat Vice President Al Gore. He said that New York would be under 20 feet of water by 1988. Yes, that is correct, 20 feet of water. That did not happen. And it will not happen.

The climate will change all by itself as it always has regardless of what mankind does. But this fact is totally lost on our Democratic politicians because they are so obsessed with power and money. Remember you are not hearing the truth and information that contradicts Democrat claims. These are lies by omission, by hiding facts Democrats do not want you to know.

Also, our military is not dangerous. These are disgusting words for people who protect our freedoms and our lives from those who wish to destroy us. And believe me there are many. Iran for just one example keeps chanting "death to America". President Obama and climate supporter sent them $150 Billion in case during his last two weeks as president. What do you think they are spending that money on?

Think about that. Our Muslim president Barack Obama cut our military and the result was chaos in the Mideast and in Eastern Europe. We need our military to protect us in this dangerous world we live in. To say our military is dangerous is totally un-American in wretched ways.

Democrats the Party of Abortion

Abortion Political Rhetoric:

On February 5, 2019 president Donald Trump gave his State of the Union address in the chambers of the house of representatives. In that address he talked about how pro-life he was and how we should focus on providing adoption services instead of abortion. This preserves sacred human life. He talked about how especially late-term abortions were wrong because babies can feel pain.

After the president's state of the Union speech Nancy Pelosi said:

"banning late-term abortions is really quite a sad thing", she went on to say *"I hope that in his (Donald Trump) family, he never has to face that crisis"*. — Source: Daily Wire February 6, 2019

Nancy Pelosi thinks that having a baby is "quite a sad thing". She considers birth to be a "crisis." Is this what Nancy Pelosi has come to? Right out of her mouth. Shocking!

The state of New York was involved with a law allowing abortions within minutes of a child being born. In other words, a situation where a mother is about to give birth and the baby can still be legally killed. And recently Democrats proposed in the name of women's reproductive rights killing a freshly born baby **after birth** in New York. Please research this on your own.

"Bernie Sanders declares abortion is a 'constitutional right." [119]

So crazy Bernie says that killing a developing fetal human being is a constitutional right. Yet if someone other than a doctor or the mother were to take a knife and kill the baby, it would be murder.

Freedom of Choice:

Women do indeed have the right to choose like all other of God's children. All of God's children are given the sacred gift of freedom. But that right to choose occurs before a woman rolls out her welcome rug with a fertile male. It is at that point she has complete freedom to choose yes or no. Every woman has both the freedom and the responsibility of how she uses the body God gave her. So too for men. Men are far more irresponsible than women. Every woman knows that playing with reproduction without precautions is a stark gamble on becoming pregnant. God gave all women this responsibility. If a woman says no. Fine. If a woman says yes, then she is playing with mother nature and human reproduction. She knows she is taking a chance of becoming pregnant. Simple really. Everyone understands this.

---

[119] Alex Pappas | Fox News, https://www.foxnews.com/politics/bernie-sanders-abortion-a-constitutional-right

Mother nature operates consistently every time. If you don't like gravity don't fool with it by walking a tight rope over a deep canyon. Gravity operates no matter what you think of it. If you fall off the rope, you do not get any do-overs. Women have gotten pregnant tempting mother nature with her laws of reproduction. Just like gravity, it is just that simple. A woman's choice is free and open, but it occurs before she decides to engage in reproduction acts with a fertile male without precautions. There is no excuse. She made her choice. Just like the tightrope walker, she must now live with the consequences of her free will choices.

Since 1973 our Judeo Christian country has killed approximately 50 million developing fetal human beings. Our completely immoral Democrats call this a "woman's reproductive right", "a woman's freedom of choice" and "women's reproductive health". These are all damned lies right out of Satan's mouth.

Yes, I fully support a woman's right to choose and what happens to her body. But once a scientifically proven human life is developing within her body, called a developing fetal human being she has already made her choice. She has already made her choice and now like everything else in life she must live with that choice and its consequences. The alternative is murdering a developing fetal human being and violating the laws of Almighty God. When you think of this it is really clear. A women's rights stop where another human's rights begin, just like men, just like everybody. We are all equal!

Doctors have said repeatedly that there are almost no legitimate medical reasons for abortion. It is only out of convenience to murder a developing fetal human being.

The Use of Innocent Phrases to Mislead:

This is the stock and trade of Democrat salesman and politicians. They call abortion in their platform, "reproductive health care" or "women's reproductive rights". They support "a woman's decision to have a child". Both of these phrases sound innocent enough don't they? Reproductive health care, what they really mean is abortion. Killing fetal human beings. Democrats hide truth by using phrases like reproductive rights, reproductive health care and so on.

They never mention "silent fetal human rights" because they can't vote. Again, this is an evil perpetrated under innocent sounding phrases targeting shallow thinking people that should certainly know better and take responsibility for their actions. If any woman tells me, it is her body therefore it is her choice I will puke on her foot. It is one of God's children inside of her.

Lastly, I fully support a woman's right to choose to have a baby or not. BUT! Her decision point again occurs before the possible pregnancy. It occurs at the time of her choice whether or not to engage in sexual relations with a fertile male. It occurs before she hangs out her welcome rug. That is when her choice is made, not when the baby is already forming inside her. That is how she, the now mother, has been designed by God.

Once you are pregnant, you are pregnant. Once you jump off a cliff, mother nature does not grant do-overs. If she wants to play with reproduction, she might pay the price of being called mommy. This is no different than trying to go against gravity. Nature wins every time. Taking precautions is fine. It's like using a parachute for gravity or other appropriate devices depending on your activity. But if you lose your bet, don't kill someone for it. They call that murder. Democrats call it reproductive health. Like the Nazi's called the murder of 6 million Jews "The Final Solution".

The Medical Truth:

It is never necessary to intentionally kill a **fetal human being** to save a woman's life. [120] Let's deal with truthful medical facts. First, we need to use correct vocabulary. We are indeed talking about a developing fetal human being inside a mother's womb. We have a living developing human being inside the womb. Why cannot some people see that or refuse to see that? From the moment of fertilization, a human being meets all of the scientific criteria for a living human organism. [121]

Saying abortion is health care is a complete damned lie. It is NOT. The fetal human being is completely distinct from the mother's body. Abortion is not healthcare either. Get that complete lie out of your head. Just a few questions. Is the fetus alive? Yes. Is the fetus human? Yes. Is it developing? Yes. So, it is an alive developing fetal human being. Done. End of story.

In cases where the mother's life actually is in danger in the latter half of pregnancy, there is not time for an abortion... "We can, and do, save the life of the mother through delivery of an intact infant in a hospital where both the mother and her newborn can receive the care that they need." There is no medical reason to intentionally kill that fetal human being. [122]

The above is what is completely lost, confused, glossed over in our mainstream media, fogged and hidden from public view. We do not have to do abortions. We do not have to

---

[120] https://www.thepublicdiscourse.com/2019/02/49619/
[121] IBID
[122] IBID

kill developing fetal human beings. They are done strictly for convenience. They are done because two people acted irresponsibly for a few minutes of whoopee and refuse to deal with it. You have people like evil Democrat New York Mayor DeBlasio saying "Live your own truth" which is a completely Godless lie of monster proportion and adolescents believe it. So, they have the fetal human being murdered. The little one is out of sight and it is quick and clean. Done.

This is one of the reasons Democrats MUST HATE CHRISTIANS!

Democrat Propaganda Against Christianity:

This is evil with people saying things like this:

"I have to confess that it's crossed my mind that you could not be a Republican and a Christian". — Hillary Clinton

This human female uses Christian words, "confess" and "cross" to demonize those people who are Christian and do not agree with her. This is a velvet shive shoved into 70% of our population who profess to be Christian. The reverse should actually be asked. How can you support the Democratic propaganda on abortion and still be Christian?

We must stop thinking of the individual and start thinking about what is best for society. — Hillary Clinton

God made us all as individuals. She acknowledges this but willfully ignores it as that is not consistent with her socialist dream. This is direct evidence of domination. Hillary looks upon us only as a source of revenue to be controlled for her personal political dreams of dominion over us. I wonder what God will do with her in a few years when her time comes?

We now have arrived at the point in our country thanks to Democrats that it easier to abort an American developing fetal human being than it is to deport an illegal alien.

If you are a Christian and voted for Hillary Clinton in 2016, you made a big mistake. Do not make the same mistake in 2020.

Clarity on Gun Control

The Nature of All Weapons:

There are so many reactions to guns and rifles in our society today. As for me, I qualified at 14 years old as an Air Force Civil Air Patrol cadet to be a sharpshooter using an M-1 Garand combat rifle. It was loads of fun at Mather Air Force Base in California with B-52s taking off and landing in the background. I will use the term gun to include all handguns and rifles and anything else that fires bullets.

First, we must realize that guns are a completely inanimate object. They do nothing, absolutely nothing of their own volition. They are an inanimate object just like every other inanimate object, a tool to be used by human beings for different purposes. This is no different than a hammer, a saw, an axe, a car or an airplane. All these items do not move 1 inch without a human being controlling them. They only do what the human being wants them to do.

Like all other inanimate objects, they perform according to the will, the morality, the ethics and mentality of the human being controlling them. These are undeniable facts of the way in which our objective reality has been created. No one can deny that a gun is an inanimate object and left alone for a very long length of time it will slowly decay into a lump of metal. These are simply the facts and nothing more.

All the hate and fury that comes about regarding guns in our society are due to not the guns themselves but rather what a few human beings do with them. It is the human being that is in control of this inanimate object. So, the Democrat term "gun violence" needs to be thrown out the window. Guns do not do violence. Humans do. Guns are a "method of violence" just like knives, hammers and so on. So, we should call it human violence using a gun.

The Necessary Use of Weapons:

"Guns Save 2,191 Lives Each Day in the US: FBI ~ 32 Guns Purchased Every Minute in The US"—Volubrjotr • 24 Sep 2014 [123]

So, I now have established the fact that guns are a tool to be used by humans. Do God's children have the right to protect themselves from violence. YES! Since their lives are a

---

[123]   https://politicalvelcraft.org/2014/09/24/everyday-in-the-usa-2191americans-use-their-gun-in-self-defense-fbi-there-are-32-guns-purchased-every-minute-in-the-united-states/

sacred gift from God it is obvious that we have the right to protect ourselves. Self-defense is indeed a God given right. It is the right to life. The second amendment to our inspired Constitution gives us this legal right in our country. We have the legal right to protect ourselves and that shall not be infringed.

What happens when our rights are abolished? Australia did just that. They banned all guns. This is the result: [124]

1. Armed robberies increased 69%

2. Assaults with guns increased 28%

3. Gun murders increased 19%

4. Home invasions increased 21%

Handguns were banned by England following the U.K. Dunblane massacre. The result after the ban was that crime using handguns increased by 40%. [125] Only an adolescent Democrat would expect anything different.

Self Defense Using Guns:

Here are some facts: [126]

1. 2.1-2.5 million times a gun is used to stop a crime each year

2. Brandishing a gun is usually enough

3. Less than 8% require shooting

4. 500,000 cases occur away from home

5. 10% involve women protecting themselves

6. The above means between 1 in 105 to 125 people will use a gun this year for self-protection.

---

[124] IBID

[125] https://politicalvelcraft.org/2011/07/18/gun-control-myths-murder-rates-sky-rocket-in-gun-controlled-england-whereas-americas-murder-rates-are-dropping-significantly-with-shall-issue-laws-gun-ownership/

[126] https://scholarlycommons.law.northwestern.edu/cgi/viewcontent.cgi?article=6853&context=jclc

Our founding fathers viewed weapons as the last means of defense for the people to defend themselves from their own government and criminals. Were it not for guns in the hands of our patriot's and founding fathers we would be nothing more than a British colony today eating hot faggots and spotted Dick for lunch. Yes! These are two dishes that I personally ate in Pinewood England. Hot faggots are strips of beef with gravy served over bland mashed potatoes. Spotted Dick is custard with raisins in it. Yuck.

What we do not keep are records of how many times guns are used to avert crimes being committed just by their presence. Statistics do show a decrease in crime when people have guns.

Yet we keep no official government records. This is outrageous. As it turns out the Center for Disease Control (CDC) indeed did a study of the defensive use of guns in the United States but purposely DID NOT release it to us the public! Again, outrageous! However, *"An unpublished Centers for Disease Control and Prevention (CDC) study confirms Florida State University criminologist Gary Kleck's findings of more than two million defensive handgun uses (DGUs) per year."*[127] Critics to the Kleck & Gertz report have failed to produce any empirical data.

So, it is obvious to see that our government has covered up the legitimate use of guns by citizens to protect themselves because they want to continue the lie that there is no real use for them. They want to continue the lie of gun control against the American people. That is until the Florida State University study of gun defense was conducted. Then the truth of things was forced out into the open. Now you are among the few who know the truth of another government lie.

We as a nation also have the responsibility to keep guns out of the hands of criminals and those who were seriously mentally ill and so on. Democrats want to ban all guns. This is completely insane. They did this in London and what happened was murderers skyrocketed using knives. Nothing improved. Now the mayor of London wants to ban all knives. When will that stop? It is not the tool. It is the deranged human mind. You do not restrict person B for something person A did or might do.

---

[127] https://www.breitbart.com/politics/2018/04/21/unpublished-cdc-study-confirms-2-million-annual-defensive-gun-uses/

Horror When 'We the People"
Cannot Protect Themselves from Government:

Lenin and Stalin:

Stalin overthrew Czar Nicholas II. The first thing Lenin did was abolish private ownership of weapons in 1929. Stalin became unquestioned leader of an extremely oppressive regime. From 1929 to the year Stalin died, many tens of millions of so called "dissidents"or anyone the leadership suspected of being a threat to Stalin's government was arrested and murdered or put into a labor prison camp till they worked them to death. [128] They had no way to protect themselves from the government murdering them.

Stalin created two national collectivization programs in order to make the country an industrial power. But both programs were characterized by murders on a massive scale. Stalin created a vast famine by increasing the grain quotas the peasantry had to give to the Soviet state. This killed a little less than ten million people by starvation. His so called "Five Year Plans"for industry were horrifically brutal leading to the deaths of millions of convict dissident laborers. Stalin has been quoted as saying, "If the opposition disarms, well and good. If it refuses to disarm, we shall disarm them ourselves".[129]

Do not ever think that it could not happen here in the USA. There are forces at work right now that are trying to disarm "We the People". Also, never think that our military or police will protect us. Just the opposite. They will be the instruments used to eliminate the undesirables in our own country. These people will simply say, I am just doing my job. Who do you think murdered tens of millions of Soviet citizens? It was the military and police just doing their jobs. Never think it cannot happen here. It can.

Adolph Hitler:

Hitler established gun control in 1938. In a very short time, he implemented his slaughter of a total of 13 million total. 6 million Jews and the rest were other perceived inferior races. It was German military troops that carried out Hitler's orders. Also remember uncounted millions of people were also killed in Hitler's war against other nations in Europe. Who did the killing? Hitler's military. If you believe it cannot happen here, there is a mountain of history that says you are wrong.

---

[128] http://www.gendercide.org/case_stalin.html
[129] http://www.thenagain.info/WebChron/EastEurope/OctRev.html

"This year will go down in history. For the first time, a civilized nation has full gun registration. Our streets will be safer, our police more efficient and the world will follow our lead into the future"—Adolf Hitler 1935

Mao Zedong:

In 1935 the Chinese government established gun control. From 1935 to 1952 about 20 million citizens were murdered by the government. Mao Zedong launched his Chinese Cultural Revolution from 1966 – 1976. They killed millions of people and inflicted "cruel and inhumane treatments"on hundreds of millions of people. The death toll was so great that even today, the actual death count is a highly classified state secret.

Pol Pot:

After we lost the Viet Nam war and pulled out, Pol Pot issued a total gun control edict. Shortly after this his regime murdered about one million "educated people". Tyrannical governments do not like smart educated people. They are far harder to control. It was Pol Pot who created the"killing fields". Pol Pot wanted to reduce the Cambodian population from 7 million to 1 million. The slaughter and suffering was beyond understanding. Those people had no way to fight back.

Why Have Weapons:

We have the right for protection against all those who seek to do harm to us and others. During world war II Japanese Admiral Isoroku Yamamoto famously said the following:

"You cannot invade the mainland United States. There would be a rifle behind each blade of grass."–Admiral Isoroku Yamamoto

Our Constitution acknowledges our inalienable God given rights to life, liberty and the pursuit of happiness. We cannot have these rights unless we have the means to protect them and our physical person.

Above I have demonstrated why Democrats are insane with a demonic agenda regarding guns. They violate our Constitution, Bill of Rights and the will of God for protecting His children. There are more big genocide events in history not listed here. Lots MORE!

Democrats Just Are Not Capable of Understanding:

Here are a few examples of the idiotic things Democrats have said about guns.

1. "Banning guns addresses a fundamental right of all Americans to feel safe." [130] . — Dianne Feinstein

2. His completely violates the rule of gun safety "If I could have gotten 51 votes in the Senate of the United States for an outright ban, picking up every one of them... 'Mr. and Mrs. America, turn 'em all in,' I would have done it." — Dianne Feinstein

3. "Well, you know, my shotgun will do better for you than your AR-15, because you want to keep someone away from your house, just fire the shotgun through the door." — Joe Biden

This completely violates the rules of gun safety. Joe is a complete idiot to tell people to fire a weapon blindly without knowing who is there. Joe is completely insane beyond belief. It is creepy the way he treats women in public. Smelling their hair, putting his hands on their shoulders while standing behind them. Creepy Uncle Joe...

4. " Some of these bullets, as you saw, have an incendiary device on the tip of it, which is a heat seeking device. So, you don't shoot deer with a bullet that size. If you do you could cook it at the same time." [131] Patricia Eddington Assembly Woman D-NY, July 2007

5. "This is a ghost gun. This right here has the ability with a .30-caliber clip to disperse with 30 bullets within half a second. Thirty magazine clip in half a second." - Kevin de Leon D-CA

6. "We have federal regulations and state laws that prohibit hunting ducks with more than three rounds. And yet it's legal to hunt humans with 15-round, 30-round, even 150-round magazines." - Dianne Feinstein D-CA Senator

7. "The Second Amendment only protects the people who want all the guns they can have. The rest of us, we've got no Second Amendment. What are we supposed to do?" - Louise Slaughter D-NY

---

[130] https://www.brainyquote.com/authors/dianne_feinstein
[131] http://blog.joehuffman.org/2018/02/11/quote-of-the-day-patricia-eddington/

This woman was a state representative making laws in New York. Her statement testifies the fact she has no idea about the law. She is completely ignorant. Typical. Both sad and very dangerous.

There are dozens and dozens more quotes I could add to this list, but space does not allow. My advice to all Democrats: Strive to avoid big mouth small brain disease. It is contagious! If you want to research this further, I suggest you buy the book"The War on Guns" written by John L. Lott Jr. it presents objective facts that are not mutated by Democrat socialist ideology.

Lastly, in concert with the theme that Democrat are mostly psychologically adolescents, we have a very famous psychologist saying the following:

"A fear of weapons is a sign of retarded sexual & emotional maturity." — Sigmund Freud

The Democrat Party is Against Border Security

The Democrat party goes really against Judeo-Christian morality regarding border security policy. If you are surprised at this statement, please continue reading.

I find it appalling that the Democratic Party's political position goes against the very first reason that we have government to begin with. No matter who is in government, it is their first and foremost responsibility to protect the American people from outside forces and undue influence. There is no getting around this fact. This is why we have a military, and this is why we have borders.

Remember there are protections for God's children that live in heaven. There is a gate to control who gets in with strict entry requirements. This is a Judeo-Christian country. But the Democrats violently oppose protecting the citizens of this country and want no entry requirements from anyone who decides to come here. On top of that, who gets here automatically gets lots of free benefits paid for by the overtaxed taxpayers of this country. This goes against every fiber of Christianity from one end to the other.

Please do not say that we are a nation of immigrants. Yes, we are. The problem is that the immigrants of the past came here legally, registered with our government and started productive lives. They asked for NOTHING, just a chance to work hard and make their own way in life.

The illegal aliens on the other hand are nothing of the sort that immigrants of the past were. These people come here illegally breaking our laws to get in. They then get taxpayer benefits just because they fooled our ICE people at the border and snuck in against our laws. So, Democrats want to reward them with our hard earned money. Why? These illegal aliens will vote Democrat.

"Nancy Pelosi invited illegal aliens to the State of the Union. President Trump Invited victims of illegal aliens to the State of the union. Let that sink in."— Anonymous

Illegal Aliens Commit Terrible Crime Against US Citizens:

Besides the direct cost of illegal aliens by giving them government benefits ($214 Billion per year) there are violent crimes committed against American citizens. One illegal alien caught in Louisiana was responsible for 100 different sex crimes against children. He had been deported before and came back here.

1. In two years, there have been 4,000 Americans killed by illegal aliens

2. 100,000 violent assaults committed by illegal aliens against American citizens

3. 30,000 Sexual assaults committed against American citizens

4. Many times, these criminals are protected by the laws of sanctuary cities.

5. 90% of the deadly illegal drugs come into our country across our southern border

Source: Fox News April 5, 2019 Tucker Carlson

Here are a few more statistics that you have not heard on our mainstream media.

1. 23% of illegal aliens deported were previously arrested for DUI

2. Congressman Steve King (R-IA) estimates that illegal alien drunk drivers kill 13 Americans every day — that's a death toll of 4,745 per year. [132]

3. More than 43,000 illegal aliens were convicted of drug offenses

4. The non-violent crime grouping of larceny, fraud, and burglary totaled 7% of illegal aliens

5. More and more guns are being confiscated from illegal aliens in Arizona

6. Sheriff Paul Babeu, Pinal county Arizona, said, "Pinal County has seen mass murders, execution-style slayings, sexual assaults, kidnappings, shootings, armed robberies, burglaries, and more — all tied to illegal immigration."

7. Government Accountability Office study of 55,322 illegal aliens, analysts discovered that they were arrested at least a total of 459,614 times, averaging about eight arrests per illegal alien: 70 percent had between two and 10 arrests, and 26 percent (about 15,000) had 11 or more arrests. Drug or immigration offenses accounted for 45 percent of all offenses, and approximately 12 percent (over 6,600 illegal aliens) were arrested for violent offenses such as murder, robbery, assault, and sex-related crimes [133]

Source: www.constitutionparty.com

Democrats Fight to Keep This Situation Hidden and Want to Do Nothing:

Democrats fight every effort to protect American citizens from all this horrific crime. For me, they are directly responsible for all these murders, sexual attacks and assaults against American citizens. Only people with no morals or Godly principles can do monster things like this.

Every nation on the earth has borders and they protect them from outsiders coming in without proper government approval and law. Taxpayers pay to government between

---

[132] www.wnd.com/2006/11/39031/#cjEhV0wE8KWZZZ5B.99

[133] https://www.constitutionparty.com/illegal-alien-crime-and-violence-by-the-numbers-were-all-victims/

35% and 40% of their productive lives in the form of taxes that are confiscated from us to pay for this protection.

Today we have 22 million illegal aliens in this country. They are not supposed to be here. They are citizens of other countries. They are supposed to be in their own country right now. All other countries that I know of put these people in jail and deport them quickly back to their own country. Illegal aliens by definition have broken US law. Of this there is no question.

It is easy to see that the Democrat party looks at these people and wants them to vote Democrat so the Democrat party can gain power in our government. It is also easy to see in our news that illegal aliens have been, currently are and will be a threat to American citizens, their lives, their property and their financial well-being.

Let's face the facts. Taxpayers in the United States are already completely overburdened and saturated with taxes of all kinds. Currently American taxpayers are paying for the illegal aliens already in our country. Studies have shown that illegal aliens are a significant drain on our common resources such as healthcare, social services and other programs that were designed only for American taxpayers. Democrats want American taxpayers to pay ever increasing amounts of money out of their productive lives and away from supporting their families and their own personal well-being.

Current Net Cost of Illegal Aliens:

The cost to American taxpayers goes something like this. The total national cost to support illegal aliens is $137 billion. Total taxes paid by illegal aliens is $19 billion. Net cost to the American taxpayer is $116 billion per year. These amounts of money are assuming there are 12 million illegal aliens in this country. Other reliable estimates put this at 22 million illegal aliens. Adjust in the above net taxpayer cost for illegal aliens from 12 million to 22 million, the net cost to our overburdened taxpayers rises to $212 billion. This number is rising each year that our government does nothing to stop illegal aliens from coming into the country. Many presidents both Democrat and Republican have looked the other way and let this problem fester into a national crisis.

These costs are not the totals either. What is not included is the costs of enforcing the laws by crimes committed by illegal aliens. This is substantial. The overcrowding of common health facilities pushing out citizens that pay for all of that. The increased traffic accidents by illegal aliens with no insurance. The increased crime like the murder of Kate Steinly in San Francisco, murdered walking with her dad near the wharf. All the illegal drugs (90%) coming into our country causing overdose deaths, 50,000 dead last year alone. It can be accurately said that democrats want these deaths to continue because of their support of open borders.

Another risk to American citizens is health. Right now, there is a large break out of measles in New York. It is a sanctuary city with lots of unvaccinated kids. Measles is highly infectious. Elite liberals are not affected as their kids go to private schools.

Elite Liberal:"Don't let unvaccinated kids into our schools!"

Same liberal:"Let millions of unvaccinated illegal aliens in!"

The Democrat party chooses to ignore all of this so as to hope to get more voters for them and their free give away programs that will destroy our once great nation.

Judeo-Christian Morality Regarding Illegal Aliens

This is not consistent with Judeo-Christian morality and ethics to ask of God's children to stop providing for the health and well-being for their own families and give this money confiscated by the government to people who should be in their own countries in solving their own problems. Almighty God allowed them to be born in these countries for spiritual reasons that we cannot know of. It is right and just to give to the needy, but it is better to teach them to support themselves. My parents and grandparents, all devoted Christians, have always said that charity begins in the home and family. But Democrats want us to spend ourselves into the same poverty that already exists in other countries. What good will that do ultimately?

This kind of thinking is what will spell the end of our democratic constitutional republic. There just are not enough resources within our country to properly take care of our own people and anyone else who decides to come here and plead poverty. We have so many people in our own country who are poor. We cannot even take care of our own military veterans properly.

This may seem hard to people who think in a shallow manner but remember no Christian is asked by God to give all their blood to someone who needs it only to kill themselves in the process. This is fundamentally what this whole thing boils down to. And remember also when our Lord and Savior Jesus Christ was here walking among us, he did not heal everybody on the planet. He did what he could within the limitations of being a human being. He did not drag himself down into the gutter for all the wonderful miracles he performed.

But this is what the Democrat party demands that we do. This is part of their adolescent mind set and dangerous shallow thinking. Lastly remember that this country is the most charitable country in the history of mankind. We shall not and should not feel guilty about taking care of our own people first. There are 6.7 billion other people in the world that would like us to give them what we have, we cannot and survive ourselves. It is that simple.

Pres. Donald Trump wants to put an end to this because of the increased violence and crime against American citizens, the drain on our national resources and restore the principle that every nation in the world has sovereign rights to protect its borders from outsiders coming in and outside influence. It is in the Constitution that this is a federal government responsibility. Anyone who says different is either totally ignorant or has a hidden agenda with money or power involved somehow. These reasons constitute a disaster for God's children who pay taxes in our country.

Other facts that are getting lost include:

The law allowing for the separation of children from their parents who cross the border illegally was signed by Bill Clinton in 1997, why is it a problem now?

68 people were killed in mass shootings in 2018. Did you know that about 2,000 people were killed by illegal aliens?

All of this are reasons to never ever vote for a single Democrat in 2020.

Unconstitutional Democrat Attacks and The Mueller Collusion Investigation:

What Trump is Guilty of:

He is guilty of being lawfully elected. Many members high in the Democrat party did not accept and are rebelling against the election of 2016. Before Donald Trump was inaugurated as president, there were already calls from members of the Democrat party to impeach him. Maxine Waters Democrat from California launched her "Impeach 45" campaign against Pres. Trump. This is completely obscene because they are attempting to overturn a legitimate presidential campaign and they will of the people, citizens of the United States, children of God.

We have an electoral college in this country. All presidents are elected NOT by popular vote, but by the electors in each state. This electoral college is designed so that the states with small populations are not constantly dominated by the bigger states that have different needs from government than the smaller Midwest states for example. Thus, it has happened in the past that presidents are elected without winning the popular vote. Our electoral college brings stability to our countries by providing all our states with solid representations to the federal government. If it were only based on the popular vote, then our entire nation would be dominated by the very liberal east coast and the west coast. All other people in between would not have a voice in government. The United States would no longer by united.

Specifically, this has happened four other times in our history. [134] The election of Donald Trump is the fifth time in our history this has happened. But these normal workings of our constitutional elections are now being attacked by the adolescent Democrats only because they lost the election. So, they did what adolescents do. The scream that we need to change the election rules and process as defined in our constitution is shouted within the Democrat party.

This includes horrific insults against the children of God who voted for Mr. Trump, calling them "the deplorables"by Hillary Clinton." What kind of mindset, what kind of psychological and emotional issues are running rampant within the minds of people who want power so badly they want to cancel an election for president and demean with horrific comments against those who voted differently than what they wanted? This is further demonstration of hateful adolescent behavior and it is destructive power to our society, our culture and our form of government.

The Biggest Hoax In American History:

Their Mueller investigation horrifically violated the Constitution of the United States. How did they do that? First, it is the rule of law in this country that there must be clear evidence of a crime before the FBI can investigate who committed the crime. By the way and surprisingly collusion is not a crime. [135] There is no law against collusion. Other actions in the process of collusion can be illegal but not collusion. But this did not stop the Democrat Party. There were corrupt people in place, appointed by Barack Obama that bypassed our Constitution and started investigating Pres. Trump using Mr. Mueller and 13 sworn Democrat prosecutors. Before you investigate you must have evidence. There was no evidence. They did all they could to cloud the things they did.

The Mueller investigation into collusion allegations against Pres. Trump is a myriad of interconnected people and money with agendas hostile to the president. This whole thing originated with a lawyer representing the Hillary Clinton campaign doing opposition research against Donald Trump. This then involved people from other countries.

The now famous dossier funded by the Clinton campaign was written by a former British spy named Christopher Steele. Later work was funded by the Democrat National

---

[134] https://www.quora.com/How-many-times-has-the-United-States-Presidency-been-won-without-the-majority-of-the-popular-vote

[135] https://nationalparalegal.edu/ViewNews.aspx?intTakeOnNewsID=129

Committee. It was well known within the Democrat power structure that this dossier was a fake full of lies. But using Democrats in high places like James Comey, Loretta Lynch, Peter Strock and other operatives, the fake documents became the reason to launch an investigation that was really an attempted coupe against a sitting duly elected president. In my view people in the Democrat party committed treason against our country.

This led to a two-year investigation by Robert Mueller appointed as special counsel to investigate president Trump on the allegations in the dossier which now have been proven false. No evidence has been found after all the following resources, emotions, hostile media coverage of the president, wasted effort from Congress and a boatload of citizens who fell prey to constant anti-Trump propaganda from both the Democratic National Committee, Democrat politicians and the media. All to get to a not guilty because of a no evidence result. How much did this cost our nation? Here is a summary.

1. The investigation lasted 675 days

2. 19 attorneys work full-time

3. $25.2 million was spent

4. 42 people were interviewed or testified before a grand jury

5. 26 Russian citizens were indicted for unrelated crimes

6. 40 FBI agents, intelligence analysts, forensic accountants and other professional staff were used

7. 2800 subpoenas were issued

8. 500 search warrants were issued

9. 230 orders for communication records were issued

10. 13 requests to foreign governments were issued

11. A total of 500 witnesses were interviewed.

This is what adolescents do when they have power. They trample on everything to get their way. All of this was originated by a lawyer representing the Hillary Clinton campaign. Subsequently, it was funded by the Democratic National Committee. Christopher Steele was paid to create the false dossier under the guise of investigative intelligence. All of this to arrive at something many of us already knew in the very beginning. It was nothing more than a monster political attack against the Republican presidential candidate. Then after losing the election they attacked the president through all sorts of false accusations and allegations that were knowingly and willfully spread through the news media with no evidence whatsoever.

Remember this, every person that you saw on TV accusing the president of collusion knew, yes, they knew that they had no real evidence to say the hostile things they did. These people knew they were lying because they knew there was no legitimate evidence. How do I know they knew that they had no evidence? Simple.

After two years Robert Mueller said there was no evidence. The behavior of these human beings and the positions they are in whether it's media or politician is disgusting beyond belief and in my opinion they all should be removed from their jobs permanently. They should be fit with orange jumpsuits adorned with silver bracelets. There must be a large cost that is proportional to the monster disruption they have caused in our nation. We as a nation must enforce our rule of law. If we do not it will disintegrate into nothingness. Therefore, strong punishments must be meted out to those people who participated in this gargantuan farce. Nothing less will do. This is a low point in our history as a Judeo Christian nation.

If we are to continue as a constitutional republic based on Christian foundations, then we must uphold the rule of law in this country and prosecute those people responsible for initiating this monster attack based on nothing at all those people who participated in the dissemination of all the lies and contempt and hate directed at president Donald Trump.

If we do not hold people responsible for their actions like yelling impeach 45 for two solid years then we will certainly go downhill into a Third World mentality where the rule of law will be discarded and all of our liberties, our freedoms and even our economic system will fall prey to the misinformed, to the snake like liberal politicians and end up being a totalitarian state just like China is today and just like North Korea is today.

Yes, it can happen here in this monster investigation based on no evidence and false accusations is the first step in that direction. Why can it happen here? Because any culture with principles is only one generation deep. If a generation never bothers to instill in the next generation the knowledge of their heritage along with the benefit of knowing what foundational principles need to be honored, then the next generation with have no rudder and will become volatile.

Here again is further reason to never vote for any Democrat in 2020! They turned this country upside down purposely following a fake dossier paid for by Hillary Clinton to smear a duly elected president of the United States. In the process they ruined many people's lives and drove them into bankruptcy with lawyer bills defending themselves from allegations made against them even when they were not the target of the Mueller investigation.

Democrat Hate Speech

Psychologically speaking, we must remember that the majority of Democrats attitudes, speech and actions correspond very well with the characteristics of adolescent behavior. We covered that earlier regarding Carl Gustav Jung, James Fowler, and other renowned psychologists. Current psychological research is founded upon these psychologist's research of decades ago.

As a reminder, their hate speech is be a product of the following adolescent behavior:

1. "their actions are guided more by the **emotional and reactive** amygdala and less by the thoughtful, logical frontal cortex". [136]

2. When this is combined with "adolescents", they are **less likely to think before they act,** pause to consider the consequences of their actions", [137] you get the volatile mixture we all see on CNN, CNBC, CBS, MSNBC's and all the other liberal outlets in the mainstream media. Yes, you can have 70 year old adolescents. Just look at Hillary and Bernie.

3. Many people in our society have not advanced beyond adolescence do to the hard requirements of being an adult. Nonetheless, when these adolescents walking around looking like adults achieve political power, they are in a position to do serious damage to our society, culture and country. The Democrat party seems to be a natural attractant for adolescent minds.

4. One feature of adolescence is believing you are right without the knowledge to inform yourself that you are wrong. This produces a steadfast belief in indeed being right while being very wrong. They naturally resist all attempts to show they are wrong.

5. Adolescents many times have a short fuse when challenged and act out anger and call those who challenge them with insults and names. We see this every day on

---

[136] American Academy of Child & Adolescent Psychiatry No. 95 September 2016
[137] IBID

our news with all the name calling against President Trump. It comes from so many different people in the Democrat media.

Hate speech is particularly damning. I ask you very plainly and clearly do you really want people like this running our Judeo-Christian country? If you vote for Democrat, you have not understood the existential threat these people present to our country.

The widespread use of accusations of racism, bigotry, white supremacy, hate speech, toxic masculinity, Islamophobia, homophobia, and a cocktail of many other accusations including all the other this-a-phobias and that-a-phobias that have destroyed the normal and necessary communication between competing ideas that should lift up our society to higher ideals.

In my research on "liberal hate speech" I simply went to a search engine and typed in those three words. Oh God! I immediately found out there are 21 different categories of liberal hate speech against anybody you can think of. Additionally, there is a full 135 references to additional websites that contain further material about liberal hate speech. So below are only examples to give you a whiff of the stench of these low-grade human creatures or psychologically some form of adolescent that turned to the dark side and got filled with hate.

Hate Speech Examples:

Case 1: There are three terms Democrats always use. They are "male toxicity" and "white privilege" and "white supremacy. This is combined with what former Pres. Barack Obama said when he emphasized to business owners, "you did not build that". And Hillary Clinton saying, "businesses and corporations do not create jobs". These four phrases are nothing but pure hate speech and lies.

The term "male toxicity" demeans all men in our country. This term is intended to put females above males because males are somehow dangerous and infected. You never ever as a Christian put one group of people above any other group of people. That is completely sinful. This is the identical sin that Lucifer committed sometime after Adam and Eve. We know the result of this. He became Satan author of all evil and lies and was thrown out of heaven with all of his angelic followers who became demons and who are now attacking Christians on this earth through the Democrat Party and Islam.

The term "white privilege" demeans and attacks all white people just because we were born white. This is heinous and hateful against God's children. It is disgusting beyond belief yet Democrats spray around this term of "white privilege" every day of the year.

There is no author other than Satan of this sinful speech. Democrats are infected with it through and through. Again, if any Christian votes Democrat, you are complete idiotic fool!

Case 2: This is just one snowflake example out of a blizzard of incidents that happen in the news every day. CNN commentator Angela Rye said the red "Make America Great Again" hat from President Donald Trump's 2016 campaign is just as upsetting for her to look at as a Ku Klux Klan hood. "Forget Donald Trump for a moment and just think about the symbol of that red hat," Rye told Chris Cuomo. "When I see the Make America Great Again hat now, Chris, I am triggered. I'm so triggered." [138] In a tweet she went on to say the MAGA hat is intolerant and claims her black ancestors built the United States. I assume you know what the word "triggered" means.

She forgets that it was the democrats that helped form the KKK. She forgets that the top three Democratic public officials in Virginia including Gov. Ralph Northam, Attorney General Mark Herring and Lt. Governor Justin Fairfax did black face and now are being asked to resign from office.

Angela is waging spiritual war against a symbol of a Judeo-Christian country, America. It says so right on the hat. There really is no other way to make sense of what she is saying. She hates America and what it stands for which is Christian values, the very foundations of our country. This is hate speech dear friends. Additionally, this is not news. Somehow CNN considers this hate speech as news. Why? We need to recognize it for the dirt it is. She finds fault with others when her own house is filthy.

Remember what Jesus Christ said: Luke 6:42 How can you say to your brother, 'Brother, let me take the speck out of your eye,'when you yourself fail to see the plank in your own eye? You hypocrite. In Christian spirituality hypocrisy is one of the worst sins you can commit.

From a psychological perspective she is projecting her own hate on to the American symbol of the MAGA hat. Her claim that her ancestors built America is also classic adolescent behavior is due to a departure into pure fantasy away from reality. This is common in adolescent behavior. People project their inner feelings onto others when they cannot or refuse to recognize those feelings coming from themselves. This is very sad to see for CNN is using this woman with her adolescent mental state of hate against America to propagandize their agenda as they are told to by the higher up big money people.

---

[138] https://www.theblaze.com/news/cnn-maga-hat-kkk-hood

Case 3: "I want to go up to the closest white person and say: 'You can't understand this, it's a black thing' and then slap him, just for my mental health". [139] "We say that Reparations is the defining human rights issue for the 21st Century. They stole us, they worked us, and they owe us. A crime has been committed, a people have been injured and compensation is due." [140] New York city councilman Charles Barron

Well that is a snoot full of racial hatred against white people. This man is hatred on two feet animated by a big mouth. The picture of Mr. Barron on his website shows him with a defiant smirk on his face with his clenched fist held in the air. Again, here is dark side adolescent behavior, a mixture of emotion, talking without really thinking about consequences, highly reactive to things that did not even happen to him but expects to be compensated for. He completely ignores the fact that if person A does a rotten thing 150 years ago, person B today is not responsible for that. This adolescent fantasyland councilman in New York does though. And I am sure he convinced himself that all whites are racist which is just a psychological projection of his hatred that he will never admit resides within himself.

Case 4: MSNBC Talk show host Ed Schultz called Fox news host Laura Ingraham, "Yeah, she's a talk slut."[141]

I cannot believe that these kinds of people get paid for say these kinds of things on radio or TV. This has been a very hard book to write due to the sludge I have had to encounter. I do remember the days when politicians actually talked about issues. Not saying asinine things like "Walls don't work" Chuck Schumer. OK then remove the walls around your house, Pelosi's house and the White House too.

Case 5: "F*** God D*mned Joe the God D*mned Motherf*cking plumber! I want motherf*cking Joe the plumber dead." -- Liberal KGO talk show host Charles Karel Bouley on the air. [142]

Here is a man capable pure hatred of another child of God only because he asked Barack Obama a tax question and disagrees with him on this issue. That is the source of

---

[139] https://townhall.com/columnists/johnhawkins/2010/03/30/violent-liberal-hate-rhetoric-fifteen-quotes-n1126185

[140] https://nyassembly.gov/mem/Charles-Barron

[141] https://dailycaller.com/2011/05/25/unhinged-msnbcs-ed-schultz-calls-laura-ingraham-a-right-wing-slut/

[142] https://townhall.com/columnists/johnhawkins/2010/03/30/violent-liberal-hate-rhetoric-fifteen-quotes-n1126185

Charles Karel and his explosive hatred of Joe the plumber. Adolescents can indeed have explosive behavior. And I have seen it many times in high school.

In June 2004, Karel opened his weekend KGO program with a clip of The Wizard of Oz song, "Ding-Dong the Witch is Dead!" as a "tribute" to former President Ronald Reagan, who had died earlier that day. The disdain and hatred that bubbles within this man's soul is a putrid expression of dark demonic forces at work.

Case 6: During the 2016 presidential campaign, Hillary Clinton call all of the Trump supporters "deplorables". Enough said on that.

Case 7: The ever famous Kathy Griffin decapitation of President Donald Trumps bloody head. Who can forget that picture? This captures the sum of most of the adolescent behavior characteristics I have researched and jammed it into one smelly can of sardines. We got the fantasy of her hoping he gets his head chopped off. We got a departure from reality. It will not happen. We got utopian thinking where she thought she would generate positive buzz for her sagging career. We got an angry adolescent here. They are very susceptible to anger issues. Kathy displays this perfectly. Watching one of her performances will convince anyone of that. We got not thinking about consequences before taking action. We got not taking responsibility. Afterward she blamed the president for all her show cancellations proclaiming, "A sitting president of the US ... is personally trying to ruin my life forever." [143] Yep we got it all right here in one picture. Thank you hate filled former wannabe comedian Kathy Griffin.

Case 8: Other names include: Nancy Pelosi called the GOP "Legislative arsonists", democrat Jay Carney called the House GOP budget "blatant extortion", Harry Reid (D-Nevada) said that Republicans "have lost their minds", D-Debbie Wasserman Schultz called the GOP "unhinged arsonists", Hillary Clinton's former running mate Tim Kaine called for Democrats to "fight in the streets against Trump." Lastly BuzzFeed writers openly called for Trumps assassination, director of social media at BuzzFeed said, "Maybe someone will assassinate him".

To be fair, President Trump does much the same thing. But the quality is different in that most of his name calling is somehow related to what the other person has done for failed to do. Elizabeth Warren falsely claimed to be a native American to get into Harvard

---

[143] https://www.news.com.au/entertainment/celebrity-life/kathy-griffin-claims-bullying-by-donald-trump-and-family-after-decapitated-head-joke/news-story/42f56fa03e002a9237d6e2fe13ed58c9

and lived that lie until DNA forced her to tell the truth. So she got the well-deserved name of Pocahontas. Other names Trumps has used in the past include Marco Rubio as "little Marco", Ted Cruz as "Lyin Ted", Jeb Bush as "low energy Jeb", Hillary Clinton as "Crooked Hillary", Bernie Sanders as "Crazy Bernie" and Elizabeth Warren as "Pocahontas". The list goes on.

One thing to be said about Trump's insults is that they are not accusatory of serious crimes or death as the Democrat insults are. On the whole it appears to this writer that the Democrat insults are more damaging to our body politic than Trumps. Ideally, none of this would be happening.

Case 9: Willful and purposeful lying about people is a form of hate speech. When a person willfully lies about another person that is just plain sinful and hateful. As one example, Bernie Sanders, Democrat hopeful for president of the United States in 2020 continues to lie about the taxes paid by wealthy people. He and all other Democrats characterize wealthy people, especially the famous top 1%, of not "paying their fair share". He never defines what that term means. Why does he not say what fair is? Here are the facts: [144]

1. The top 1% of income earners paid 37.3% of all income taxes. Source: IRS

2. The top 5% of income earners paid 58% of all income taxes: Source: IRS

3. 44% of income earners pay ZERO income taxes. [145]

Further, Bernie is a millionaire. Nancy Pelosi is worth $125 million. Colossal hypocrites both. Enough Said.

Case 10: Lastly, we have Don Lemon. Appropriate last name, I think. A true sourpuss. "We have to stop demonizing people and realize the biggest terror threat in this country is white men, most of them radicalized to the right, and we have to start doing something about them."— Don Lemon on CNN (October 29, 2018) [146]

In summary I want to close with one final thought about Democrat hate speech against America and what it stands for, foundational Judeo-Christian values. There is a

[144] https://www.foxbusiness.com/personal-finance/heres-how-much-wealthy-americans-pay-in-taxes
[145] https://www.taxpolicycenter.org/taxvox/closer-look-those-who-pay-no-income-or-payroll-taxes
[146] www.prweb.com/releases/former_us_navy_seal_ephraim_mattos_responds_to_cnns_don_lemon/prweb15885914.htm

spiritual war going on. It envelopes the entire earth. Satan was thrown down here. I have personal experience with being attacked multiple times from him. It was hair curling scary awful. He preys on the weak of us. That includes all adolescents whose minds are susceptible, like most Democrats from a psychological adolescent perspective. It is my feeling that for those with a predisposition toward anger, that is being used against others of God's children to spread hate as far as Satan can to foster chaos and destruction. The causes of what we see run far deeper than we would normally suspect.

Regarding the attacks against America from Democrats, George Washington said this:

"Citizens by birth or choice of a common country, that country has a right to concentrate your affections. The name of American, which belongs to you, in your national capacity, must always exalt the just pride of Patriotism, more than any appellation derived from local discriminations."— George Washington, Farewell Address, September 19, 1796

"Why are people on the left so angry? There is a reason. Know what it is?" — Anonymous

Democrat Lies to the American People

First, both Republicans and Democrats lie to all of us. There is no escaping this ugly fact. But in the last two years we have been bombarded with a complete blizzard of lies regarding President Trumps so called collusion with Russia. That was a monster pack of lies the likes of which this country has never seen before in our history as a nation on the earth.

I predict that with Joe Biden entering the Democrat sweepstakes for the presidential nomination of the Democrat party, there will again be monster lies about the "Obama economic recovery" when he was vice-president. That was a recover that never happened. It was a ghost recovery that did not have any meat to it and did not really help the people in our country.

But those facts will not stop the Democrats from celebrating the recover that never was. Here are 9 charts from the Governors of the Federal Reserve Bank that tell the accurate story. In the coming months, observe how the Democrats lie about the Obama recovery and remember these 9 charts when they do. Joe Biden does not want you to know this.

Source: ZeroHedge, Tyler Durden, Wed, 09/16/2015

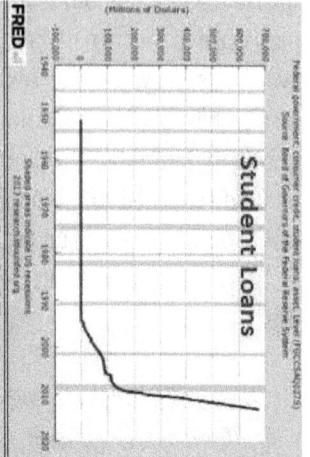

Student Loans

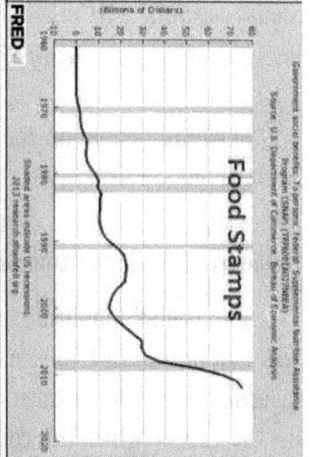

Food Stamps

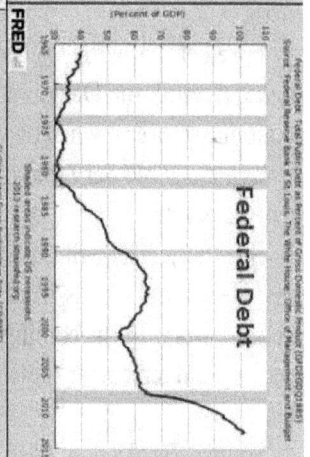

Federal Debt

Money Printing

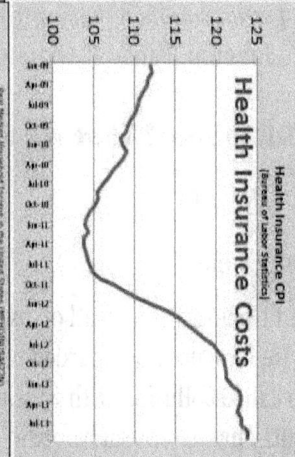

Health Insurance Costs

Labor Force Participation

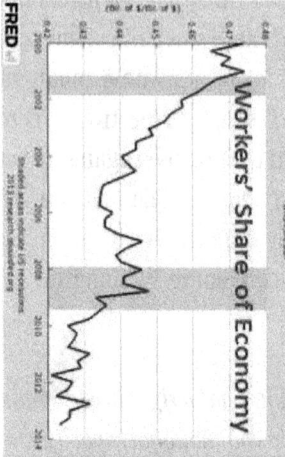

Workers' Share of Economy

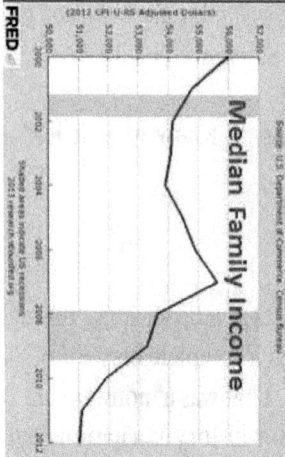

Median Family Income

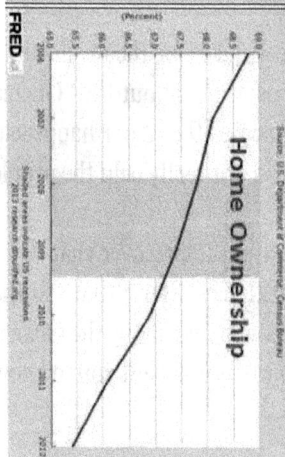

Home Ownership

The Bigotry of The Democrat Party

Democrats like to paint themselves as being very tolerant and open. This is not true. Their actions and words are the opposite of what they want you to believe about them. Here are a number of topics that show just how bigoted against the children of God Democrats really are. I wish this was not true, but it is the truth and we must deal with Democrats as they really are, bigoted.

Catholics and Christianity:

"Senators Mazie Hirono (D-HI) and Kamala Harris (D-CA) raised concerns about membership in the Knights of Columbus while the Senate Judiciary Committee reviewed the candidacy of Brian C. Buescher, an Omaha-based lawyer nominated by President Trump to sit on the United States District Court for the District of Nebraska."[147] Sen. Mazie Hirono (D-HI) stated to Buescher, "the Knights of Columbus has taken a number of extreme positions. For example, it was reportedly one of the top contributors to California's Proposition 8 campaign to ban same-sex marriage."[148]

Sen. Harris described the Knights as "an all-male society" and asked if Buescher was aware that the Knights of Columbus "opposed a woman's right to choose" and were against "marriage equality".

Senator Cory Booker (D-NJ) asked "why should a litigant in your courtroom expect to get a fair hearing from an impartial judge in a case involving abortion rights?"[149]

During confirmation hearings, Supreme Court nominee Judge Amy Coney Barrett, Democrats "grilled Barrett over how her Catholic faith would affect her views on court precedents concerning abortion cases".[150]

Sen. Dianne Feinstein (D-Calif.) and Sen. Dick Durbin (D-Ill.), in particular, showed what Catholic League President Bill Donahue called anti-religion "animus" during their questioning of her religious beliefs.

Wall Street Journal columnist Kimberly Strassel noted that it "doesn't matter, though, who the candidate who is picked is going to be." "They're going to make this into a smear because it's going to be their best and only shot to try to stop someone because

---

[147] https://www.catholicnewsagency.com/news/senators-quiz-nominee-about-membership-of-extreme-knights-of-columbus-78683

[148] IBID

[149] IBID

[150] https://www.lifezette.com/2018/07/anti-catholic-bias-called-lefts-last-acceptable-prejudice-in-scotus-hysteria/

they can't do it on the basis of arguing they're not qualified for the court,"Strassel added, noting that the"most convenient way to go against Barrett"is to target her faith. [151]

Vermont Sen. Bernie Sanders slammed President Donald Trump's Office of Management and Budget (OMB) nominee Russell Vought as a religious bigot. Vought had said that Muslims stand condemned because they do not know Jesus Christ. This made Sen. Bernie Sanders fly into a rage saying, "In my view," Sanders declared, "the statement made by Mr. Vought is indefensible, it is hateful, it is Islamophobic, and it is an insult to over a billion Muslims throughout the world." But Vought is totally correct. Muslims do not know Jesus Christ. Islam targets Christians for extermination of this there can be no doubt. The ideology of Bernie Sanders blinds him completely to the truth of things.

There is much more regarding the Democrats Anti-Catholic and anti-Christian mindset. Space does not allow for more, but there is. I urge you to do your own research on this topic of anti-Christian bias with Democrats.

Whites Especially White Males:

By omission you could say Democrats are bigoted against whites particularly white males. Their political emphasis is always on women, blacks, people of color and illegal immigrants. Nowhere in their 2016 campaign platform do they single out whites for any kind of special recognition or treatment or priority. They forget completely that it is European white people that started this nation and built it from the ground up. This is not a racist thing to say because it is historically and objectively true. They never speak of supporting white people. Speaking of racism, slavery in the South was absolutely against any and all rule of law and against the will of God.

What people never ever talk about is who sent all those poor black people to North America. My research indicates it was a combination of Blacks and Muslims in North Africa. Please do your own research on this for further knowledge. Democrats never talk about the total picture regarding slavery in the world. To this day Muslims engage in slavery of all kinds. [152] Do your research on this as well. You will find it to be true, ugly as hell but true. Democrats never mention this truth.

Another thing Democrats never talk about is the historical fact that white males from the north led by Republican President Abraham Lincoln defeated all slavery in our nation. He was assassinated by Democrat John Wilkes booth. It was a monster ugly war

---

[151] IBID

[152] https://en.wikipedia.org/wiki/History_of_slavery_in_the_Muslim_world

where many men died and were crippled for life. Why don't Democrats honor the sacrifice of these people? I have never heard them do so. It is because the historical facts do not fit their ideology. That in and of itself is also ugly. If you are a Christian, why the hell would you ever vote for a Democrat?

Nonetheless, the totem pole of Democrat priorities puts white people and especially white males at the bottom. In a sense you could call this "discrimination by omission". "Clearly, the latter half of the 19th Century, and for much of the early half of the 20th Century, it was the Republican Party that was the party of choice for blacks. How can this be? Because the Republican Party was formed in the late 1850s as an oppositional force to the pro-slavery Democratic Party."[153]

Now let's take an honest look at the relationship between the Democrat Party and black people.

White Supremacy:

This brings us to the topic of white supremacy and what Democrats say about it. From the above discussion it is very plain to see that historically Democrats have strongly supported white supremacy. Their segregation policies have proven this beyond any doubt. Now however they blame white people for being white supremacists. When in fact they have been exactly the same thing that they accuse other people of. Psychologically speaking this is known as "projection". This is where people will accuse other people of doing what in reality exists in their own minds, especially in their subconscious. The famous psychologist Carl Jung identified this a long time ago.

As I have stated before, a huge portion of Democrats are indeed adolescent in their psychological development. They show all the signs of this and what they say, their tone of voice when they say it and what they do. I have covered this in far more detail elsewhere in this book.

Regarding white supremacy the best thought that I have come across describing this from the Democrat Party is from Dinesh D'Souza, a bestselling author on current political topics. I suggest you purchase a few of his books that provide very deep thought on our current political situations.

Regarding white supremacy accusations from Democrats today, Dinesh said, "But today's Democratic Party is different from the past. Today the Democrats affirm every type of ethnic nationalism—black nationalism, Latino nationalism, Asian

---

[153] IBID

nationalism—except white nationalism. So, whites can't show up to the multicultural picnic, because all these other nationalisms are mobilized against white nationalism. Whites have become the bad guys."[154]

In other words, Democrats have labeled white people as white supremacists when they speak out for nationalism Democrats accuse them of white supremacy. You just have to listen to the news today from more objective sources such as Fox News and other outlets that do not include CNN or MSNBC or even CBS. As an example of horrific bigotry in CNN here is a quote from one of their news hosts.

"We have to stop demonizing people and realize the biggest terror threat in this country is white men, most of them radicalized to the right, and we have to start doing something about them." Don Lemon on CNN (October 29, 2018) [155] How do you feel about that my fellow Christians?

These news agencies I have found are not objective and censor the news by not including any items that could shed negative light on leftist liberal Democrat policies or statements. This amounts to the second kind of lie, it is lies by omission. It is lies by just not speaking the complete truth of things. Almighty God will hold them responsible for this when their time comes.

This small section outlining just a few examples of Democrat bigotry is another reason that Christians should never vote Democrat in 2020.

The Perversion of Our Vocabulary

Example of Democrat doublespeak abound throughout all the thing they say. Their vocabulary is designed to make the thing they say sound good. The problem is that what words they use really mean much different and sinister things when it come to the truth and implementing their policies. Here is a table that summarizes many more leftist liberal doublespeak terms and their real meaning in our country today. I found a translation table that shows what they say and what they really mean when it comes to acting on those words. [156] Please see Appendix C. You may be surprised. I give akdart.com full credit and attribution for this table. I have shortened it some to fit in the space for this book.

---

[154] https://www.foxnews.com/opinion/dinesh-dsouza-democrats-big-lies-about-white-supremacy
[155]
www.prweb.com/releases/former_us_navy_seal_ephraim_mattos_responds_to_cnns_don_lemon/prweb15885914
[156] http://www.akdart.com/libspeak.html

In the book "1984" George Orwell talked about government taking control of the vocabulary. Many words were outlawed in an effort to control peoples thinking and minds. The above is very reminiscent of that where "Big Brother" controlled every aspect of our lives. Changing our vocabulary is serious business when you think about it. Again, thank you to akdart.com for putting this table together. I wish I had space to include all of it.

Leftist Censorship of Free Speech:

But we as Christians must thoroughly recognize the serious threat that the Democratic Party and leftist liberal thinking poses to us as a free people. Just one example of this is the increasing censorship by high-tech companies within social media. I see more and more You Tube channels being terminated due to "violations of standards of content" than ever before. Channels I subscribed to that I know by watching them are NOT a violation in any way. This is a disgusting and evil action that stems from Satanic impulses within the leftist liberal minds of the people in the tech industry. I myself have been censored by both Facebook and YouTube. This censorship is real and is a clear and present danger fomented by leftist liberal thinking and the Democrat party and their hopes of getting more votes and power to control all citizens of the United States all of whom are children of God.

What Facebook, Twitter, YouTube and the rest are doing is not only unconstitutional violating the first amendment in the Bill of Rights, they also are violating the second of the two Great Commandments. They are putting themselves up above us as judges for what we say in social media. Whenever you put yourself higher than anyone else, you have violated this Great Commandment and have done exactly the same thing that Lucifer did against God.

Not only do leftist liberal Democrats want to control what you say but also what you wear, the clothing you decide on. There is this new concept for attacking people. It is called "cultural appropriation". This means that if you wear an article of clothing that seems to be identified with a culture other than your own, you are guilty of cultural appropriation. You have automatically demeaned the other culture and you are a bad person for doing that.

Kim Kardashian accessorized a church outfit with what appears to be traditional Indian maang tikka head jewelry. There was an uproar from leftists for violating cultural purity it seems. [157]

---

[157] https://www.foxnews.com/lifestyle/kim-kardashian-blasted-for-cultural-appropriation-in-sunday-service-outfit

Summary of Why Democrats Are the Biggest Threat to America

Just what are Democrats for?

1. Democrats want to increase your taxes from the current 35% to 40% to God knows what.

2. Democrats love socialism. They have been the driving force for the past fifty years in our country for all the social programs that have caused all the monster tax increases we have seen in our country during this time. This has been the root cause of why it now takes two incomes to support a family. Before when I was small, it took only one. Now actually, even two incomes is not enough because our government has gotten so good at confiscating money from citizens in so many hidden ways. With both parents out of the house working all the time, no wonder kids being kids get into trouble with no parent there to guide them. Government is a very corrosive force that destroys what is good in life. Children need parents and government has destroyed that all in the name of social programs.

3. In favor of abortion where babies can be purposely killed minutes AFTER they are born. Thank you, Gov. Cuomo. The code phrase is women's reproductive rights or health. Alyssa Milano is the poster girl for a sex strike to support women's right to kill their babies. Well, good. There will be less murder of developing fetal human beings that way.

4. You have no right to buy personal health care insurance. Force everyone to buy government insurance. Obamacare on monster steroids with no way out. Government will control every cell and function of your body in other words. It's like the people at the DMV or Post Office controlling your bladder and all other bodily functions.

5. They want felonious convicts to vote in our elections even when in prison. Never mind that the damage they did lives on forever. I bet they will make careful informed decisions.

6. We should have no borders to protect US citizens. Illegal aliens should also be given the right to vote. Theoretically, this means people in Africa, the mid-east, China, Russia and so on all should have the right to vote in our elections if they make it past our open border. This is completely

unconstitutional and completely demeaning to every citizen who pays taxes in this country.

7. Democrats want illegal aliens to vote in our elections but hate Trump for a hoax they created regarding Russian collusion meddling in our 2016 elections. Sound contradictory with number 6 to you? It is.

8. They want to limit free speech based on their wishes, already one person went to jail for using a wrong politically incorrect pro-noun.

9. They soundly reject God given individual identity, freedom of action and sovereignty

10. They only think of people in groups, not individual expressions of divine love

11. They want to confiscate all our weapons, only the government should have weapons, total control over your life

12. They soundly reject Judeo-Christian principles, but Islam and Allah are just fine

13. They want the New Green Deal which would mean

   a. No fossil fuels in 10 years

      i. No cars

      ii. No airplanes

      iii. No trucks

   b. No more nuclear power

   c. Government will be employer of last resort which means being guaranteed a government check if you work or not.

   d. Only electricity by wind and solar will be allowed, hope the sun shines and wind blows

   e. Full in on climate change based on an enormous hoax, not real science

14. Democrat leadership actively hates God. Democrat's goal is a purely secular society with no God in sight that is governed by only what feels good at the time as the law of the land.

15. The replacement for God in the minds of the Democrat party is a monster adolescent driven government that controls every aspect of the lives of God's children. But, history proves that mankind is unable to govern itself.

16. It has been my observation over the last 60 years that Democrats are very ignorant of science, philosophy, cosmology, psychology, logic, reason, wisdom, theology and all the other knowledge that is needed in order to produce an ongoing fruitful and sparkling society that flourishes with the grace of God shining down upon us and blessing us in our efforts to grow as human beings and as spiritual beings as well. Said differently, they are damn stupid. And their adolescent minds make them too stupid to know that they are stupid.

17. Notice how democrats seem to be angry all the time. There is a reason for this. Remember that they are on the left side of things. Remember what this means Biblically. They are the goats of life and they deep down inside know it. Minions of the underworld. Pray for them people.

"Our world is raining and dripping with ignorance, stupidity and self-delusion. All this happens on the left side of things. Stay dry and drive on the right side of the street."— Richard Ferguson

The Republicans Are Not Much Better

The Republicans are not much better than the Democrats when it comes to honesty and morality in government. They do know more however about economics and trade and tax policy in such a way that it will produce far more growth in jobs and economic stability for the people of our country. Democrats do not have a clue about how economies work. Remember they are adolescents and they do not know what they do not know. That makes them very dangerous trying to steer our economic ship of state. They are only socialist and ideologically driven.

They Republicans on the other hand will work within the current structures of our government but they will pollute it with very corrupt profit and power oriented people. They like to join secret societies and have hidden agendas within our government that work against the wellbeing of the American people. They like to keep secrets from us, and they freely use "national security" as a broadband excuse to hide all the skullduggery and evil things they are up to.

However, this retched behavior is not exclusive to republicans. I know of one Democrat president who kept secrets from the American people and used a false attack on one of our destroyers to get us into the Vietnam War. That Democrat was Lyndon Baines Johnson. He was a bully of a megalomania that went so far as to control how our naval pilots would attack certain targets in North Vietnam. He would issue presidential orders regarding which direction our pilots would attack from. The North Vietnamese caught on and put all of their antiaircraft guns along the path our pilots were forced to take by President Johnson. Many pilots lost their lives or became prisoners of war directly because of Democrat Lyndon Baines Johnson. I know this personally because a good friend of mine was an A-4 Skyhawk pilot that flew these bombing missions. There is a good reason Johnson had a big nose. He stuck it into everywhere.

Republicans Love the Defense Industry:

The Republicans are exactly what Pres. Dwight D. Eisenhower warned us about in his farewell speech. They love the profits for well-placed individuals in government and industry.

President Eisenhower's farewell address to the nation, January 1961: "...in the councils of government, we must guard against the acquisition of unwarranted influence, whether sought or unsought, by the military industrial complex. The potential for the disastrous rise of misplaced power exists, and we will persist. We must never let the weight of this combination endanger our liberties or democratic processes. We should take nothing for granted. Only an alert and knowledgeable citizenry can compel the proper meshing of the huge industrial and political machinery of defense with our peaceful methods and goals so that security and liberty may prosper together.

He said for us to be wary of the military industrial complex for it will expand greatly and become a huge power within our government that will end up being uncontrollable. This is precisely what has happened. We now have a deep state government that is not answerable to us the American people. The tentacles of our defense industry and all the black projects for military hardware continue onward without any approval or knowledge of the American people. This is a horrible situation, but it exists today.

Coincident to the huge military industrial complex that exists within our federal government, $21 trillion of unauthorized spending by the US government was discovered in 2017. It apparently was spent somewhere between 1998 and 2015. [158] [159] This money apparently was spent by the Pentagon purchasing unknown amounts and kinds of weaponry and other items from our defense industry.

There are large black budgets within the Pentagon and our military that continue onward regardless of who was in the White House, Democrat or Republican.

There are many articles that I researched talking about the "deep state." There are many things that go on in our federal government that even the president of the United States does not have sufficient security clearance to know about. This is just damned awful but there are just too many articles and evidence to think otherwise.

Stupid Immoral Actions:

Ronald Reagan was a good president regarding his handling of our economy and winning the Cold War without any bloodshed with Russia. This was a huge achievement and a complete blessing for us the American people. However, his Iran-Contra scandal surely tainted his presidency. His senior administration officials secretly facilitated the sale of arms to Iran. They did this outside the normal structure of our government with its checks and balances. This is the country where they keep screaming "death to America." Was that in the best interest of God's children here in the United States? No!

How can we forget president Richard M Nixon's Watergate scandal? This was a third rate burglary in June 1972. At his direction his operatives broke into the Democratic National Committee headquarters at the Watergate office complex in Washington, D.C., and the Nixon administration's attempted to cover its involvement. This became infamous known as the Watergate scandal. He was forced to resign and left office in disgrace saying the infamous words, "I am not a crook". Yeah right! He earned his nickname as "tricky Dick."

Not only that, President Nixon had compiled an "enemies list". Shows the mentality of the man. "The official purpose, as described by the White House Counsel's Office, was to "screw" Nixon's political enemies, by means of tax audits from the Internal Revenue Service, and by manipulating "grant availability, federal contracts, litigation, prosecution, etc." John Dean, (August 16, 1971). [160] "Dealing with our Political Enemies". There were about 20 people on the list which changed over time. A longer second list was made public by Dean on December 20, 1973 during a hearing with the

[158] https://www.rt.com/usa/413411-trillions-dollars-missing-research/
[159] https://www.truthdig.com/articles/the-pentagon-cant-account-for-21-trillion/
[160] https://en.wikipedia.org/wiki/Nixon%27s_Enemies_List#cite_note-dean1971-5

Congressional Joint Committee on Internal Revenue Taxation. [161] This is the same tactics that Barack Obama used with the Republican Tea Party scandal and other things Obama did.

These kinds of things are so far removed from our Judeo-Christian morality and ethics. I can only think these people and so many others in Washington are sociopaths and psychopaths. Research says this is true. [162]

There are a lot of Republicans in Congress who were charged with all sorts of scandals and crimes. They include such things as, wire fraud, using campaign funds for personal use, conspiracy to commit securities fraud, lying to the FBI, mail fraud, use of public funds to settle a sexual harassment charge, using money from a fake charity for personal use, an antiabortion congressmen urging his mistress to seek an abortion, sexual misconduct, solicitation for sex on Craig's list, lying to the House of Representatives, bribery, extortion, racketeering, money laundering, possession of cocaine, domestic violence and the list goes on and on and on ad nauseum. You get the picture.

Protecting Our Legitimate Military Secrets:

Usually it is things that politicians do that are terribly dishonest and play havoc on the children of God in the United States. But, in the case of keeping our military secrets away from hostile nations like China and Russia, both Democrats and Republicans are guilty of ignoring the needs of our people to keep our high technology away from our potential enemies. Frankly I believe our government is better at keeping secrets from the American people that should not be secrets than protecting our technology secrets from hostile nations. They do a lousy job of keeping technical secrets away from China and Russia. How is it that China quickly developed a new stealth fighter, the J-20, [163] aircraft that looks almost like our F-35 stealth fighter. [164] Analysts say it was because they stole it using Internet access.

There are many more examples like this not only in many different areas of the military technology but also in commercial products. Since the Republicans are so focused

---

[161] IBD

[162] https://www.politico.com/magazine/story/2018/06/23/washington-dc-the-psychopath-capital-of-america-218892

[163] https://www.dailymail.co.uk/sciencetech/article-3893126/Chinese-J-20-stealth-jet-based-military-plans-stolen-hackers-makes-public-debut.html

[164] https://www.cnbc.com/2017/11/08/chinese-theft-of-sensitive-us-military-technology-still-huge-problem.html

on the military-industrial complex, why is it they are so lax in protecting our priceless technology from our adversaries? I cannot believe that we do not have the capability to keep our secrets away from the prying eyes of China for example.

I do have a very dark terrible feeling that deep down inside tells me tells me that there is some kind of global plan to allow the Chinese to keep pace with the United States and our technology so as to justify far more spending within the military-industrial complex. Remember our defense industry is very profitable for those people positioned high up in the defense industry many of whom have been in government. This sinister and God awful feeling just makes too much sense to me not to ignore it. Can I prove this? No. But this thought somehow fits in with my general distrust of our federal government and all the hidden shenanigans that we as Americans deep inside know are going on. Maybe I'm a conspiracy theorist on this one, you be the judge.

One look at President Bush's vice president Dick Cheney when he growls at people adds credibility to what I just said. His involvement as a war hawk before the war with Iraq is another. The comic Lewis Black said during one of his comedy routines that he had a chance at an event to stand next to Dick Cheney. Lewis said in a videotape I saw, "now I know what it is like to stand next to pure evil." Remember it is also Dick Cheney that went hunting and shot one of his friends, Harry Whittington with 200 pellets, in the face with birdshot from his shotgun. [165] Why is it that Henry ended up apologizing to Cheney? ""My family and I are deeply sorry for all that Vice President Cheney and his family have had to go through this past week." [166] What the hell is going on with that? Cheney never apologized either. What kind of Judeo-Christian character does this show about president Bush's vice president Cheney? How about none.

This is why I propose a 12 member civilian counsel that makes the final decision on what should be kept secret and what should not. We need to take this away from our career political appointees that are way too tempted to engage in their own agendas. The members of the civilian counsel should rotate in and out on a two-year service basis. Rules can be written to ensure members of this Council are fair-minded, intelligent, just and have foundational values that are consistent with our countries foundational Judeo-Christian values. This Council should also have the power to fund cyber warfare defense against foreign intrusion into our military secrets. The current people whoever they may be are completely failing at this task in my opinion.

---

[165]   https://thehill.com/blogs/blog-briefing-room/269143-dick-cheney-has-yet-to-apologize-to-the-man-he-shot-in-the-face
[166] IBID

Gaming Our Laws and System:

As this book was being written the Mueller investigation regarding Donald Trump and collusion with the Russians has turned up other unrelated crimes by a few members of his campaign team. Paul Manafort headed up his campaign for a number of months before resigning. The Mueller investigation looked at all of Manafort's financial dealings and tax returns and lobbying for other countries. Ended up pleading guilty to tax fraud, other counts of fraud and violating different laws governing lobbyists. For this he was sentenced for seven years in federal prison. The defense regarding his crimes wiped out all of his financial wealth estimated at $24 million. Nothing about collusion.

It has been my experience that Republicans are the ones that are most likely to commit crimes such as this. Besides sex crimes they engage in money oriented crimes to enrich themselves in a variety of ways from their positions in government. Of course, Hillary and Bill Clinton are the superstars of this stuff. As I've said before Republicans also like to keep lots of secrets from the American people so they can use government power to conduct wars and other horrific nasty things. They also have fallen in love way too much with our military and defense industries. Lots of profits to be made from our defense industry. Just ask vice president Dick Cheney during the Bush administration and his deep connections with Halliburton, a very large defense contractor. These kinds of crimes are more the style of the Republicans. But yes, Democrats do the same damn thing.

Using the NSA to Spy on the American People:

December 16, 2005 by the New York Times.

WASHINGTON, Dec. 15 - Months after the Sept. 11 attacks, President Bush secretly authorized the National Security Agency to eavesdrop on Americans and others inside the United States to search for evidence of terrorist activity without the court-approved warrants ordinarily required for domestic spying, according to government officials. [167] Why is it President Bush could not use our system of checks and balances to protect the American people from unwarranted spying on them?

This action by President Bush is completely unconstitutional and illegal but he did it anyway. Every president needs an excuse. This time it was terrorism. The American people have lost a lot of civil liberties under the banner of "fighting terrorism." They use the attacks on the twin towers of September 11, 2001 as their excuse for clamping down on emails and phone calls from average citizens in United States in the way that George

---

[167] https://www.nytimes.com/2005/12/16/politics/bush-lets-us-spy-on-callers-without-courts.html

Orwell predicted in his book titled "1984"by big brother. Thank you big brother George Bush.

This behavior of this president Bush falls well outside of our Judeo-Christian morality and ethics. The children of God have every right to expect privacy when they sent emails and make phone calls. I have other things to say about 911 and another section.

NSA Spying on Americans Rises Sharply In 2017 according to Reuters. The U.S. National Security Agency collected more than 500 million phone call records of Americans last year, more than triple gathered in 2016, a U.S. intelligence agency report released on Friday said. The sharp increase to 534 million call records from 151 million occurred during the second full year of a new surveillance system established at the spy agency after U.S. lawmakers passed a law in 2015 that sought to limit its ability to collect such records in bulk. The reason for the spike was not immediately clear.

This is an existential threat to the freedom of every man woman and child living in the United States. This will be the mechanism for the government to track everything you say and will hold that against you. This is part of the preparation for tyranny in the United States. This goes completely against Almighty God for children of God do NOT spy on other children of God.

Regarding spying on Americans, police cars now have automatic license plate readers installed. They can surveil you driving down any street and highway. They log in your identity, where you were, the direction of travel, the time of day. With a series of these intrusions collected, the government can create a picture of all your activities, where you friends live, where you go to ship and all other sorts of privacy invasion information. God's children have a right to privacy. Our government is violating our constitutional rights blatantly every day.

Is It Bad Judgement or Stupidity or Both?

George H. W. Bush: First, he was a graduate from Yale and a member of a secret society called Skull and Bones. Secret societies by definition are never a good thing. I repeat never, ever a good thing. If something good is going on why do you want to keep it a secret? John Kerry who put together the worst deal in the history of the United States with Iran regarding nuclear weapons is also a member of Skull and Bones. Get the idea? This is not bipartisanship. John Kerry suffers from terminal pot brain disease. This man cannot think his way out of a wet paper bag.

One huge problem that George H. W. Bush decided not to foresee was NAFTA. NAFTA was negotiated by his administration. Clinton signed it into law. Critics were right when they said it would increase corporate profits at the expense of American working people. Bush turned a blind eye to it. Experts said it would produce large trade deficits. It did. Our current nonpolitician president Donald Trump said on October 1, 2018 at the White House,"Since NAFTA's adoption, the United States racked up trade deficits totaling more than $2 trillion."We all know about the political fallout regarding all the jobs that flowed out of our country and all the factories that were moved offshore because our presidents just did nothing about it. At least not until Pres. Trump. Why did they do nothing? Why did they let things deteriorate and American workers suffer so badly? When corporations move factories outside the US, the corporations profit and American workers lose badly. That's what NAFTA did to our country and its follow-on CAFTA. [168] [169]

Something had to be going on behind the scenes. Someone was making a lot of money. This seems to be one trademark of Republicans, secrecy and profit. Actions using government structures but against the best interest of God's children that live here. Corporation profits went up while American workers suffered badly.

The American people were being shafted silently and our government was remaining silent about it. The very people who we hired to protect our best interest. Remember, not telling a meaningful truth is the same as a lie. It is called a lie of omission. This is simple foundational Christian morality. Republicans negotiated NAFTA. Americans suffered. Its that simple.

And we all wondered why life was getting harder. Our money was gushing out of our country to enrich other countries that were potential enemies like China. Jobs were also being lost here and being transferred to other countries.

Bush and Iraq:

Our 41st president was not above playing war games with real people's lives. Bush lied to the American people when he said that Iraq invaded Kuwait "without provocation or warning". He lied by omission by not telling us that the U.S. ambassador to Iraq told Saddam Hussein "we have no opinion on the Arab to Arab conflicts, like your border disagreement with Kuwait."This was a clear green light to Saddam to invade. [170] [171]

---

[168] https://www.epi.org/publication/ib214/

[169] https://www.workdayminnesota.org/articles/reject-flawed-cafta-union-leaders-tell-congress

[170] http://representativepress.org/LiesAboutIraq.html

[171] https://www.projectcensored.org/6-no-evidence-of-iraqi-threat-to-saudi-arabia/

Then president Bush fabricated intelligence along with the pentagon that there were 250,000 troops on the border threatening a key U.S. oil supplier. This lie was discovered when Jean Heller of the St. Petersburg Times got her own commercial satellite images of the Saudi border showing only empty desert. NO IRAQI TROOPS. The entire reason for Bush sending in troops just did not exist. President Bush lied to the American people. The result was our military dropped 88,500 tons of bombs on Iraq and Iraqi occupied Kuwait. This also resulted in awful civilian deaths and dismemberment. Our bombing also destroyed critical Iraqi infrastructure including power plants, water treatment facilities and food processing plants for civilians. President Bush is no more than a mass murder cloaked in presidential clothing.

Later military planners admitted that their "intent was to destroy valuable facilities and infrastructure that Bagdad could not repair without foreign assistance."[172] Bush as commander in chief wanted more "leverage" over Saddam Hussain by using our military to destroy and kill people in order to get it. Does this not appear to you as terrorism? The final result of commander in chief Bush according to a Harvard public health team was "acute malnutrition and epidemic levels of cholera and typhoid with the Iraqi people.[173] Yes, president Bush 41 was the cause of all of this for his political gain. We also know that our military industrial complex defense contractors profited from this as well. Worse, you and I were forced to pay for this through confiscation of our money in taxes. I do not know what happened to this man after he died. But I know his actions as president were not even in the same galaxy as our Judeo-Christian values and ethics. So sad. And in the end, he was glorified and honored is a great man during his funeral.

President Bush also told all the American people to "Read my lips no new taxes ". That is what got Bush elected president. New taxes came anyway. He openly did not keep his word to the American people. And the people voted him out of the White House and rightly so. So, he lied to the people and paid the price. Not the brightest bulb in the box.

In keeping with an awful so called presidential tradition, president Bush during his last days as president pardoned six senior government officials from felony convictions regarding the Iran Contra scandals. These guys were guilty as sin, but the good old boy club was operating effectively. I do not know how many people died because of these felons that Bush pardoned. The sin was open for all to see using presidential power in your face to American people and gave real criminals a get out of jail free card. Disgusting.

---

[172] https://theintercept.com/2018/12/01/the-ignored-legacy-of-george-h-w-bush-war-crimes-racism-and-obstruction-of-justice/

[173] IBID

Republicans Are Not Above Petty Scandals:

Other recent scandals involving people on the right mention three.

"In New York, Rep. Chris Collins has been indicted for insider trading. In California, Rep. Duncan Hunter is also facing charges for allegedly using his campaign's cash to pay for a lavish personal lifestyle. In Iowa, Rep. Rod Blum is under investigation by the House Ethics Committee over his role in an internet company whose work is directly related to the federal government." [174]

Notice this is consistent with Republicans. They fool around with lots of money money and more money. Not like the Democrats who like perverted sex and kill developing fetal human beings under the banner of "women's reproductive rights."

Chris Christie GOP's poster boy 2016 presidential nominee created "Bridgegate." Christie collaborated to create traffic jams in Fort Lee, NJ, along the George Washington Bridge, as simple revenge against Fort Lee Mayor Mark Sokolich for not endorsing Christie in the 2013 gubernatorial election. Good God, this is elementary school stuff.

Over many decades of observation, it is this writer's opinion that this is the mode of operation of immorality on the right hand side of our political spectrum is either election rigging which both sides do in very amateurish ways or has to do with moolah and boatloads of it. On the other hand, the left side already has sex covered in an entertaining wide assortment of ways and positions depending on your particular preferences. The top Democrat Virginia State Officials including the governor all democrats are under investigation for sex and racial crimes as of the time this is being written. So, the only thing left is money for the right side to indulge in.

George W Bush:

Well, here we have another war story, George W. Bush our 43rd president. His father George H. W. Bush went to war against Iraqi leader Saddam Hussain kicking him out of Kuwait lying about all the nonexistent troops that were stationed at the Saudi and Kuwaiti border. Now his son George W. Bush was ready to finish the job. Don't worry dad, I will pick up where you left off.

In an article published by Sidney Blumenthal on September 6, 2007 [175] he categorically states that CIA director George tenet briefed Pres. Bush in the Oval Office on top secret intelligence that Saddam Hussain <u>did not have weapons of mass destruction</u>

---

[174] https://www.vox.com/2018/11/5/18064466/republican-corruption-scandal-midterms-2018
[175] https://www.salon.com/2007/09/06/bush_wmd/

according to two senior CIA officers. President Bush unilaterally dismissed this information as worthless. What was going on here?

This information was not included in documents given to Congress that needed to vote on the authorization to use our military force in Iraq. This was never told the American people either. Rather there was an orchestrated campaign to do quite the opposite which was to paint a picture that Saddam Hussein had many weapons of mass destruction including chemical biological warfare and SCUD missiles to deliver them. [176] I remember all of this.

As for his part Mr. Tennant knowing the real truth of things kept his mouth shut and allowed the charade and lies to Congress and the American people to continue and the march toward war to continue onward as well. There were people within our government pushing for war with Iraq. Later George Tennant did say, "his agency was under pressure to justify a war that the administration had already decided on."[177]

An article written by Peter Taylor on March 18, 2013 said, "Much of the key intelligence that was used to justify the war was based on fabrication, wishful thinking and lies - and as subsequent investigations showed, it was dramatically wrong. Saddam Hussein had no weapons of mass destruction."[178]

President Bush for reasons unknown had already made up his mind and would not listen to anything else other than to pound the drums of war. He was obsessed on going to war with Iraq and overthrowing Saddam Hussain. Then a new report about Saddam Hussain was written by unknown sources by someone in the CIA. They knew what the president wanted so they gave it to him. The report contained all the falsehoods that the president wanted and stated that, "Saddam was aggressively and covertly developing nuclear weapons and that he already possessed chemical and biological weapons."

The following is a subtitle on an article written about President Bush and Dick Cheney regarding their lies to the American people pushing us into war with Iraq.

On "Hardball," Michael Morell concedes the Bush administration misled the nation into the Iraq War. [179]

From the appearances of things Bush wanted dominion over this part of the middle east. It is never ever a good thing to want dominion over anything. This is the way of evil,

---

[176] https://newspunch.com/declassified-cia-document-reveals-iraq-war-had-zero-justification/
[177] https://www.theguardian.com/world/2003/jul/17/iraq.usa
[178] https://www.telegraph.co.uk/news/worldnews/middleeast/iraq/9937516/Iraq-war-the-greatest-intelligence-failure-in-living-memory.html
[179] https://www.motherjones.com/politics/2015/05/michael-morell-bush-cheney-iraq-war/

the way of Satan. It is the way of attempting to put yourself higher than other people, of other children of God. It is what Lucifer did or try to do eyed as a result he was cast down to this earth and hell.

Do any of you really wonder what will happen to the person that caused all this or the people that allowed all this to happen. It is just as bad to allow evil to occur and watch it happen as it is to be perpetrated. Think about that. Christian morality is very much involved in all of this. It is a wise person that learns from the mistakes of others so they do not have to learn the hard way as the others will. Mr. Tennant will have to answer to God just as much George Bush will.

The Attack on The World Trade Center 9/11/2001

George W. Bush was president and Dick Cheney was vice president at this time. Cheney is known to have deep connections within our military industrial complex now known as the defense industry. There are many "black" projects going on within this industry.

Signs of a massive coverup and hoax regarding the 911 attack abound. How is it that we "knew" that Osama bin Laden was responsible on the same day of the attack? How did we know the identities of the 19 hijackers within hours after that? How is it that flight 93 that crashed into the field had no bodies or parts of an aircraft? How is it possible for a Boeing 767 make only a round hole in the side of the Pentagon like it had no wings? How is it that our on patrol fighter jets that morning were ordered to fly east off the coast appearing like someone wanted them out of the way. If you believe the public explanations of what happened, you are believing a story that is impossible. It is because that story breaks many laws of physics, not just suspicious circumstances.

It is impossible for jet fuel to melt steel for example. The melting point of high strength steel is far higher than where jet fuel burns. No steel building has ever collapsed due to fire. Why did everything "turn to dust"? Concrete crumbles into chunks. It does not dustify. This list goes on. There is a very good book that presents a complete forensic analysis of the 911 attack. It proves that what we were told about 911 is physically impossible. The book is "Where Did the Towers Go?" by Judy Wood. [180]

I bring this up because this is the greatest hoax ever perpetrated on the American people. It changed all of our lives. It gave rise to the TSA, the NSA spying on our phone calls and a host of other freedoms lost in our lives. It was a seminal event in the history of

---

[180] Where Did the Towers Go?, Judy Wood, The New Investigation, 2010

the United States. I urge all of you to do your own research on this and get a copy of the book mentioned above.

Now, I cannot believe that the White House did not know anything about all of this. If they did not know anything, how did they know who did it almost instantly? Why were our fighter jet ordered out of the way? Things like this. Remember George W. Bush is a member of the Skull & Bones secret society. I am not planting a conspiracy theory here, but you should read the book by Judy Wood. You will see that our Republican led government under George Bush lied to us in horrific ways. How deep that goes I do not know.

The Deep Hidden Industrial Military Defense Industry:

Donald Trump:

I think president Trump is on the whole doing a great job for the American people. A great job. He has defused the North Korean nuclear threat and has ongoing talks with them as this is written. They were testing ICBM's capable of delivering nuclear warheads to the United States. They were testing nuclear bombs as well. They were rattling their military sword against the United States when President Trump took office. As this is being written, things are quiet, and we are negotiating to bring North Korea into the world of nations in a peaceful manner.

Somehow, watching TV it is apparent that the Democrats do not like this. Anything president Trump does is automatically hated by Democrats, no thinking involved. Adolescents are good at not thinking.

He has reversed our country's financial hemorrhaging in trade with the rest of the world so we can keep our created wealth here at home where it really is needed. No other president in the last fifty years has done this. Thank God he has done this. But I hold responsible previous Republican presidents for ignoring their responsibility to the American people, to our created wealth and to our well-being as children of God. They ignored this vital area and our country has greatly suffered because of it.

I don't blame the Democrats as much because you can't get blood out of a turnip. In their adolescent minds they are just too busy with their demented and evil social programs to pay any attention to the well-being of the United States on the international front.

Thank God Pres. Trump is doing that for the wellbeing of us and our children. He has also appointed many people to high positions in our government including the judiciary that fully support our Judeo-Christian foundations of this country. Democrats are screeching, moaning and gnashing their teeth to stop this and are holding up more than 200 nominees from starting to work for the American people. Why? Because they do not support killing developing fetal human beings and are Christians. That is unconstitutional and illegal, but they do that anyway.

However, Pres. Donald Trump supports the civil asset forfeiture laws. This is outright awful and must be stopped immediately. It pits the police state against the children of God in this country. This is what it means. This government schemes to deprive Americans of their liberties—namely, the right to property—is being carried out under the guise of civil asset forfeiture, a government practice wherein government agents (usually the police) seize private property they "suspect" may be connected to criminal activity. Then, whether or not any crime is actually proven to have taken place, the government keeps the citizen's property. [181]

Did you know that police consider it illegal and suspicious to have a significant amount of cash on you if you are stopped by them? They automatically think you are a drug dealer and confiscate it. No proof or drug evidence is needed. Nope. They steal your money anyway. I have read multiple articles where ordinary citizens are stopped by police for a traffic violation. They end up having cash and other valuables seized by the police under asset forfeiture laws when they have committed no crime and no charges are ever brought against them. This is an absolutely heinous crime against God's children in this country and it continues on to this day. Shame on Donald Trump for supporting this.

On another note, it is estimated that at least 30,000 drones will be airborne in American airspace by 2020, part of an $80 billion industry. Lots of profit going on here. Although some drones will be used for benevolent purposes, many will also be equipped with lasers, tasers and scanning devices, among other weapons—all aimed at "We the People."[182] This is just more of the government encroaching on our privacy and fishing for possible crimes that have not yet been committed. In London they have horrific surveillance using cameras. That has not stopped the high murder rate there using knives because guns have been outlawed. It's like the police looking at you on every step you take as you walk down the sidewalk. Disgusting! Somehow republican like this sort of thing.

---

[181] May 1, 2018 | John W. Whitehead | The Rutherford Institute
[182] IBID

Republican and Individual Privacy:

Republicans seem to love the idea of big brother, big government, spying on its citizens using high technology to invade American citizen's privacy. They like to use all sorts of surveillance technology and spying to monitor our every activity, even driving down the road peaceably not violating any traffic laws. Today police cruisers have a high tech device that can read people's license plates from quite a distance. This information is then transferred to a database to record where you were, the time of day, the speed you are going, what direction you are going in and other things. This is none of their damned business.

Our courts are no help right now because they keep shifting what constitutes what they call "our expectation of privacy". It's getting so that no matter where you are in public is going to get recorded by our damned government. This is not government of the people and by the people and for the people. This is government controlling and monitoring the people.

You can expect a great decline in your privacy once facial recognition software gets wide distribution within law enforcement agencies. You can expect this invasive software to analyze you at every public place, airports, bus stations, train stations etc. The police will say that it helps them catch the crooks. Do we really want this in our society? Privacy is a God given right that should never be taken away. Will they catch more crooks? Probably but is that worth the government knowing everything you did today? My answer is no!

In Pittsburgh California they already have installed license plate readers on police cars. "According to city documents, the project was inspired by Pittsburg's use of video cameras and a license-plate reader project, which were installed in police cruisers." [183] California and other states are very active installing automatic license plate readers both in police cars and street poles. They say the following:

"sophisticated cameras mounted on squad cars and street poles that read license plates and record the time, date, and location a particular car was encountered." "By matching your car to a particular time, date and location, and then building a database of that information over time, law enforcement can learn where you work and live, what doctor you go to, which religious services you attend, and who your friends are." [184]

---

[183]   https://www.eastbaytimes.com/2017/12/11/regional-freeway-license-plate-reader-network-coming-to-highways-4-and-80/

[184] https://www.eff.org/cases/automated-license-plate-readers

I am sure that the Democratic Party is going along with this in my opinion. But surveillance including the NSA activities monitoring American citizens domestic phone calls and emails are something consistent with the Republican mindset I believe. This activity is completely against our Judeo-Christian morality and ethics because it puts government above God's children, the citizens of our country. This is the same thing that Lucifer did when he rebelled against God and got thrown out of the heavenly kingdom. He tried to put himself above God. Government is our civil servant, not our monitors, not our personal surveillance people and certainly not people who control every aspect of our lives through surveillance.

Conclusion:

My conclusion about the Republican Party, it's mindset and how it appears to operate is something like this. Republican certainly are not involved too much with changing our social morality regarding such things LBGQT, so called special rights for small special interest groups, and special women's rights. Republicans do not believe in violating our Second Amendment under the guise of "gun violence". Republicans do not engage in such horrific name-calling as Democrats such as racist, homophobic, Islam phobic, white supremacy, white privilege, mail toxicity and all these other idiotic hate speech terms designed to demean members of God's children.

Republicans do however engage in unconstitutional acts very much like Democrats. Republicans do put American citizens first before citizens of other countries especially illegal aliens who have penetrated our borders breaking our laws. Democrats love these people because they viewed them as future Democrat voters just like Democrat Lyndon Johnson did with black people in the late 1960s.

Republicans do tend to stick more towards our Judeo-Christian foundational principles the Democrats do. Democrats view Christianity as a roadblock to their socialist dreams that will result in horrific suffering pain and agony and even death to our American children of God.

It was Republicans that supported black people and ended slavery in spite of hateful resistance from the Democrat party during the time of Abraham Lincoln who was shot and killed by a Democrat named John Wilkes Booth.

I have never heard a Republican publicly speak against Judeo-Christian morality and ethics like the Democrats actively do. Nor have they used religious anti-Christian litmus tests against nominees for public office as the Democrats have demonstrated so well recently.

Republican support the human rights of developing fetal human beings in a mother's womb. Democrats want to kill them for pure convenience under the banner of "women's reproductive health care and rights."

In summary Republicans have some real and dangerous problems with money, power and conducting wars for what appears to be profit. This is damned awful. But in total when all things are considered it is the Republicans, awful as they may be in the above-mentioned areas, are better in the long run for God's children that live in the United States of America and our democratic constitutional republic. The only compliment I can give them is that they are the lesser of two evils.

So, in a manner of speaking pick your poison. Choosing Democrats will result in the disintegration of our culture, our society as we know it in the willful and purposeful destruction of our Judeo-Christian foundations as a people of God and children of God. Republicans will keep the structures of our democratic constitutional republic intact. Republicans will respect our constitutional laws far greater the Democrats will. Democrats given the chance will modify our Constitution in such a way as to degrade it into nothing more but a piece of historical paper.

But Republicans will indeed flood the structures of our society and government with people with their own agendas that seek profit and power including what appears to be war for profit against convenient enemies of our nation. The poster boy for immoral war and profit is Dick Cheney, vice president to George Bush in my humble opinion.

Summary of the Right Wing Republicans

1. Republicans seem to have a very spotty and inconsistent relationship with God. It has been my observation for the years that some right-wing politicians are magically able to to church on Sunday and then on Monday continue leading unnecessary wars in foreign lands. In my opinion Jesus Christ view these people worse than he did the Pharisees. He called these people whitewashed tombs that look good on the outside but are full of vermin and filth on the inside.

2. Right-wing politicians certainly know that war is profitable. It is profitable for the mega military industrial complex that Pres. Dwight Eisenhower warned us about in 1958. In my opinion there is not a new weapons system that these people do not like. Yes, our country definitely needs a strong military. But the United States spends more money on our military that all the rest of the countries in the world combined. Where does all this money go? In the last few years the Pentagon has lost trillions of dollars that they cannot account for. That is our money people. That money came from the sweat and labor of all of us and they misplaced it somehow. Why is there not an investigation on this?

3. Republicans are different Democrats. Instead of trying to tear down our existing social order, the structure of our government, our election process because they lost the election, continue to kill developing fetal human beings, invite the worlds poverty-stricken poor into our country and sanctuary cities, being in love with disastrous socialism and monster catastrophes for our country, the Republicans instead our existing society and government structures and processes. However, they are very good at populating our government with people like the Democrats, are very good at lying to your face. President Bush told the nation Saddam Hussein had weapons of mass destruction. No, he did not. This did not stop Bush from invading that country and killing many tens of thousands of people mostly innocent civilians. Civilians suffered horribly with starvation and disease after our military got done with them. All because President Bush lied to our country. I wonder how many times President Bush went to church during the Iraqi war.

4. Republicans do want to control the entire population. They do not want to do it through socialism's laws and regulations however. They would rather be very sneaky about it. This is why the NSA has been allowed to spy on all public

communications including email, phone calls and other such activities like recording your license plate as you drive through town or on the freeway with photo ID for your license number on your car. This information is stored to be used against you if they ever want to hang something. We can can do this that Republicans are not very much in favor of individual privacy. Not good.

5. These days the government has reserved itself the power to confiscate wealth if in any way shape or form they can conjure up out of thin air a suspicion and only a suspicion that the money might have, may have, could have been result of illegal activity. You do not even need to be charged with a crime. Your wealth is confiscated, and you can do anything about it except hire expensive lawyers in an effort to get part of your money back. This is called being guilty until proven innocent at great expense. Pres. Trump supports this obscene police power. The Republican Party has remained silent on this complete abuse of innocent God's children.

6. Unlike the Democrats, the Republicans are not so hot for sex like Harvey Weiner. Instead they like money a lot. Things like wire fraud, appropriating public funds to settle lawsuits against Republican politicians and using money from charities is far more the Republican style.

7. Republicans have the image of "strong on defense". But frankly they are lousy at protecting our defense secrets from potential enemies like China. The Chinese stole our F– 35 stealth fighter technology through the Internet. How stupid can you be?

8. The one good thing about Republicans is that I do not detect their psychological development to be only adolescent. This means that they have more ability to be conniving, dishonest and successful in hiding hidden agendas.

9. They do not speak against our Judeo-Christian morality. But again, they ignore that when it seems convenient to do so.

In summary, as voters we get to pick the flavor of our poison. In the case of Democrats it is moral and ethical rot that will result in pain, suffering and agonizing death through starvation, poverty and very high crime rates.

In the case of Republicans, it will be more and more defense spending until we are blue in the face. Republicans will take our military into space in that realm of existence will become another battlefield. Let's face it, we already have weapons space in my opinion. It is just that our government has decided that we as God's children should not know about that. Republicans will lead us down the path of blowing up more people more efficiently. Somehow they think that is a good thing.

Life Threatening Dangers to Our Country

For the first time in the existence of our democratic and constitutional republic we now face real existential threats from both inside and outside our nation. These are very serious threats to not only our way of life, the structure of our society and culture but our very existence as a people of God. It terrifies me to say this but in my search for the foundational truth this is what I have found. Before we had enemies outside our nation as in the Revolutionary war, World War I, World War II and communism with Vietnam and Korea. Now we face a double barreled threat from both inside and out.

From the Outside:

Russia:

From the outside we have the following. Russia continues with its aggression throughout its region wanting to re-create the Soviet empire. This is very serious business. That country is one where no American would want to live. Living standards are much lower than here. That is why vodka is so popular. Basically, due to the weather they can survive providing for themselves. But it is their oil and gas that they sell on world markets that provide them the money to fund their military, and their space programs, their rocketry, missiles and nuclear weapons. It was once said by a senior official in the federal government that the Soviet Union was basically a Third World country with a gas station. That is very crude but essentially true. That is one threat we face and must deal with constantly.

China:

Over the years I have observed our trade with China. Many years ago, if a product appeared on a department store shelf and said made in China it meant cheap and no good. That was true back then. Over the years however two things have happened. First, they learned how to make better and better products. Due to our lax trade policies and their very low labor cost, they provided the American consumer with quality goods at a low price. This provided China with very high profits. They smartly used these profits to build up their infrastructure like the three gorges Dam. It is really something to see. To China frankly, individual people are expendable. They do not value individual human lives. This goes directly against the will of Almighty God. Remember that and to them one size fits all, no such thing as an individual. That's communism and socialism. Everyone must wear size 10 shoes. Too bad if it does not fit. Complaining is an insult to the state.

As things went along their profits kept increasing and increasing. Then, the second thing occurred. Through the use of high technology when it became available, they started to maneuver and steal our intellectual property in both commercial and military areas, especially the military. They used our blueprints to reproduce our designs and sell them either on commercial markets or use them in their military to one day confront us in a war that they are already planning for. Yes, that is true. Our trade balance with China has been ignored by many of our federal government administrations both Democrat and Republican. Both are guilty as sin. As far as I am concerned both border on treasonous behavior against the American people who trusted them to protect us against exterior threats. But our government looked the other way and did not do a damn thing. For the first time now, our current president is addressing these issues. He does deserve the full support of the American people. He is trying to protect us from future Chinese aggression and war with them.

This is the biggest threat to the United States in the near future. It is coming and it will happen unless we change things immediately. The current administration under Pres. Trump is doing everything that is right and proper to stop the hemorrhage of the well-being of all American citizens. It is just that simple.

Immigration:

Even protecting our country from being invaded by millions of citizens of other countries that do not belong here, properly called illegal aliens, many liberal democratic politicians roll out the red carpet for them and want to give them health care, food, housing, and all the necessities of life. This is at the expense of the already overburdened American taxpayer and children of God. Along with these people come in enormous amounts of dangerous drugs that we know kill American citizens. Human trafficking of poor young women into sex slavery occurs on an everyday basis. Extremely violent members of gangs that have the slogan "rape, murder, kill " come into our country with these illegal aliens and are greeted or ignored by our liberal democratic politicians.

Democrats have set up many sanctuary cities for people like this and our country. This makes Democrats an existential threat to the health and wellbeing of the people in our country. Our liberal democrat politicians cannot see any difference between a citizen of the United States and a citizen from Nicaragua. Do you really want to vote for someone like that? Always remember what the new governor of California has said, "I am willing to make bold decisions and glorious mistakes." And he is doing it with your money and your life. People voted for this lunatic adolescent.

Democrats accuse people that disagree with them saying that we are violating their illegal alien's human rights if we try to stop them. It is simple. Illegal aliens have human rights. They do not have constitutional rights. Those are reserved for being a citizen of this country.

Democrats ignore the slavery they are imposing upon the taxpaying people of the United States, God's children. They are taking God's children's lives away from them. They are taking away from our citizens their rightful opportunity to explore, to learn, to gain knowledge, to grow closer to God in many different ways of their choice within this physical realm.

They ignore the crowding effect on our health facilities where our own citizens depend on for their health needs. They ignore all the social services that become overwhelmed that are here for our citizens. They ignore all the crime, rape burglary murder that comes with many of these illegal aliens. They ignore the stress it puts on our police and judicial system to handle these people that should never have been here in the first place. Barack Obama has been quoted as saying his goal was to "Make America like all the other nations in the world." No more would we be the shining city on the hill that Pres. Ronald Reagan described. Rather, we would have Third World problems just like everybody else courtesy of the Democrat party and Barack Obama. In my opinion, the underhanded actions of Obama are acts of treason.

All of that is thrown into the gutter because we must put our nose to the grindstone to work for more money to pay the higher taxes that the Liberal Democratic Party wants to spend on these illegal criminals coming here to the United States.

Why you ask do Democrats do this to the American people? It is for the same reason that Lyndon Johnson stated so clearly on Air Force One in 1968 before he signed the civil rights bill when he said, "I will have all those nig%ers voting Democratic for the next 200 years". This quote is referenced and footnoted earlier in this book. It is all about political power.

I truly hate to say the following. It is dismal. It is awful. But I believe it to be truthful. I have come to the point in my research where I believe that my opinion is now that the liberal left Democratic Party would rather rule and control over a dung heap than participate in a sparkling successful Judeo-Christian society. This statement is the result of many years of education in science with degrees and chemistry, physics, business, theology, pastoral ministry and observing our politics during the last 50 years and how it has evolved from cooperation between liberal and conservative ideals into nasty and barbaric name-calling. Disagree if you wish, but all the evidence points otherwise.

The only ones that lose in this current situation are God's children, the American people no matter who they are, no matter where they are. Everyone loses, every child of God loses no matter where they fit on the political spectrum, because of the hatred, the disgust, the mistrust, the I will get you attitude, the I will use my government powers against you attitude, the I will override the Judeo Christian-based Constitution of the United States so I can do what I want attitude.

The widespread use of accusations of racism, bigotry, white supremacy, hate speech, toxic masculinity, Islamophobia, homophobia, and a cocktail of many other accusations including all the other this-a-phobias and that-a-phobias that have destroyed the normal and necessary communication between competing ideas that should lift up our society to higher ideals. That has been destroyed. The environment has become so toxic because of the liberal left and its love of attack and accusations that reasonable discussion has disappeared from the public marketplace of ideas. This cornerstone of Democratic and constitutional republic government has been successfully destroyed by them. We are now weakened as a nation, a culture and a Judeo Christian society. That must STOP NOW!

Our founding fathers said that they were leaving us a system of government that required a populace that was intelligent, educated, thoughtful and engaged with government. In these respects, we have failed and failed miserably in the last 50 years. Now we're seeing the results of our failures. It shows in our liberal left Democratic politicians every day we turn on the TV. It shows what is being taught to our children in school such things as common core and liberal ideas about marriage and so forth. In these areas it is like termites eating at the foundation of your house. It is silent, you do not notice it until the walls start crumbling down. Then it is too late.

Islam And Its Threat to America

It is said that Islam is the third Abrahamic Religion. It is a religion of peace. Muslims claim that the Bible has been corrupted and it is Islam corrects this through the last prophet Mohammod. They even go so far as to say that Jesus Christ said there would be one more prophet after him. They say that the Bible was corrupted after it was written, and Islam corrects those mistakes. Therefore, the Islamic posture is one where they claim superiority over all things Jewish and Christian. BS!

All these claims are totally false with no factual evidence behind them. This is awful from the very beginning. Just the idea that Islam is superior to Judaism and Christianity is a shortcut to hell. They are putting themselves higher than God's children. This is precisely what Islam claims, that they are the final word from God. Judaism and Christianity somehow got corrupted and it is Islam that is the only legitimate word of God. BS!!!! I have noticed in my study of Islam that Muslim apologists never mention any specific example of any Biblical corruption that the Koran has corrected. This is because there are not any.

I highly encourage you to get a copy of the booklet "Islam Religion of Peace or War?" from CBN.com. This is another Christian source in addition to the footnoted ones in this section. This will give you an excellent start in understanding Islam and answer the questions about why Muslims behave the way they do.

Who is Allah? [185]

Allah means "the god". It is not the pagan's god's name. It is derived from the name "al-ilah", meaning the chief and most powerful god of the pantheon of the local 360 pagan gods or deities in Mecca. In Mecca Allah replaced their existing moon god Hubal as the lord of the Kabbah. The name al-illah was originally a phase of the moon god, the god of Mohammad's tribe when he lived in Mecca. Each Arab tribe had its own pagan god. Mohammad did not create the name Allah. This god was Allah, known well before Mohammad was born.

There are also astral elements connected with the god al-ilah or Allah. It was the moon and stars. Allah is possibly represented by the black stone in the Kabbah in Mecca. In those times, Arabs thought large stones or boulders were sacred. Allah is considered the lord of the Kabbah. When Mohamud proclaimed Allah to be the only one god, he was really saying not much new. Only that this one god was the only god. So, Mohammad morphed his tribe's moon god into Allah and proclaimed this god as the only god. This angered many people in Mecca, and they turned against Mohammad.

"The religion of the Arabs, as well as their political life, was on a thoroughly primitive level...In particular the Semites regarded trees, caves, springs, and large stones as being inhabited by spirits; like the Black Stone of Islam in a corner of the kabbah at Mecca, in Petra and other places in Arabia stones were venerated also..."[186]

---

[185] http://www.bible.ca/islam/islam-allah-pre-islamic-origin.htm
[186] IBID

There is more regarding all the gods in ancient Mecca, no space to get into all the details. For further research the footnote above is a good starting place. But as we can see, Allah is not in any way related to our Judeo-Christian God. It has been derived actually from what you would expect in those primitive cultures as shown in the above quote. Now, what you have just learned is something that 99% of Muslims DO NOT KNOW.

Islam is More a Political and Personal Lifestyle, Not a True Religion: [187] [188]

Islam is more of a complete lifestyle dictated by the details of the lifestyle of Mohammad and his attitudes than worshiping their god. If you count all the verses in the Koran, you will find a full 2/3's is devoted to secular relationships with non-Muslims, the infidels and kafirs, not spiritual thoughts or worship.

It is Mohammad that started violent jihad against all non-Muslims killing, raping and destroying as they conquered much of the mid-east and into much of southern Europe. All this is documented in the Koran, the Hadith and the Sira. It is thee three books of Islamic literature that documents all of this. It is their own writings and their own heritage. These statements are not my opinions. This is history and Islamic commands to modern day Muslims on how to behave as recorded in the three major writings of Califs written in ancient times who knew Mohammad and some who knew those who did. The Koran instructs all Muslims to wage jihad against all non-Muslims.

Mohammad is considered the perfect example of how a person is to live their live on earth. He is to be copied by Muslims in all aspects of how he lived including his attitudes toward all other people. You can read all about Mohammad's lifestyle in the Sirah. The problem is all the crimes he committed and people he killed. Here are some historical facts about Mohammad provided to us by the Egyptian Jesuit father Henri Boulard: [189]

1. Mohammed had slaves and traded them (Sahih Muslim 3901.
2. He commanded his followers to stone adulteresses (Muslim 4206).
3. He personally decapitated 800 Jewish men and children. (Abu Dawud 14:2665)
4. He ordered the death of women. (Ibn Ishaq 819,995)

[187] https://www.politicalislam.com/author/
[188] https://bible-quran.com/uthman-collection-quran/
[189] Crusade magazine. Islam and the suicide of the West. Interview with author *Luiz Solimeo May/June 2019*

5. He killed those who insulted him. (Bukhari: 56:369, 4:241)

6. The jihad raises someone's position paradise 100 times (Muslim 4645)

7. In the last 10 years of his life, Mohammad led 65 Illa Terry campaigns and attacks, he killed captives taken in battles. (Ibn Ishaq 451)

8. Mohammed encouraged his men to rape and enslave women. (Abu Dawood 2150, Koran 4:24)

9. He ordered his men to kill apostates.

He is the model for what we see Muslims doing today. He promoted jihad not peace. He wanted Islam to subjugate the entire world. Muslims are still trying to do that today though jihad...killing innocent people.

During his time in Medina, he raised an army 10,000 strong. They attacked caravans on trade routes to and from Mecca for example. He came to hate Christians and Jews because they rejected him in Medina. This is the reason you see all the violent jihad and terror coming from Muslims and Islamic countries against the Judeo-Christian world. Mohammad waged war against Christians and Jews in his attempt to conquer the world. He did conquer much of what was the Roman empire. Think of all the killing, rapes and all the blood that was spilled, the killing, and the subjugation that went on after Mohammad's death.

Is this a man of God. NO! Mohammad in his sayings actually projects his human hateful, just like himself emotions onto Allah. One example, Allah can hate people for what they may do. Allah metes out punishments on this earth to people and wants them put to death. Basically, Mohammad anthropomorphizes Allah and makes him a bully with anger issues just like himself. There is no redemption in Islam. The list goes on.

Islam is Opposite to Christianity:

Also, unlike all other religions in the world, Islam has no golden rule. They have no principle that says you must treat all other people as you would want them to treat you. There is nothing like that in all Islamic texts. In Christianity, we have the two great commandments. Love God first and above all else. The second is like the first. Love your neighbors as you love yourself. There is nothing like this in the Koran, the Hadith and the Sirah. Instead Mohammad instructed all Muslims to conduct jihad against all non-Muslims especially Christians and Jews. Muslims are instructed to kill the kafirs wherever you find them.

Islam claims that Christianity is a polytheist religion. They say that our Trinity is actually three Gods, not one within a Triune. If there is no Trinity, then Jesus Christ cannot be the incarnation of the Word or the Redemption. Mother Mary would no longer be the mother of God. Our Christian churches would lose all meaning and there would be no redemption mankind. They also say that Jesus Christ was a lesser profit and he came in order to announce the arrival of Mohammed who is the last and greatest prophet.

Therefore, there can be no reconciliation between Islam and Christianity. The above beliefs in Islam and Mohammed's hatred of Jews and Christians are the root causes of all the bombings, the killing, the beheadings and all other terrorist activity in our Western world. If anyone ever tells you that Islam is a religion of peace, I think I would spit on their shoes.

The Koran instructs Muslims to treat all non-Muslims as second class people. It outlines the details of how to do this. All other people are to pay Muslims the jizya, a monthly tribute in money to buy protection from Muslims killing you.

How the Koran Was Created:

Completely unlike the Bible, the Koran in use today is the product of one singular Caliph who was two steps removed from Mohammad, Calif Uthman (574-656). There were many hot disagreements about what should be contained in the collection of Islamic texts and sayings that should appear in Calif Uthman's final version of the Koran.

Many fragments of text were assembled along with the memories of Islamic fighters who survived their campaigns of war and conquest. His task was to put everything together in some coherent fashion. Calif Uthman did so and in doing that created many enemies. To rid the Islamic community of so many arguments, disputes and fights about what should be contained in the final version Calif Uthman did the following:

"Uthman decreed that all personal Mushafs differing from his own should be burned." [190]

He was assassinated by fellow Muslims in 656 A.D, a common way for Muslims to solve disputes. Do you trust the word of a single Arabic man from 1,400 years ago that is known to be deadly hostile to all non-Muslims including all Christians and Jews? Do you trust an Arab man that ordered the deaths of all Muslims that disagreed with him, killing

---

[190] https://bible-quran.com/uthman-collection-quran/

them by burning them to death? For further study I recommend the following book. "The History of the Quranic Text from Revelation to Compilation, by Muhammad Mustafa Al-Azami"[191]

The important thing to remember is this: The Koran in the hands of Muslims today is the result of one man, Calif Uthman, who selected what sayings and teachings would be in the final version of the Koran. Uthman had all other texts available to him burned so as to ensure there would be only one version of the Koran, his version. This is completely unlike Biblical texts. Christian texts have been written by many people over thousands of years. So, Muslims today are unknowingly taking the word of a single human being about what Mohammad said 1,400 years ago. Would you do that?

Is Islam a Religion of Peace? NO! It Never Was and Never Will Be:

Islamic Wars of Conquest:

During the last 1,400 years Muslims in their lust for world domination have killed approximately 270 million people on this planet. [192] There were about 548 documented battles of Islamic religious conquest. [193] This compares with 17 different crusades of different sizes in an attempt to regain Muslim conquered holy lands such as Jerusalem. Not for conquest but to regain what was already Christian until Muslims came, killed untold thousands of Christians to seize the land and subjugate the people under Sharia law against their will.

The first Muslim conquest of a Christian holy site was Jerusalem in 638 after a siege of about 4 months. Abu Ubaidah, the Muslim commander-in-chief conducted this war against Christians. Abu settled the conquest without much bloodshed under one major condition, that the Christians pay the Islamic jizya tax to them. This is a monthly tax so as not to be killed. For reference, this is the same thing mobsters in places like Chicago enforced on people and businesses to leave them alone. They called this "protection" money. Then…

---

[191] https://www.amazon.com/History-Quranic-Text-Compilation-Comparative/dp/1872531652?tag=duckduckgo-d-20

[192] politicalislam.com

[193] IBID

In approximately 750, the (Islamic) Caliph destroyed the walls of Jerusalem, leaving it defenseless... [194]

There is a huge difference between invaders subjugating a people through making war on them, forcing them to pay Muslims their jizya protection money, making them second class people versus trying to set them free to practice Christianity again. Anyone who legitimizes Muslim wars of conquest compared with the crusades does not understand history or has a demonic agenda against Christians.

World Religions:

Religions in the world all have peaceful messages and various forms of the golden rule or the second great commandment in Christianity.

- *Christianity: Do unto others as you would have them do unto you. Matthew 7:12*

- *Judaism: What you do not wish for yourself, do not wish for others. Talmud Shabbat 31.A*

- *Buddhism: Do you offend others as you would not like to be offended. Udanavarga 5.18*

- *Confucianism: What we do not wish to be done to us, let us not do it to others. Analects 15.23*

- *Brahmanism: Never do unto others what would hurt you if done unto you. Mahabharata 5.15*

- *Bahai Faith: If you seek justice choose for others what you would choose for yourself.*

- *Taoism: Make: as yours the profits of your fellowman as well as his loss. T'ai-shang Kin-ying P'ien*

- *Maya: You are myself. We are all one.*

- Islam does NOT. There is no equivalent to the second great commandment or golden rule in Islam.

---

[194] http://www1.cbn.com/churchandministry/1400-years-of-christian-islamic-struggle

Islamic Violence

First, YES, most Muslims are peaceful. But the percentage of those who are not is disturbingly high from antidotal evidence. We never hear from peaceful people, only the violent ones. I do not know how peaceful Muslims ignore all the violent commands in the three holy books of Islam and still consider themselves Muslim. But I give them my heartfelt thank you that they do.

On the other hand, I keep running into stories like the following. On Fox news, May 3, 2019, Lou Dobbs show there was a video showing a group of Muslim children about 10 years old at their school singing the following lyrics.

"The blood of martyrs protects us. Paradise needs real men! Those who reject oppression are [--ne] ones who assert their existence, we will defend the land of divine guidance with our bodies, and we will sacrifice our souls without hesitation. We will chop off their heads, and we will liberate the sorrowful and exalted Al-Aqsa Mosque. We will lead the army of Allah fulfilling His promise, and we will subject them to eternal torture."

The video was taken in Philadelphia, Pa. The Muslim American Society Islamic Center. So, you be the judge. Is Islam a religion of peace? For me I think not. There is just too much hatred and violence in the name of the pagan god Allah and for Mohammad.

I have personal involvement with the malevolent hatred and violent deeds of Islamic jihadists. My father-in-law was kidnapped by Muslims on the island of Mindanao in the Philippines. They were going to kill him unless they were paid $250,000. The family scraped up the money and paid them to rescue my father-in-law. It is this way and other ways that Muslims fund themselves.

I also contribute substantial amounts of money to an organization that helps Christians recover from ISIS Islamic jihadist attacks in Iraq, the Iraqi Christian Relief Fund. These attacks not only kill people, they also make certain they destroy all the infrastructure so that no one can live there after they leave. Islamic jihadists are like locusts, they steal everything they can, kill all the people and destroy all the infrastructure like water wells so that no one can live in that town again. They are especially famous for destroying any artifacts and religious symbols.

Currently the organization I support is rebuilding the water supply system for a Christian town which ISIS went out of their way to destroy. I am helping to fund that effort. You will never hear about this in our mainstream media. This kind of thing happens continually every day of the year. Their complete hatred against Christians and

Jews goes beyond description. I do not have time in this book to cover everything. I will only be able to describe some important highlights to give you a taste of Islam. I am very happy that the people I fund are making very good progress in restoring what ISIS destroyed so the Christians and other people can return to their town in Iraq.

Islamic jihadists are in our country today. Muslim population in this country has grown substantially over the last 10 years. This is largely due to the willful and purposeful actions of Barack Obama. Obama is indeed a Muslim if you did not know. I have videos of Obama talking about "his Islamic faith". These Muslims create enclaves within the United States and have no interest in assimilating into our society. They are forbidden to do so by the Koran, the Hadith and the Sira. Do not ever believe any politician that goes soft on Islam for they are only looking for votes if they do that. That can only be part of a hidden agenda. They are not protecting the best interests and well-being of God's children in the United States of America. It hurts to write this. But I must do this for the sake of truth and God's children.

Abrogation:

There is one bit of Islamic history and the Koran on that you MUST understand. 99% of people today including Muslims do not understand this. It is the concept of abrogation. This means replacing old texts with new ones. The new violent ones were written in Medina and afterward. They replace the old peaceful spiritual ones written in Mecca. The Quran was written in two places, Mecca and Medina. In Mecca Mohammed spoke peaceful and loving things. There however he failed as a preacher. When he was kicked out of Mecca, he was forced to go to Medina or be killed. It is there things changed 180° and no longer did he preach peace and love. Rather he became a warlord and preached domination, submission, destruction, conquering Christian and Jews by the sword. He was rejected by the Jews and Christians.

The verses he wrote in Medina of violence and domination over the infidels are intended to replace the peaceful versus written in Mecca. This is why there is so much confusion about the Koran with both peaceful and hateful versus contained in it. Bottom line, the hateful ones through abrogation are intended to replace the peaceful ones. Terribly sad but nonetheless true.

This says two very important things.

1. Islam is NOT a religion of peace. Rather is preaches violence against all non-Muslims. Two thirds of its texts preach about jihad against non-Muslims called infidels and kafirs.

2. The Koran is a human document. Yahweh is perfect who we call Almighty God. He called himself, "I Am" when Abraham spoke with Him at the burning bush. God never has to do things twice. It is perfect the first time. But Islam has to do things over again and replace their first attempt. This can only be from the hand of man, not God.

None of Our revelations do We abrogate or cause to be forgotten, but We substitute **something better or similar.** *Knowest thou not that Allah Hath power over all things?* Surah 2:106

Because it is so important, I say again, the mere existence of abrogation or substitution in Islamic texts proves without any doubt that Islam is NOT FROM GOD! Why? When "I Am" says or does something it is perfect the first time. In all Biblical literature we NEVER see replacement texts that supersede older ones. This Koran can only be a product of man, not of God. Always remember this. It also proves that there are only two Abrahamic religions today, Judaism and Christianity. Period!

We see the result today in our news, and all the terrorist attacks across the world, in the subversion of our own federal government courtesy of Barack Obama. Shockingly I have multiple videos of Obama referring to his own Muslim faith. These videos are available to you on the Internet. Do your own research and you will confirm this. His presidency was the biggest hoax ever perpetrated upon the American people.

The Koran:

Christians and Jews: [195]

8:12 *Then your Lord spoke to His angels and said, "I will be with you. Give strength to the believers. I will send terror into the Kafirs' hearts, cut off their heads and even the tips of their fingers!"*

33:60 *They [Kafirs] will be cursed, and wherever they are found, they will be seized and murdered. It was Allah's same practice with those who came before them, and you will find no change in Allah's ways.*

---

[195] https://www.politicalislam.com/sharia-law-for-non-muslims-chapter-5-the-kafir/

9:29 *Make war on those who have received the Scriptures [Jews and Christians] but do not believe in Allah or in the Last Day. They do not forbid what Allah and His Messenger have forbidden. The Christians and Jews do not follow the religion of truth until they submit and pay the poll tax [jizya] and they are humiliated.*

Quran (9:30) - *"And the Jews say: Ezra is the son of Allah; and the Christians say: The Messiah is the son of Allah; these are the words of their mouths; they imitate the saying of those who disbelieved before; may Allah destroy them; how they are turned away!"*

Sira and Hadith

Sahih Muslim (1:33) - *the Messenger of Allah said: I have been commanded to fight against people till they testify that there is no god but Allah, that Muhammad is the messenger of Allah* [196]

Tabari 9:69 *"Killing Unbelievers is a small matter to us"*. The words of Muhammad, prophet of Islam. [197]

Killing Christians and Jews Today:

Christian persecution close to 'genocide levels,' largely ignored due to 'political correctness': report [198] — By Caleb Parke | Fox News, May 7, 2019

"I believe the death of most people suffering today is truly because of political correctness, because the world turns a blind eye to this, and when we are politically correct, we are sympathizing with those terrorists that are destroying communities and erasing history," Taimoorazy said. [199]

Please do not think that just because you do not hear about all the killings of Christians and Jews by Muslims that they have magically stopped. They are an ugly daily occurrence around the world. The reason we fight in various parts of the world is to

---

[196] https://www.thereligionofpeace.com/pages/quran/violence.aspx
[197] IBID
[198] https://www.foxnews.com/world/christian-persecution-close-to-genocide-levels-largely-ignored-due-to-political-correctness-report
[199] IBID

prevent them from gaining strength and to then come here. But many are already within our United States. Remember the Muslim training camp found in New Mexico. [200]

Wife Beating:

Men are the maintainers of women because Allah has made some of them to excel others and because they spend out of their property; the good women are therefore obedient, guarding the unseen as Allah has guarded; and (as to) those on whose part you fear desertion, admonish them, and leave them alone in the sleeping-places and beat them. [Quran Verse 4:34] [201]

Here is a propaganda piece that purports to show what "proper wife beating should look like". [202] Muslims cannot run from this so they make it look as harmless as they can in this video.

Hadith and Sira

Sahih Bukhari (72:715) - *A woman came to Muhammad and begged him to stop her husband from beating her. Her skin was bruised so badly that it is described as being "greener" than the green veil she was wearing. Muhammad did not admonish her husband, but instead ordered her to return to him and submit to his sexual desires.* [203]

Sahih Bukhari (72:715) - *"Aisha said, 'I have not seen any woman suffering as much as the believing women'" Muhammad's own wife complained Muslim women were abused worse than other women.* [204]

Sahih Muslim (4:2127) - *Muhammad struck his favorite wife, Aisha, in the chest one evening when she left the house without his permission. Aisha narrates, "He struck me on the chest which caused me pain."* [205]

---

[200] https://gellerreport.com/2018/08/new-mexico-polygamist.html/

[201] https://controversialislam.wordpress.com/wife-beating-quran-verse-434/

[202] https://www.memri.org/reports/qatari-sociologist-abd-al-aziz-al-khazraj-al-ansari-demonstrates-correct-wife-beating-islam

[203] https://www.thereligionofpeace.com/pages/quran/wife-beating.aspx

[204] IBID

[205] IBID

Sahih Muslim (9:3506) - *Muhammad's fathers-in-law (Abu Bakr and Umar) amused him by slapping his wives (Aisha and Hafsa) for annoying him. According to the Hadith, the prophet of Islam laughed upon hearing this.*[206]

Here is a video link showing an imam and an interviewer discussing wife beating. The cleric says that Islam honors women by not allowing them to have their faces beaten. Watch in horror. [207]

Sharia Law and Human Rights:

Many respected bodies, including the European Court of Human Rights, have concluded that Sharia is incompatible with accepted modern standards of human rights.

In 2003 and 2004, the court [European Court of Human Rights] ruled that "that sharia is incompatible with the fundamental principles of democracy" (13/02/2003), because the sharia rules on inheritance, women rights and religious freedom violate human rights as established in the European Convention on Human Rights. [208]

Freedom of Speech

Islam does not allow the adoption and propagation of 'Freedom of Speech' as propagated by the west since this would include the promotion of such ideas that clearly contradict Islam, such as usury, obscenity under the guise of entertainment and separation of Islam from life's affairs. [209]

Non-Muslims (Kafirs, People of The Book)

Kafirs are non-Muslims. People of the book are Christians and Jews. We too fall under the name of kafir. A Muslim is to behave exactly the way Mohammed did. They are to hate what Allah hates and to love what Allah loves.

40:35 They [Kafirs] who dispute the signs [Koran verses] of Allah without authority having reached them are greatly hated by Allah and the believers [Muslims]. So, Allah seals up every arrogant, disdainful heart.

---

[206] IBID
[207] https://www.youtube.com/watch?v=EGHAFxwI2qU
[208] https://wikiislam.net/wiki/Islamic_Law
[209] https://www.islamicity.org/8653/freedom-of-speech-an-islamic-perspective/

h8.24 It is not permissible to give zakat [charity] to a Kafir,

47:4 When you encounter the Kafirs on the battlefield, cut off their heads... (Keep in mind modern day Muslims consider the entire Earth as a battlefield.)

Violence Against Non-Muslims [210]

Quran (2:244) - *"Then fight in the cause of Allah and know that Allah Heareth and knoweth all things."*

Quran (3:56) - *"As to those who reject faith, I will punish them with terrible agony in this world and in the Hereafter, nor will they have anyone to help."*

Quran (3:151) - *"Soon shall We cast terror into the hearts of the Unbelievers,*

Quran (4:76) - *"Those who believe fight in the cause of Allah..."*

Quran (8:67) - *"It is not for a Prophet that he should have prisoners of war until he had made a great slaughter in the land..."*

Quran (8:65) - *"O Prophet, exhort the believers to fight..."*

Quran (9:14) - *"Fight against them so that Allah will punish them by your hands and disgrace them and give you victory over them and heal the breasts of a believing people."*

Quran (9:123) - *"O you who believe! fight those of the unbelievers who are near to you and let them find in you hardness."*

Hadith and Sira:

Sahih Bukhari (52:177) - *Allah's Apostle said, "The Hour will not be established until you fight with the Jews, and the stone behind which a Jew will be hiding will say. "O Muslim! There is a Jew hiding behind me, so kill him."*

Sahih Bukhari (52:73) - *"Allah's Apostle said, 'Know that Paradise is under the shades of swords'."*

I must stop here. But there are so much more terrible contents within the Koran, the Hadith and the Sira. I urge you to do your own research but beware. There are many websites seeking to reconcile Christianity and Islam they paper over the underlying truth

---

[210] https://www.thereligionofpeace.com/pages/quran/violence.aspx

of things and try to paint a picture that is filled with peace and compassion. But this does not at all reconcile with what is going on in the world and the activities of Muslims against Christians and Jews and other non-Muslims.

Remember this last fact. There are four different forms of jihad.

1. The first is what we are most familiar with, that of violence, slaughter and murder.

2. The second is of speech. When a Muslim speaks defending Islam that too is considered a form of jihad.

3. The third is giving money to support the activities of jihadists.

4. The fourth is praying for the jihadists to reach their ultimate goal of world domination. This is the openly stated goal of Muslims across the world, world domination. Christians and Jews will then be required to pay monthly taxes to Muslims. It is called the jizya. Remember this.

We have here in our political structure a number of Islamic apologists, those who make excuses for all the horror Muslims do to other people. Here are a few.

"Islam is the fastest-growing religion in America, a guide and pillar of stability for many of our people." — Hillary Clinton

"The future must not belong to those who slander the prophet of Islam"[211] — *Barack Obama*
"The sweetest sound I know is the Muslim call to prayer"[212] — Barack Obama

"Islam has a proud tradition of tolerance."[213] — *Barack Obama*
"Islam is not part of the problem in combating violent extremism – it is an important part of promoting peace." — *Barack Obama*

---

[211] https://conservativefiringline.com/compare-contrast-40-obama-quotes-islam-christianity/
[212] IBID
[213] IBID

"As we hear these words from John 13:15 and 17, we know that this message, this command of love, is not confined to New Testament. The same message stands at the center of the Torah and the teachings of the Prophet Mohammad too. [214] —Nancy Pelosi

If you dismiss this and think that this is just another political statement, you really need to think again! I have not encountered a quote from a Republican that praises Islam. Think of this too dear child of God.

"About sixty-one percent of the contents of the Koran are found to speak ill of the unbelievers or call for their violent conquest; at best only 2.6 percent of the verses of the Koran are noted to show goodwill toward humanity. About seventy-five percent of Muhammad's biography (Sira) consists of jihad waged on unbelievers." [215]

This last quote agrees completely with other sources I have found. Sources like Bill Warner at Political Islam. [216] Dr. Warner has devoted his life to the objective study of Islam. His research explains why they do what they do and say what they say. During my research for this book I spoke with him at length. Space does not permit me to include them all. I implore you to do your own research on Islam. But the least you can do is to never ever believe what Democrats say about Islam. They are lying through their teeth.

Everything said above explains why we continue to have serious problems with Muslims. As we allow more Muslims into our country, the more intense our problems will become in this country that was built by Christians. I will leave it up to you to determine how all of this fits in with Christianity and biblical prophecy and the book of Revelation.

---

[214] https://eaglerising.com/29907/nancy-pelosi-quotes-mohammad-and-pushes-islam-at-the-national-prayer-breakfast/

[215] http://www.truthbeknown.com/islamquotes.htm

[216] https://www.politicalislam.com/

Part 5

Fixing Things Back To Our
Judeo Christian Foundations

Washington DC Needs a Gigantic Enema

As Christians we have provided the Judeo-Christian foundations for the success of this country up until about the late 1960s. From there things started to go bad! The up rise of anti-this and anti-that became stronger and stronger and the Democratic Party somewhere along the line decided to detach itself from its long-held position as defender of the working class family. Now they appeal to all the radical leftist groups and illegal aliens that want to destroy this country.

Additionally, the Republicans during this time have firmly entrenched themselves within the structures of government and the military industrial complex that Pres. Eisenhower warned us against to promote wars that we have no business dealing with.

President Eisenhower's farewell address to the nation, January 1961

"In the counsels of Government, we must guard against the acquisition of unwarranted influence, whether sought or unsought, by the Military Industrial Complex. The potential for the disastrous rise of misplaced power exists and will persist. We must never let the weight of this combination endanger our liberties or democratic processes. We should take nothing for granted. Only an alert and knowledgeable citizenry can compel the proper meshing of the huge industrial and military machinery of defense with our peaceful methods and goals so that security and liberty may prosper together.

But we did not listen to the president. Instead our government and the defense industry got deeply intermingled with each other. Black budgets blossomed with bountiful amounts of billions of dollars paid by you the taxpayer. And you the taxpayer have no idea, you have no right to know how your money, your earnings your hard work has been spent by your government. The coming election in 2020 will be probably the most important election in this nation's history. It is because we need to accomplish two things.

Number 1. We need to rid ourselves of the socialist infestation in the minds of our people which will lead us to complete disaster as it 100% of the time always has in the history of mankind. The Leftist radical democrats that support, abortion, the Green New Deal, pay without work, eliminating cattle because cows fart too much, eliminate airplanes in 10 years, eliminate all gas powered cars in 10 years, do what the looney 22 year old democrat in Chicago named Ugo Okere said where "government controls every aspect of our lives".

This is completely opposite of what God intended when He created mankind on earth. I covered this earlier in this book. These young people are so very ignorant with adolescent minds that they really do not have any idea what they do not know. So, they think they know everything. This is a broad psychological trap many people fall into. These democrats think they have all the answers when in fact they do not have even the knowledge to ask the right questions.

Given the chance they will indeed destroy this great country and bring pain, suffering, misery and death to this once great country. They will do it with great fanfare and then when that does not work, with the ugly force of guns aimed at our citizens which is what has happened 100% of the time in human history. We of the Judeo Christian heritage must rise up against these know nothings and set them aside where they belong for the betterment of our entire nation. We need to do this NOW! These people are half our problem.

Number 2: Now the other half. We also need to flush out all those people with deeply entrenched interests, financial interests, and our military war making machine that produces tremendous profits for very many companies. Some people call this the deep state. It is people in very powerful appointed positions in government that deal with many different things such as, trade, healthcare pharmaceuticals, weapons for our military, weapons research and other dark budget items that are hard to find.

But they also are in visible positions high in government where they pretend to do their constitutional duties when in fact, they accomplish the opposite. These people are deeply entrenched inside government and can leak selected information to outside media in order to affect public opinion. They are sworn to be neutral but are not and have chosen winners and losers in the political realm. You see these people on the news all the time.

This is absolutely not in any way shape or form what our founding fathers have intended for us. Secrecy is bad. Secrecy is always bad no matter the excuse. Don't tell me it's for national security. That is bullsh&t. If the American people pay for it, then the American people have a right to know. When the government tells you it's for national security, remember that is putting themselves higher then you. That goes directly and explicitly against the will of God for all of his children on this planet.

Additionally, the government is our servant not our masters. Legitimate power comes to God's children from God directly. We lend that power to our representatives in government to do our bidding guided by the way we vote. Things have gotten backwards in the last 50 years. That needs to change as well.

So, what I am telling you is that in the history of our nation we have arrived at the point where we will lose what we take for granted and think we will have forever. It just is not so. The Democratic Party is proposing gargantuan changes to our entire way of life in their idiotic Green New Deal. It is a monster that will swallow all of your income completely. It will force you into indentured servitude at the end of a rifle pointed directly at you. It always has in the history of mankind. ALWAYS!! It is horrifically this bad. Horrifically true.

The interior of our social structure, our way of life, our individual freedoms, our freedom of movement, our freedoms to purchase whatever we wish, our freedoms to do whatever we wish, and all the other freedoms that we take for granted today that we think stay forever will vanish into a regime of rigid rules and regulations that you dare not disobey. Remember the 22 year old Democrat wacko running for a councilman seat in Chicago. That half brain wants every aspect of human life controlled by the government. Worse yet, the ignorant adolescents in Chicago will vote for him. This is what we are up against.

The other half of our problem is the entrenched powerful people in government whose names you never hear of. They do not act in the best interest of the American people. Rather they act according to their own agendas with others in government so as to profit from the decisions they make.

We as Christian citizens of this country have ultimate sovereignty over government. It is you and me as individuals who must make changes. For one thing never vote for a Democrat especially in 2020. The following is a list of items we need to enact to protect the futures of all our children and grandchildren and their grandchildren too.

How We Need to Fix This Nation

Simple but Hard Solutions for The United States:

1. Our founding fathers set term limits on federal offices. We must greatly expand this concept to far more offices within the federal and state governments so that there are no more career politicians that serve more than eight years. After that they must reenter the private sector. Period. This is the way it was originally intended and will eliminate hidden entrenched money powered interests from controlling our government.

2. Political appointees should also have total service time limits as well to avoid entrenched deep state dark government control that we have today. No person shall serve in a capacity above a certain rank to be determined for a total service in all capacities of more than 8 years as well.

   Remember this: "Politicians are like diapers, they need to be changed often and for the same reason." ~Mark Twain, 1903

3. Age requirements:
   a. Change the age requirement for president from the current 35 years old to 50 years old. This also applies to the vice president and the first four people in the line of succession. The reason for this is that when our founding fathers created the age requirement of 35 years old, people did not live as long as we do now. Additionally, life was much simpler then. There was not nearly the complex problems then as now. Now it just takes more life experience to run a country.

   b. Change the age requirement for the house of representatives to 40 years old. The same reasons apply here as above.

   c. Change the age requirement for the senate to 45 years old. Since this is supposedly our deliberative body in congress, w must have people old enough to have the ability to see both sides of an issue.

4. To fix the under the table bribery and hidden agendas in congress we must make that very hard to do. Within our current voting system, we need to do the following:
   a. Instead of one single congressman and one single senator we need to replace every one of these bought and paid for representatives with a triad of three elected people. Each triad would continue to have one

vote as is currently the case for the individual representative we have now. Three people must debate and come to a conclusion and then cast their single vote.

b. The way the one triad vote is determined is within each triad, they would vote within the triad. Two out of three determines how they would cast their single vote in congress.

c. Each member of a triad would be elected for a term of two years like the current term of the house of representatives.

d. Among the triad members, elections would be held on a rotating basis where only one member would be elected every two years.

e. The eight year rule would apply to each member of a triad. After eight years, each member would be thanked for their service and be ineligible for further service in congress.

f. Current voting districts as per the house of representatives would apply to each triad.

g. Establish an easier method to recall representatives of the triad by an off cycle vote of each district. Therefore, each triad member would be always subject to recall at any time.

h. BENEFITS: The benefits of this triad system would be:

    i.   Much harder for lobbyists to corrupt the triad versus a single person.

    ii. Each member would not have time to create a mini political network with other members and corporations.

    iii. We the People would then have more exposure to their representative when congress is not in session. There would be three instead of one to canvass the will of the people.

    iv. We the People would enjoy much better representation by giving the people a far easier way to recall any triad member applicable at any time.

5. Eliminate the Federal Reserve Bank completely and replace it with one something like the supreme court but with more directors and transparent

plainly visible deliberations. All deliberations should be public. It is the people's money and so the people have every right to see what is going on. Ever since the Federal Reserve Bank was established, the dollar has lost 98% of its value and we have had many recessions and depressions when they raised interest rates "to control inflation" which they created. Remember what Henry Ford said: *"Depressions aren't acts of God; like wars, they are the work of a small group of men who profit by them."* Later on President Dwight Eisenhower would say the same thing about our war machine calling it the military industrial complex.

6. Establish a department of economic education that favors the Austrian School of economics. Keynesian economics is stupid. This is the foundation for cyclical business trends with recessions.

7. No person entering government service shall exit same service substantially wealthier than they entered monitored by appropriate boards of accounting. This includes any third party financial institutions they may have control of such as corporations or foundations etc. No one shall get rich off the government service. If so, that will be a felony with prison time. Hello Hillary, hello Bill.

8. Once you leave government service, thank you, you are gone for good. You may not secure any job that requires interaction with any former government contacts you worked with while inside government.

9. There will be no lobbying organization headquartered within 25 miles of the capitol.

10. All senators and representatives shall have pinned on their jackets the top 10 donors to their last political campaign. Yes, I am not kidding. Think NASCAR

11. In case you did not know, it is illegal to lie to the government! You may NOT lie to a police officer if you are stopped in traffic. This is why you MUST KEEP YOUR MOUTH SHUT! They fish for information by seemingly being friendly. It is a trap. But the reverse is NOT true. It is legal for the government including the police to lie to you! Look at what they did to Paul Manafort. They accused him of lying and put him into solitary confinement, a punishment reserved only for hardened criminal already in prison. They wanted to totally destroy him so he would invent stories against President Trump. Evil abounds in the ranks of our government. This "truth law" will end such horrors.

This MUST change to SAVE our country. WE MUST MAKE IT A CRIMINAL FELONY for any government employee to lie to an American citizen. They are our civil servants. They are NOT our masters. They used to be our servants but over the decades that has mutated into some form of godhood. NO MORE! Doing this will end tyranny in its tracks. No longer will it be "legal" for the police to lie to a citizen in order to entrap that person. If a senator or congressman lies to the American people, it is a felony with prison time. Period.

12. Reduce the federal government payroll by 10%. Barack Obama laid off "non-essential" workers in a political move so we know they are there. Private sector companies do this all the time. Government is no different regarding the machinery of things. These people are our servants, not special untouchables that are sanctified. We pay them to do things for us efficiently. They do not. After 5 years, reduce payrolls another 10%.

13. Change rigged accounting rules to eliminate lying to the public. Eliminate the rules that create a lie where if something is budgeted to increase by 20%, then if the increase is reduced to 10%, DO NOT call that a 10% decrease. It is now a 10% increase.

14. Reinstitute and require in ALL public school's early morning Pledge Allegiance to the Flag of the United States of America. If you do not like that, go somewhere else. If you take part in the benefits of this blessed country, then you will take on also the responsibilities of it too.

15. Work aggressively toward assimilation of all aliens that come here legally. Treat them with love and respect. Show them how to be good American citizens. If they do not want to, kick their ass out the door. Forget religious exemptions too.

16. Congress should be made to live under the same laws that they make for us citizens to live under. This means they should get the same health care, same social security, no more same salary as they got in congress for the rest of their life as they do now and so on.

17. Voting: There are two things:

a. If you pay no taxes, you cannot vote. This ends the robbery and viciousness of robbing Peter to pay Paul. This is completely evil at its very core. I do not care what label of sympathy you want to paste on it. You cannot confiscate another person's hard earned wages from him in order to feed your own pockets. It must be at the discretion of other people who pay taxes and by our very nature as God's children are charitable, compassionate and loving toward our fellow man. This is the very nature of the American citizen to begin with. We need to remember this for the United States is the most charitable nation in the history of mankind. We will not refuse our own citizens. Anyone who tells you different must be someone other than a child of God.

b. Harebrained adolescents full of hormones with no life experience should not be able to vote. They are way too susceptible to being propagandized by political interests that make things sound good but underneath it all it is rotten to the core. The only way to combat this is to have more life experience in order to see through the sham that it really is. Therefore, I believe we should increase the minimum voting age to 25 years old. It is at this age where people have settled down, started families, started careers and have a direction in their life. They are mostly out of wacko adolescent behavior. They mostly have the minimal life experience necessary to make sound choices regarding those people who we will lend our God-given powers to lead us.

What Can I Do as An Individual Christian?
Good question. There are a number of things.

1. Do your own research on the topics I have presented here. This is important for you to become familiar with our current mess of a political situation.

2. When you find facts and figures, NOT PROPAGANDA, send this information to people on your email distribution list. Add your own commentary as well.

3. When you are at a social gathering or after mass, mention your concerns about what is happening in our country as a conversation starter. Tell people what you know.

4. Call into radio talk shows and express your concerns and opinions. Don't be afraid to do this. If you need to write down the statements you want to make and the questions.

5. As you are doing these things, read more from websites that look like they are telling the truth. One indicator are sites that post real data and research. Avoid opinion only sites for they are full of propaganda and stupid opinions based on nothing.

6. Not necessary to talk to your pastor or priest. I have found from personal experience that the clergy is very disconnected from real life especially living in the real world. They are sequestered from paying taxes, going grocery shopping, do not experience the real day to day hardships of children going to school,

balancing budgets and so on. They also tend to be ignorantly liberal due to not living in reality the same harsh way the rest of us do. I have had a lot of experience dealing with clergy and lay spiritual direction people.

7. Bug your senator, congressman, city council and all government officials that are supposed to represent your best interest, wellbeing and financial security. Write letters to these people. Make appointments to see them personally. Let your opinions be heard by these people.

8. Come the 2020 election, get active for conservative candidates. It is these people who will save our country.

9. Teach your children about the mess we are in and who caused it by the awful anti-Christian policies they have implemented.

10. Write articles for publications and submit them. Do not be afraid to do this.

11. Do what I have done, write a book of your personal experiences and what things need to be changed.

We Need to Learn from Other Cultures:

Regarding this age limitation, we need to take a lesson from Asian societies. They honor their elderly people for their gathered wisdom and seek their advice in matters of life. We here in this country have a lot to learn from Asian cultures in this way. These cultures have been around for thousands of years. We have been around only a few hundred. We have much to learn. It is the wise person who learns from another person's life experience. And so too we as a nation can learn from other nations experience. The Chinese culture has been around for about 6000 years. They are still here today.

I tell you through personal experience having been married fortunately to a Filipino woman for almost 40 years and now a half Chinese woman for six years. They have much to offer our American society on how to behave in the long-term and be successful. We need to look to them as a guiding light to provide not for next quarter's profits, but rather for our long-term health and well-being is a sparkling Democratic constitutional republic and culture. If we do this and enact age limits such as I have described, we will be far better off as a nation, as a culture, as a society, and will regain the honor, the trust, and the eagerness for the well-being of each other knowing that we are all brothers as children of God.

Liberal Political People Are Very Hostile Against Changing Things:

The people who will scream the most, the people who will pull out their hair the most, the people who will squeak, rattle, roll on the floor, throw fits, tantrums, and all the other nasties of both personal and political behavior will reveal themselves when they read this. And verily I say unto you, it is these same people that you surely do not want leading us in government positions with political power over all of us.

By their very behavior they disqualify themselves as reasonable, clear thinking, levelheaded, adults that are able to tackle the serious problems we as a nation faced today both internally and externally.

To save our nation this must stop by measures like the ones above. They are simple but boy will the fur fly, teeth will gnash, and the wailing be loud. And it will all be about money and control. Those who scream the loudest are identifying themselves as in most need of replacement.

Conclusion:

I do leave you with these thoughts. This physical reality that we live in today with all of its sham and drudgery, pain, suffering and disappointment is but a small part of all creation. The far larger and vastly more important part of creation is all within the unseen Divine spiritual world. It is there from which we came, and it is there to which we will return.

From this literary work here are the main points you need to take away as truth and remember:

1. We all are spirit beings born within the loving arms of Almighty God. It is there that each of us has been bestowed a unique blend of gifts and graces not possessed by anyone else in the kind and proportion that God has given us individually.

2. God prepared each of us for our physical lives here on earth, telling us how it would be, the loving opportunities, the challenges, the hardships and suffering we would endure. The purpose of this life is to learn to love both God and all our brothers and sisters in the human brotherhood in more intense and unique ways that cannot be accomplished anywhere else in the universe He has created for us.

3. Coming here to physical earth also provides us with a very unique opportunity to know God in a different way, through the lens of physical life, which is different than what we have experienced before coming here.

4. The earth is a very difficult place to live in. This is on purpose and for the benefit of us God's children. To succeed here we must flex our spiritual muscles to accomplish our goals for this life as ordained by God for each of us. Part of this life and its suffering is to demonstrate to both ourselves and the inhabitants of the universe that we can love others as ourselves while suffering is working against us in doing so.

5. Coming here also gives us the opportunity to demonstrate our love for God that comes first in our short lives here and never wavering from that while never falling short and putting ourselves above others of God's children.

6. We must avoid the one and only danger to our eternal life which is put ourselves above our fellow brothers and sisters so as to gain unfair advantages above them so as to exploit them for only material gain. This is the shortcut to being separated from God. This is exactly what Lucifer, the morning star, did before he was cast down out of heaven. Now called Satan, he wants to destroy all of God's children who are made in His image.

7. We must learn while we are here that we indeed have power over Satan and to never be fooled or succumb to the false attractions Satan's puts before us. If we do, we are separating ourselves from God in eternity.

8. We must learn that faith, knowledge and reason lead to wisdom, a wisdom that will help us defeat the adolescent minds within the leftist liberal Democrat party that proposes political policies that will certainly destroy us God's children and our country that we built. Obama said, "you did not build that". Ignore him as you would any other of Satan's low level minions.

9. In our earthly lives we must come to the conclusion that it is "truth" that will set us free from getting caught up in all the lies and deceit of the world and in our country. Only in this way can we build that "shining city on the hill" that President Ronald Reagan talked about years ago.

10. Pursuing the truth will allow you to see through all the sham and lies that the Democrat party has propagandized to the American people, the children of God. We must learn that this takes effort and determination so as to protect ourselves, our loved ones and our country from falling prey to the minions of Satan, the author of all lies.

11. We must always be cautious about what people in power tell us. There are many evil hidden agendas perpetrated by those who lust for money and power. They must be thrown out and punished according to their crime against us.

12. We must here on earth learn how to manifest the will of God for His Children and in doing so to reap the rewards that have been promised by God to all those who love Him first above all else.

13. Lastly, we as Christian children of God, we must rise up and MAKE OUR VOICES HEARD ALL ACROSS THIS COUNTRY. FOR IN DOING THIS WE WILL INSPIRE ALL NATIONS TO DO THE SAME, TO LOVE GOD FIRST AND LOVE OUR NEIGHBORS AS OURSELVES, TO FLUSH OUT ALL THE VERMEN DEMONS THAT EXIST IN OUR GOVERNMENT TODAY THAT HATE THIS GOD GIVEN LAND AND US AS GOD'S CHILDREN. THOSE WHO POISON THE MINDS OF OUR CHILDREN IN OUR SCHOOLS AND UNIVERSITIES AND HIDE IN POWERFUL CLOSED ROOMS OF GOVERNMENT TO MAKE LAWS THAT STEAL THE VERY FREEDOMS BESTOWED TO US BY ALMIGHTY GOD. TO THESE PEOPLE THEY SHALL BE BANISHED INTO THE DUSTBINS OF HISTORY TO BE FORGOTTEN AS WE CONTINUE ON THE TRUE PATH ORDAINED BY GOD FOR US HIS LOVING CHILDREN.

14. The first step in making our voices heard is to NEVER VOTE FOR ANY DEMOCRAT IN 2020. Also be very suspicious of all politicians. Most have forked tongues.

So please think long and hard about who you vote for in 2020. This will be a pivotal election in the history of our United States. We either reaffirm our country as a Judeo-Christian founded nation or we fall down the ugly path toward socialism with all its completely false promises of free this and free that.

As for me I will not vote Democrat in any way shape or form. Because Democrats are ever so anti-Christian, cannot understand money, economies and budgets, have no idea how to handle other hostile nations to the U.S., and promote completely immoral social policies. The fallout from that is horrific and totally goes against the will of Almighty God. We need to remove these people from all public offices and replace them with people that hold dear our Judeo-Christian morality and ethics. These people are immoral termites that will eat away everything it is good in our society, our culture and structures of our democratic constitutional republican government. They must do this to get to their evil dreams. Prevent that.

But I remind you again that Republicans are no picnic either. but they will do far less harm to us as a nation. We as a society need to implement far stronger laws against the kind of money and power crimes the Republicans commit against us children of God living here in the United States. This is why I strongly urge everyone to support far more stringent and widespread term limits on all sorts of federal and state governments to fight entrenched and hidden dark state power structures inside our government.

President Donald Trump is the first light in this direction. This is why he is hated so much by Democrats and the hidden powers that exist in government today. All the hatred and lies of accusations against this president are undeniable proof to the deep extent that evil dark forces live within our government both state and federal.

Additionally, I strongly feel that to lead Almighty God's children in the United States we need everyone that holds public office to publicly adhere to our Judeo-Christian foundations as a country and the Judeo-Christian principles that all of us live by every day of our lives.

In the upcoming presidential election in 2020 all hell will break loose fomented from the leftist liberals now taking over the Democrat party. Their anti-Christian attitudes must not prevail. Our children and our grandchildren depend upon us to confront this evil head on and defeat it were it ever to raises its ugly reptilian head. This is a call for all of God's children into action. Let your voices be heard across this great nation and stop at nothing to spread the word of God and our Lord and Savior Jesus Christ. Let everyone know the evils we now face to prevent it from overwhelming us in the coming years.

Basically, I ask everyone to pull the silver handle and flush out all people who speak against the Judeo Christian foundations of our country, Republican or Democrat. If we do not do this, we are letting Satan in the door and he certainly will take advantage of it using evil ways against us that we cannot comprehend.

May Almighty God keep you, bless you, bless your family, guide you in all things and may He bless and shed His grace on this wonderful country that we have built through blood sweat and tears making it the greatest country that has ever been on the face of this earth and will continue to be if only we adhere closely to His will for us in his guidance within our minds that will lead us in our speech and our actions. Amen.

APPENDIX A

Translation of leftist liberal Democrat doublespeak into the real meanings.

When they say...	They really mean...
multiculturalism, diversity, fairness, equity, inclusion, opportunity, empowerment	racial quotas, discrimination against whites, special rights and preferential treatment for protected minorities, the exclusion of white males
multicultural, inclusive	the exclusion of heterosexual male Caucasians.
diverse	whites and Christians absent
invest in the future	redistribution of wealth, spending borrowed money
"Prominent" Democrats "Greedy" Republicans	unusually wealthy people
Justice-involved youth	Juvenile delinquent
community, grassroots	low-income citizens, "victimized" minorities,
federal family	Big Brother
affirmative action, minority enterprise development, minority business development, disadvantaged business utilization, equal opportunity, diversity programs	racial quotas, discrimination against whites, minority hiring quotas,
human trafficking	21st-century slavery
terrorists	Islamist Muslim terrorists

revenue measure, deficit reduction, balanced approach, revenue enhancements, Shared Responsibility Payment, fairness	Higher taxes
troubled inner-city youth at-risk teen	gang leader, juvenile felon, thug, dope dealer, pimp, hoodlum, mugger
sex trade worker	prostitute, whore, stripper, slut, tramp, hooker, hussy, harlot
sexual minorities	sexual deviates, perverts
federal family	Big Brother
community, grassroots	low-income citizens, "victimized" minorities,
for the children, it takes a village, for our future, Goals 2000, Agenda 21, socialization, School to Work, outcome-based education, leave no child behind,	cradle-to-grave socialism, indoctrination disguised as education, collectivist group-think instead of individual achievement, conformity instead of individualism
affirmative action, minority enterprise development, minority business development, equal opportunity, diversity programs	racial quotas, discrimination against whites, minority hiring quotas, lowered standards
"Prominent" Democrats "Greedy" Republicans	unusually wealthy people
Justice-involved youth	Juvenile delinquent
human trafficking	21st-century slavery
terrorists	Islamist Muslim terrorists
troubled inner-city youth at-risk teen	gang leader, juvenile felon, thug, dope dealer, pimp, hoodlum, mugger

sex trade worker	prostitute, whore, stripper, slut, tramp, hooker, hussy, harlot
sexual minorities	sexual deviates, perverts
sustainable economy the greater good shared responsibility living wage laws economic justice giving back to the community earnings inequality	socialism Marxism redistribution of wealth
judgmental, extremist, hate speech, bigotry, prejudice, the religious right, religious extremists	religious objections to homosexuality, religious objections to abortion, any favorable discussion of conservatism
tolerance, inclusion, acceptance, open-mindedness, understanding	approval and endorsement of perverse, deviant lifestyles
assault weapons, gun reform, gun violence solutions, cop-killer bullets, saner gun policies	gun control, banning all gun ownership disarming the law-abiding populace
undocumented workers, Americans in waiting, migrants, economic-driven immigrants, DACA recipients, "Dreamers"	illegal immigrants, illegal aliens
comprehensive immigration reform	amnesty for illegal immigrants
reproductive rights, choice, reproductive choice,	abortion, fetal homicide

freedom, health care, women's rights	
progressive	liberal, radical, leftist
social responsibility	high taxes
giving back to the community	taxing the rich guilt-tripping a lottery winner, corporate executive, or overpaid athlete
human rights	Marxism, socialism
gender reassignment	sex change operations

APPENDIX B

ISLAM:

There is a booklet published by the Christian Broadcasting Network. It is the best levelheaded information about what Islam really is. It explains in detail things that every Christian needs to know regarding the increasing influence that Islamic Muslims are having in our country today.

Pres. Barack Obama was not a Christian as he claimed. There are videos on the Internet, particularly YouTube where he talks about his Islamic faith. He was a Muslim. Many Christians fell for the propaganda from the Democrat party, our mainstream media and the smooth talk out of the mouth of Barack Obama. Here are also some quotes from Obama. There are many solid websites that have the same information.

Here are some of the websites with quotes from Barack Obama on Islam. There are many more.

- https://www.online-ministries.org/barack-hussein-obama-and-his-islamic-quotes/

- https://www.azquotes.com/author/11023-Barack_Obama/tag/islam

- http://thetruthwins.com/archives/20-obama-quotes-about-islam-contrasted-with-20-obama-quotes-about-christianity

- "The future must not belong to those who slander the Prophet of Islam"- Barack Obama

- "The sweetest sound I know is the Muslim call to prayer"- Barack Obama

- "Islam has a proud tradition of tolerance."- Barack Obama

- "Islam has always been part of America"- Barack Obama

- Here is the website where you can get online a free copy of Christian Broadcasting Network's booklet on Islam.

- http://www.cbn.com/special/islambooklet/

- A Video where Obama talks about his Islamic faith:

- https://www.youtube.com/watch?v=hwdHK1zp3Bg

- Obama says he is from Kenya:

- https://www.youtube.com/watch?v=VNBsvpPeMws

- Ex-Muslim talks about her experience within Islam:

- https://www.youtube.com/watch?v=7exliTOghqE

- Three Koran quotes every Christian should know:

- https://www.youtube.com/watch?v=qKRVr_5pOVc

- Short History of Mohammad and Islam:

- https://www.youtube.com/watch?v=qKRVr_5pOVc

This is just an introduction into Islam. I urge you to learn more about Islam and why this so called religion is not in any way compatible with Judeo-Christianity. Sharia law is the most cruel and awful set of laws I have ever seen or read. Beware all Christians, Islam considers you their enemy. They openly say so.

Richard Ferguson is available for book interviews and personal appearances. For more information contact:

Richard Ferguson
info@advbooks.com

To purchase additional copies of this book visit our online bookstore at:
www.advbookstore.com

Orlando, Florida, USA
"we bring dreams to life"™
www.advbookstore.com

www.ingramcontent.com/pod-product-compliance
Lightning Source LLC
Chambersburg PA
CBHW070808270326
41927CB00010B/2350